ULF JENSEN

HOW I TRIPLED MY MONEY IN THE FUTURES MARKET

Winner Of The Robbins Trading Championship Shares His Secrets

PROBUS PUBLISHING COMPANY
Chicago, Illinois
Cambridge, England

ISBN 1-55738-584-X

Printed in the United States of America

BB

WM/BJS

1 2 3 4 5 6 7 8 9 0

Charts by Omega TradeStation

Probus books are available at quantity discounts when purchased for business, educational, or sales promotional use. For more information, please call the Director, Corporate/Institutional Sales at (800) 998-4644, or write:

Director, Corporate/Institutional Sales
Probus Publishing Company
1925 N. Clybourn Avenue
Chicago, IL 60614
PHONE (800) 998-4644   FAX (312) 868-6250

Contents

PART 4: BUILDING A TRADING SYSTEM

PART 5: GETTING THE MOST OUT OF YOUR COMPUTER

PART 6: THE PAYOFF

Preface

This book was written to help thousands of novice traders convert from losing to winning; to teach them to take profits out of the market instead of letting profits slip away; and to guide them in accumulating sufficient capital and experience to survive in the more risky world of long-term trading.

Although much of the material presented can benefit long-term traders, the main emphasis will be on short-term trading and day-trading. Logical analysis of market sentiment in real time has produced exciting new indicators, which I hope will provide fertile grounds for further research. Therefore, the chapter on the development of technical indicators will be of interest to all traders, whether long- or short-term oriented.

Naturally the methods described in this book are not the only ones that work—but they work well. If you are a successful trader, you will want to read this book for the new ideas it can give you; if you are not yet a successful trader, you *must* read this book to learn how to bring your account into the profit zone.

The section on using analytical software is both very general and quite specific. It can only scratch the surface of this fascinating software, but those "scratches" will reveal what is crucial for the busy trader. This section contains many trading tips and much valuable information for all traders, regardless of what analytical software they use, if any. It will extract those powers of the computer that will be most useful in their trading as well as research.

Introduction

Probably every successful trader in any market has written a book about "how I did it."[1-5] Notice that I said "did it," since very few traders are inclined to reveal their "secrets" until they've retired, or, in other words, until after they've become wealthy enough not to care if their system gets overused or misused.

However, that kind of abuse simply isn't possible. The markets aren't like horse racing. If you discover a way to beat the races, then go down to the track and place a $20,000 bet on a 30-to-1 long shot, and those odds will immediately change—perhaps down to 3-to-1 or less. You truly would have spoiled the chance of a big payoff for a whole bunch of little guys, the long-shot bettors. However, in the giant futures market, we individuals are small potatoes, a drop in the bucket, and with the exception of a very thin market in some commodities, our individual orders, no matter how large they seem to us, *cannot* influence the market.

For example, take one of the largest, the U.S. Treasury Bond (T-bond) market, which has a volume of 200,000 to 300,000 contracts traded daily. The day session has 6 hours and 40 minutes of trading, from 7:20 a.m. to 2 p.m. Chicago time, or 400 minutes. Divide 200,000 contracts by 400 minutes and you get 500 contracts per minute. You can see that your or my order for 1, 3, 6, 10, or even 20 or 30 contracts couldn't possibly have much effect on the price. Even if you bought 200 contracts, and as a result the price rose a little during that one minute, that effect would be gone the next minute, when new forces come into play.

The larger the number of traders who use a good system, the more stable the market becomes. If more traders do well in the market, they will likely continue to be active traders and provide more liquidity, which stabilizes the market. One benefit of this is that it's easier to monitor and predict the behavior of a stable market. I hope to contribute to this in a small way by helping my readers and users of my approach to do better.

However, let me give you one warning: No matter how good we think we're getting, the market always will find ways and times to make us humble, sometimes very humble. The market will show us who's boss, who is right, and will underscore that there will always be a need for each of us to get better!

When we speak of an approach to trading, we mean a certain method by which we perform the various tasks that comprise our trading activity. Such a method, or set of guidelines or rules, can consist of one or more simple ideas, the simplest extreme being "Buy low, sell high." Other methods become more complex. Some are sets of rules that require judgment on the part of the trader; others are purely mechanical rules such as mathematical relationships, formulas, and/or logic statements that require only direct application without the need for a trader's judgment. Most of the latter are best used with the help of a computer. Various combinations of those methods are quite prevalent, and many do enjoy a certain amount of success.

However, **there is no perfect method or system of any kind!** This is my first important observation and a fundamental part of my approach. Of course, you knew that already, but now you've heard it again. The very existence of a multitude of systems tells you that no one system "has it all." I'm sorry to burst your bubble, but at best there are systems with some degree of success, and each has a price: such disadvantages as risks, small profits, a large number of trades needed, great volatility needed, large draw-downs, and so on.

I don't intend to be a system critic, as many more qualified than I have already taken that task to heart. I will not elaborate on different types of systems and their relative merits. In this book I'll only provide an overview of what I call my approach, which will include some of my systems, and will give you a perspective of where my approach fits into the general scheme of things. As you may already have surmised, I've not been terribly impressed with any single system or approach to the futures markets, and so I've sought to compile the advantages from many, many approaches to the markets in an attempt to formulate a successful approach.

Such an approach combines the best features of many others with the results of my own analysis of the markets during more than six years of active trading. It is composed not only of the latest technical analyses, but also, and equally important, the "wisdom of the ages," as well as an understanding of the psychology of the participants. This last is extremely important, since the last time I looked, the participants were still *humans!* Perhaps by the next century, the markets will be dominated by computers and our task might be easier, but for now you'll need to know at least a touch of psychology.

In the next chapters I shall describe my approach in a chronological fashion as much as possible—a sort of guided tour of a trader's brain during a day's trading. You'll see that my system is based on what I call common sense, which must by definition come from experience, both mine and that of others. However, where other authors enumerate a long list of rules or guidelines, leaving you with the awesome task of trying to check your every thought against a huge panel of advice, my approach will apply relatively few such principles in a step-wise, almost a "cookbook," fashion that will enable you to have a greater chance of being successful immediately.

Let me emphasize that I am not unique in having arrived at a workable approach to the futures markets,[1-7] nor have I yet surpassed many fabulously successful traders who've enjoyed all kinds of lofty achievements.[1, 4, 5, 33] However, I do have one claim to make, and that is having taken a $10,000 account to nearly $35,000 in the course of six months, which constitutes nearly 250 percent profit (or 500 percent on an annualized basis), which is somewhat better than 5 percent from a savings bank! (Fig. I-1)

The fact that I have done it does not guarantee that anyone can do it, or even that I can do it again, but the likelihood of producing very worthwhile results with my approach is quite good. In fact, since I began writing this book, I again have doubled my money in only five months, and started a very successful daily market letter called *PROFIT$ NOW*, trading the most profitable commodities from all the major groups. I've also presented several successful two-day work-shops, and more are scheduled each month with just one or two attendees. A number of my highly successful indicators and systems are now available on floppy disks, ready to use if you own a computer (see order blank on last page).

Figure I-I

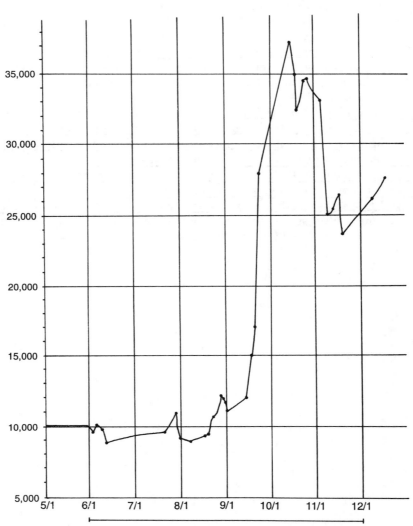

Equity curve, Robbins System Trading Championship,1992

PART
1

PREPARATION

1
Groundwork

Success in the markets depends on many factors, but the most important is the trader himself. Other important factors that cannot be ignored are: opportunity, health, time, and distractions. It is important that the reader understand the impact on his success of each of the above; therefore, let me say a few words about each.

Opportunity

To make successful trades, you must have the opportunity to do so. If the markets are closed for the Christmas holiday, you can't trade. There is no opportunity! "Of course," you say. "That's obvious!"

But even on a day before an event or economic report of some magnitude, the trading in the affected commodities often will be light or limited in price action (low volatility). There is little or no opportunity (Fig. 1-1). Yes, you could trade those markets, and obviously many do, but I choose not to. When a sudden crisis develops, you will see an opportunity! Take the invasion of Kuwait for example:

Figure 1-1

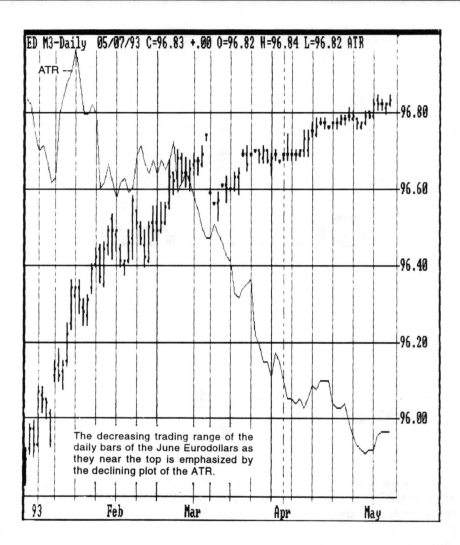

ED M3-Daily 05/07/93 C=96.83 +.00 O=96.82 H=96.84 L=96.82 ATR

The decreasing trading range of the daily bars of the June Eurodollars as they near the top is emphasized by the declining plot of the ATR.

The sudden fear of an oil shortage drove prices sky-high in a matter of days. Clearly, there are times when opportunities for profit are greater than others (see Chapter 2: "Choosing the Market").

Health

Your general health is very important. If you are down with a cold or the flu, you would not think of going out and playing a game of tennis or other competitive sport! Your lack of energy and proper coordination would soon make themselves known, and you would not do well. The markets are no different. They take constant alertness and concentration just to participate, and a higher level of those functions to make quick and correct decisions. If you are not feeling well for any reason; if you are tired from a long night out, travel, or any other reason, **don't trade!** Give yourself the best chance to compete. Wait! There will always be another day.

Time

It's been said that *time* is our most precious commodity. But they aren't trading it yet!

There are several ways you may not have enough time to do justice to your trading. You may have a profession or primary vocation that allows you only certain hours for trading. If they are predictable, you are in luck; if unpredictable, you'll have to be careful about entering the market so you don't wind up having exposure that you can't monitor properly. We'll discuss ways to deal with this problem in Chapter 12: "Stop-Loss Orders and Risk Control."

Time also is required to *study* the markets. You can't just sit down and look at a screen and place an order, you must devote some time to preparation. If you don't have that time, postpone your trading until you do.

A third aspect of time is patience. We all want to be wealthy yesterday, but I have some really bad news for you: If that's what you want to do, trading commodities is not the answer. Do not expect to "make a killing in the market." You could be that lucky, but I emphasize the word "lucky." What we are defining here is the opposite of luck, namely skill and hard work. Be prepared for a long haul of steady small profits, each of which in turn will require patience to achieve. You must give the market time to get from point A to point B. That takes time ... *and* your patience!

Distractions

Distractions are abundant, but you must be able to exert a modest control over them. If you trade at home, you'll have days when dogs, kids, spouses, phones, and the doorbell all will be vying for your attention. You'll need to develop a work atmosphere, where you are not only awake and alert, prepared and ready, but also undisturbed, and confident that this environment will be maintained and under your control for as long as needed.

These four factors are merely common sense, you say. Yes, that's basically what they are, and that's why I claim this is a common-sense approach. But do not underestimate the importance of paying attention to these four bases of successful trading! Neglect them and you will handicap all your efforts to trade.

Now let's get down to business.

2

Choosing the Market

With the basics in mind, you're now ready for the next step: choosing the market in which to trade.

Imagine you're a young surfer ready to tackle that first wave. You've prepared yourself by acquiring the latest model surfboard; you've waxed it down well; you've put on your wet suit to keep warm. You had the good sense to wait till you were over the flu and are feeling strong; you've chosen a day when you don't have to worry about work or school, and you are determined not to be distracted by other people or scenic beauty … at least not until later!

You have carefully chosen the day and the beach where the waves should be better than at any other beach for miles around. You paddle out past the surf and look around. There are lots of waves. Some look good, others better. Which should you take?

Oops, you missed a good one—well, just wait, another good one will soon come along. Perhaps it will be even better! You finally see one that looks promising—you should have gotten a sense for which ones will last the longest. You take it … you're on!

You glide smoothly down the water, but soon your board gets wobbly. Is the wave beginning to collapse? Should you continue riding or get off? You turn off and watch as the wave crashes into itself in a mass of white foam. That was a nice ride! How did you do that?

That example may be overly dramatic, but the markets *are* like the ocean: beautiful and treacherous at the same time! You can't fight them; you must always be friends with them. You always must go in their direction—*always* go with them. Does this mean that you cannot trade counter trends or reactions? No, you can trade all kinds of waves, and you can squeeze out profits, but what I am describing here is a better way to profits with less risk to your capital.

Your first task is choosing which of the more than 30 commodities you want to trade. Your goal is very simple: finding the market that will give you the most bang for your buck. Look at the daily price charts. (I assume you already have certain basic tools of the trade at hand, such as price charts—either as weekly sets from one of several sources, or from your computer and data vendor—with appropriate software for graphic display and technical analysis by various indicators, either on the price charts or from the software.) Use a 100-point move as your yardstick. Some commodities move 20–30 points between the cycle highs and lows. Some move more than this; some less.

1. Check off the commodities that are in the 50–100 point range or better.
2. Next, look at the dollar value of each point. If each point is worth only 15 cents, a 100-point move is worth only $15. Try finding two or three commodities that yield at least $5 a point, so that a 100-point move will be worth at least $500 (Fig. 2-1).
3. Finally, check the margin requirements. If one requires $1,200 per contract and another $2,500 per contract, the first one obviously will give you more price action than the second if they move roughly the same number of points. For example, if you bought one contract requiring a $2,500 margin deposit, you could have bought two of the type requiring only $1,200 per contract. Each point would then be worth only $5 to you as opposed to $10 for the two less "expensive" contracts. But beware: Both profits *and losses* will be greater with two contracts. Going with the contract having lower margin requirement will allow you to use less of your capital as margin deposit, if you were to take only one such contract. But don't confuse that with taking less risk! If you are in the market, whether with one contract or 10, your entire account could be wiped out if not handled properly (see Chapter 12: "Stop-Loss Orders and Risk Control").

Now we can quite easily put together a type of volatility index—the kind that I find most useful:

$$\text{Volatility Index} = \frac{\text{Last 10 Daily Price Moves} \times \text{Cent Value of Point}}{\text{Dollars of Margin Deposit per Contract}}$$

Figure 2-1

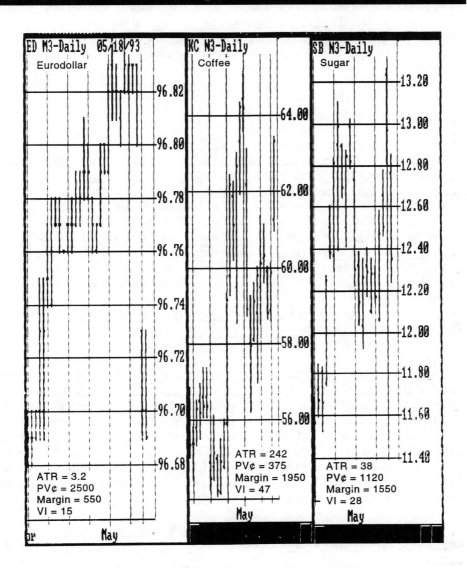

Rather than just picking one day's move, I like to look at the last 10 days (or bars) to get a more representative figure. Most computer programs now incorporate what is called the ATR, or "average true range" of the price bars. That is a 10-bar average of the high minus the low, taking gaps into account.

We can then take the ATR and the formula becomes:

$$\text{Volatility Index (VI)} = \frac{\text{ATR} \times \text{Point Value (cents)}}{\text{Margin (dollars)}}$$

and round off to a whole number.

Let's say you check your three leading contenders and find that the VIs are 15, 28, and 47. Always go for the top! Choose the 47, and you might also look at the 28, but discard anything below 20 (Fig. 2-1).

With time you will get to know the various markets like all your relatives. Some you will like, some you won't; but their characteristics will become second nature to you. After a little practice, you won't need to calculate the VIs, simple as they are; you'll know roughly what they'd be just by looking at the price charts. But, for a start, I've given you a simple formula for objectively choosing the one or two markets that will serve you best and make your efforts and risk taking most worthwhile.

Usually 8 or 10 markets have good volatility, but don't try to follow all of them closely, and definitely do not trade all of them at the same time. You would be spreading yourself too thin over too much territory. Leave that to the professionals.

That level of trading requires several well-trained assistants to help you keep track of things; two or three markets is plenty for us mortals to track by ourselves. It's nice that there are 8 to 10 markets to choose from, since that will give you a pleasant chance to choose a market that's compatible with your personality and interests. You might be more at ease with one of the foreign currencies than pork bellies, or perhaps it's the other way around if you have a background in livestock and know nothing about world finance. Go in the direction of your knowledge and fascination. You must be comfortable doing your work. Eventually you'll be at ease in all the markets, but for now get to know just a few closely.

Now let's take these ideas one step further. We've identified volatility as a desirable characteristic. Therefore, does it follow that greater volatility should be even better? You might ask, "Is too much of a good thing still good?" The answer is, "Yes, *if* you know what to do with it!"

We see this in crisis situations or perceived crisis situations. Take the currency crisis in the fall of 1992 for example. The European currencies had escalated to extreme heights not seen for many decades and appeared to be topping out. Once the decline began, the British pound dropped like a lead balloon, as much as 1,240 points in one day (Fig. 2-2).

In this kind of situation, the definition of a trader's heaven or hell becomes quite clear: It's determined by which side of the market he finds himself! Being short one contract alone, at $6.25 per point, would have returned a profit of $7,750! On the other hand, if you were long and did not sell quickly enough,

Figure 2-2

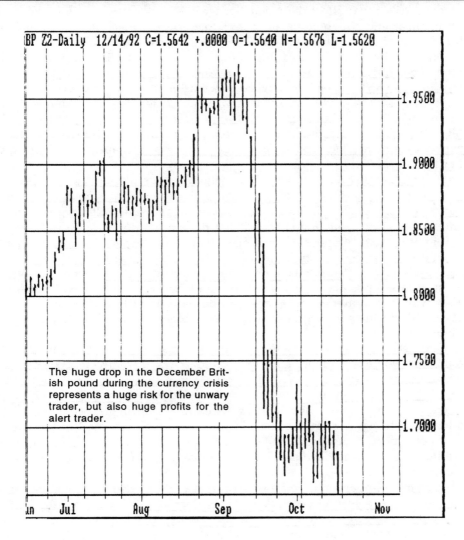

BP Z2-Daily 12/14/92 C=1.5642 +.0000 O=1.5640 H=1.5676 L=1.5620

The huge drop in the December British pound during the currency crisis represents a huge risk for the unwary trader, but also huge profits for the alert trader.

your loss would have been sizable. The point of all this is that you should be on the lookout for crises, whether they be fiscal crises that affect currencies, mine-worker strikes that affect the metals, or weather crises, such as hurricanes that affect sugar and cotton crops, or freezes that affect orange juice and coffee. All these provide great volatility.

On the other hand, here is where the often-belittled wisdom of the ages is vital. Frequently, but not all the time, prices will anticipate the effect of a crisis, if the crisis can be foreseen. Then, when the crisis finally hits, prices rebound, leaving the novice trader wondering why. (One old adage tells us: "Buy the rumor, sell the fact.") So don't always expect to be able to enter a market after a crisis hits. You must anticipate it, and position yourself ahead of time; then you can expect profits, *provided* you also get out in time (see Chapter 13: "Exiting the Market").

Having found several markets that qualify for your attention, keep close track of two or three, so that one of them will present you with a good opportunity before too long a wait. Since you must be patient and wait for the right chance to enter the market, your funds should not remain idle for long periods, as that would be a waste of opportunity to make them grow. When you are considering several markets, be sure that they are truly different markets and not related, such as T-bills and eurodollars, or soybeans and soymeal. You eventually may want to take a position in two markets, and when you do it's best to diversify. That way, if one market turns against you, you don't have to worry that the other will do the same because it was too closely related and affected by the same factors.

One last criterion for choosing a market is its magnitude. In many markets the total daily volume is a mere 1,000 to 2,000 contracts. If we divide 2,000 by a 400-minute trading day, the result is 5 contracts per minute. If you placed an order for 20 contracts, you might be waiting 5 or 10 minutes before you could get filled, and who knows what kind of price movement might occur during the attempt to fill your market order. (If you're not well schooled in the various types of orders, please study the glossary in the appendix now.) A limit order would give you some protection on the price, but you might never get filled completely.

Even more important is getting out of such a thin market. Just imagine having 20 contracts and seeing the market turn against you in a big way. By the time you enter your sell order, there are no buyers left. In a big market, there might be a few buyers around, but in a thin market, forget it! You could see several limit down moves before any buyers appeared. Your loss could be greater than your account (see Chapter 4: "Money Management"). Nevertheless, if there is a crisis looming, one or perhaps two contracts in a thin market could be very lucrative; just be wary of the low volume and get out in time—selling into strength and buying into weakness. (see Chapter 13: "Exiting the Market").

3

Choosing the Proper Timeframe

It may seem strange to you that some traders never learn which timeframe is best suited for them. But this decision has a lot to do with one's style of trading, and most traders never can settle down to a definite style. In other words, they cannot develop the consistency of style that is needed for success.

There are essentially three timeframes for trading; day-trading, short-term trading, and long-term or position trading. Day-trading means getting in and out of the market(s) on the same day, one or more times, or simply never holding a position overnight. Short-term trading means being in the market(s) anywhere from a few minutes to a few days, usually only 1–3 days, but possibly as long as 10–14 days. Long-term or position trading means holding a position in the market(s) for as long as several days to many months, usually several months.

Must you choose only one? If so, which one is best? Which one is for you? It is difficult enough to find a successful approach to the markets without trying to straddle several timeframes in the process. If you can be that versatile, great; but most people can't. Why not? It has to do with your framework of rules and guidelines for trading. Let us examine some pros and cons of each timeframe, and then see how the various rules either coincide or conflict with the reality of the markets.

To begin with, the two major camps are investors and traders. The two have quite opposite philosophies about how best to make their money grow. The investor likes to buy something and hold it for as long as possible. His grandfather probably told him to buy General Motors stock and hold on to it for as long as he could, and it would be worth more the longer he held it. There is something very wonderful about that concept, and it has worked well at certain times. If that's how you think, you're definitely an investor.

Then there are the others. That's us, fellas! We are the traders. We believe there's a lot more money to be made by going in and out of the markets many times and taking advantage of the many price swings up and down, whether they definitely head up or down or simply fluctuate inside a range. In fact, we frequently can make much more money much more quickly on a downswing than an upswing, something that the old "buy and hold" strategy would never see. It seems to take much more time to build something up than it does to rip it down; so it is in the markets. It may take three or four weeks for prices to ascend to a top, but only three or four days for them to tumble down to where they came from (Fig. 2-2). Hence much faster profits can be made when prices are plummeting.

In the commodity markets, it's easy to sell short, and investors can reap the benefit of that tactic. But, more often, they will buy and hold (or sell and hold) for the long haul, sometimes many months. For example, silver was priced at $3.45 an ounce not long ago. An investor might well say to himself: "This is the lowest price I've seen in years, and it has come up a little from the recent bottom. I'll buy 10 contracts now and sit on them for the next several years, if necessary. By then the price should be much higher, and then I'll sell. I don't have to worry about up- and downswings in between. I'll just keep enough money in my account to cover any possible downswings and prevent a margin call. A worry-free investment! He may be right, but then again, he may be wrong. A lot can happen in two, four, or six years. He may die. His needs may change. Who knows? But this investing style matches his philosophy and attitude. As traders, we look at things differently. We like to see the results of our efforts quickly. We also think we can outdo the typical investor by trading, or entering and exiting the market(s) many times over. So you see, an investor would definitely not be suited for getting in and out of the markets quickly. In and out on the same day? Many times a day? Definitely not! Let's look at a few more comparisons.

As a day trader you need never worry about events occurring after the markets close that will cause a direction reversal on next morning's opening. On the other hand, a strong trend that started one day may cause a large gap on the next opening, which will represent lost profits if you're no longer in the market.

As a day trader, your exposure to the market is much reduced. You will recall that we cannot control the market; it has a mind of its own. We can only try to join the prevailing forces and move along with them. Therefore, the less time your funds are exposed to this uncontrollable force—the whims of the market—the less risk of a loss. No matter how much you think you can anticipate the whims of the market, holding a position overnight definitely prolongs your exposure to unexpected changes in direction and possible loss. Holding a position overnight could actually set you up for a fall. In effect, you're saying: "I am right and will continue to be right." That could be a dangerous road to start on. It takes an increasing amount of discipline to get out of the market. The longer you stay, the harder it is to leave. As a day trader, you know that you should be out of the market by the close, hence you will be better focused on taking profits early, and you will be focused on "letting go" sometime during the day.

On the other hand, staying in the market overnight does make it easier to avoid the dangerous trap of "chasing the market" the next day in order to re-establish a position. You jumped off the train at the first station. It keeps on going. You drive to the next station to jump on again. Will you still make it? Under some circumstances yes, under others no. Deciding at such a time can be difficult, and you probably will make an emotional decision. You know what that means; you might as well flip a coin! You must learn to evaluate each day's action on its own merits if you are a day trader. When you can do this, you easily can avoid the trap of chasing the market.

As a day trader, you will by definition improve your entry timing, since you are planning to be in the profit zone within a few minutes, or at the most 30–60 minutes. A position trader is less concerned about optimal timing of entry during the trading day, as he expects to "ride the train" for a longer time. He may find that his entry was on the wrong side of a short swing or wave that could carry him into the loss zone during the next day or two. But he is prepared to ride out that swing through its bottom and *hope* it will retrace its move toward the eventual top. If this takes a long time (days, weeks, months?), he is prepared to sit patiently with a paper loss and wait. Day traders believe that this is a precarious position, since the environment of that market could suddenly change for the worse, and the position might never rise again.

Some say that long-term trading holds the key to huge profits, and that is quite true for those megamoves we see once in a while. A huge soybean bull market after a long drought, the several huge bull markets in sugar during the past decades, and gold going from $100 to more than $800 an ounce are several well-known examples. But try to find such runaway bull markets when you want them! There aren't very many around. To spot the next one, you'd have to watch all the markets closely, and if your funds are just waiting around for such moves, they surely will be idle much of the time. And what if you don't find one at all? Your time will have been wasted. If you want to be an active trader, don't bank on the big move; be prepared to ride it if you should find yourself aboard.[13,14]

Perhaps your temperament is best suited for long-term trading, taking one or two trades a month and staying in the markets one to two months at a time. Some markets may lend themselves to that, some won't. If you get aboard early, the long ride can be wonderful, but if you try to board at the midway station, be careful. You could be thrown from the train by a reaction to the major trend. Some markets may even change from a nicely trending market to a choppy market without a trend.

The time you have available to trade may be limited, perhaps preventing you from day-trading. This is probably the most common reason that beginning traders rarely are day traders.

In day-trading, things happen rapidly, and you need to be quick on the draw. You need to be able to make quick and correct decisions. This can make day-trading more difficult for some and impossible for others. On the other hand, you will see your results more quickly. That can be very gratifying when you're right and very humbling when you're not.

So you see, there are pros and cons to the various timeframes, and it's not easy to trade them all. Of course, you could say that you'll buy 10 contracts of silver and sit on them while you use the rest of your capital to trade as a day trader, and thus span both timeframes. But you know, I'll bet you five bucks that you'll sell your profitable 10 contracts of silver at the first top where you have a nice profit. I *know* you will after reading this book! As you will see, the logic of my approach points to day-trading and an occasional short-term trade as the most profitable and least risky style of trading. With today's excellent real-time data and the software to display it graphically, it's become possible and often easy to make a good entry and exit. I like to keep the risk of exposure to a minimum, and I like to know where I stand by closing time. After that, I don't have a worry in the world! I can start the next day fresh and sound. I don't have to worry about how great my loss might be at the opening and whether prices will be able to get me back out of the loss zone during the day.

At times a powerful trend looks like it will carry over well into the next day, and I could be persuaded by several factors (see Chapter 6: "Monitoring the Market") to hold on for the ride. If so, I probably will exit the market at the first sign of a reaction or pullback, sometimes as early as right on the opening (see Chapter 21: "Putting It All Together"). On such days, I not only can start fresh, but with a profit already in the bag!

In summary, although my approach works in all timeframes, I personally use day-trading with only occasional short-term trades.

4

Money Management

Years ago not much was written about money management. People knew it was important, but most just assumed that traders understood all about it. Apparently, that wasn't the case, for suddenly many articles and books appeared that treated the subject from all angles. Even gambling management ideas were presented. Of course, if you don't know how to trade successfully, you are in fact gambling, and you probably should use some form of gambling system!

According to such systems, you should risk only a small percentage of your capital, such as 5 percent or less, on each trade. Even if you lost every time, you wouldn't be wiped out unless you had more than 19 losses in a row. There are some fallacies in that argument, as you might need more than 5 percent of your capital to trade a particular contract, and you could also loose more than 5 percent of your capital on such a trade. However, I'm not going to discuss those concepts, since I am presuming that you will become a successful trader after reading this book. Then you won't be gambling, and you won't need to follow gambling rules.

A concept that is rarely well clarified is that the margin you post for entering a market is a *deposit* and does not in any way represent the money at risk. Your *entire account* is at risk the second you enter a market, whether long or short, with 1 contract or 10! You could post a small margin, perhaps $400, on a live hog contract, yet a sudden series of limit moves could present you with a loss of $1,200 or more, or three times your margin deposit! Hence, it is the **dollar value of the potential move** that represents the real amount of dollars at risk. This is intimately connected with the behavior of that particular market and prevailing circumstances. Certain markets are prone to sudden violent moves when a shortage or abundance of the commodity is perceived, and those moves can place the unwary trader on the wrong side of the market very quickly.

Markets such as livestock, orange juice, lumber, metals, and some grains can exhibit sudden limit moves (Figs. 4-1 and 4-2). The financials and currencies are less prone to limit moves, since the daily limits are either non-existent or very large. ("Back months," or later delivery months, may have lower limits than front months.) To develop an exact formula for the actual dollar risk to your account would involve very complex concepts and calculations, and would still remain rather theoretical. However, a reasonable assessment of risk (R) can be done by taking the size of the last intermediate move (H-L) on the daily chart and multiplying that by the dollar value of each point (P) and the number of contracts either planned to take or already held (C). Thus:

$$R = (H-L) \times P \times C$$

The value of R will shock you! (See Figs. 2-2 and 4-1)

But then, the truth has a way of doing that. Better be shocked before you start than too late, when you look at the shambles of what once was your account. Fortunately, the practical risk to your account is always less than such theoretical risk, because traders with any sense at all usually will be out of the market well before the theoretical limit is reached.

You probably have heard that you should never commit more than 65 percent of your capital to the market at any time, preferably less; and never more than 35 percent to any particular market, and preferably less. Some conservative traders have advised figures even lower than these. The idea behind those figures is to limit the number of contracts purchased, and thus limit the dollar value of a losing move. Again, I must point out two major fallacies with that concept.

1.   Even though you purchased only one contract with a $3,000 margin for a $10,000 account, a rapid move during only a 10-minute rally could easily hand you a $600 to $800 loss, and a larger rally would mean a greater loss. Dollar loss is related to more than just the margin posted.

2.   Some grain and livestock contracts have low enough margin requirements to permit you to purchase six or eight contracts without exceeding the 35-percent limit; yet a sudden move against you could wipe out the entire account. Hence, the protection given by the 35-percent limit is purely illusory! Not only that, but you actually could experience a debit balance on your account if the losses mounted higher than your equity

Figure 4-1

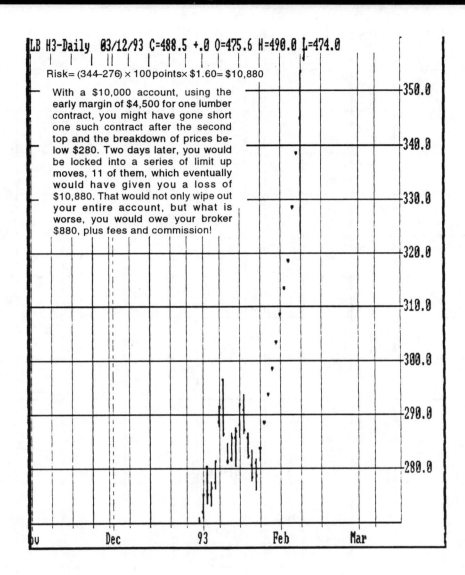

LB H3-Daily 03/12/93 C=488.5 +.0 O=475.6 H=490.0 L=474.0

Risk= (344–276) × 100 points × $1.60 = $10,880

With a $10,000 account, using the early margin of $4,500 for one lumber contract, you might have gone short one such contract after the second top and the breakdown of prices below $280. Two days later, you would be locked into a series of limit up moves, 11 of them, which eventually would have given you a loss of $10,880. That would not only wipe out your entire account, but what is worse, you would owe your broker $880, plus fees and commission!

350.0

340.0

330.0

320.0

310.0

300.0

290.0

280.0

Nov   Dec   93   Feb   Mar

Figure 4-2

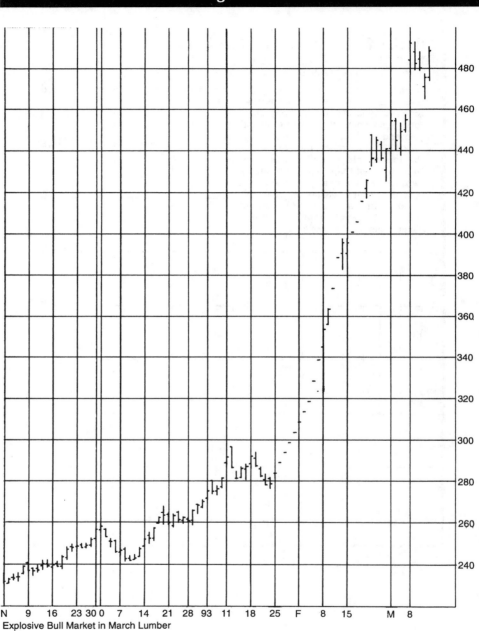

Explosive Bull Market in March Lumber

balance. Not only could you lose your entire account, but you could wind up owing your broker money!

The more contracts you hold, the greater your loss if the market moves against you. Any limitation you apply to the percent of your capital committed to a given trade will help limit such losses. But such a strategy is *not enough* to limit losses properly. In fact, such a capital limitation is not needed for day-trading if the rules are followed (see Chapter 12: "Stop-Loss Orders and Risk Control"). One disadvantage of such arbitrary limitations is that both profits and losses are affected equally.

Sometimes the worth of an idea is seen best by carrying the notion to its extreme. For example, if you wonder whether stealing just one little apple might be okay, just carry that thought to its extreme: Is it right to steal the whole apple cart? The answer obviously is no. If you carry the degree of perceived protection to its most conservative extreme, you have 0 percent capital commitment. What happens? No trading; no losses. Great! But, no trading; no profits either. Not so great! You affect profits and losses equally. We seek a method that limits only losses, not profits.

In summary, you must consider four important concepts as part of money management:

1. Successful trading is not gambling, and money management rules for gamblers should not be applied.
2. A 35 percent/65 percent limitation on capital commitment to trading will provide only an *illusion* of protection against losses. You can achieve some limitation, but your profits will be equally limited.
3. The amount of capital placed at risk when entering the market is the **entire account,** regardless of the number of contracts held or margin posted. For many, the above formula is an eye-opener!
4. Be aware of specific markets that are prone to sudden violent behavior, as well as what conditions create the potential for such violent moves.

5

Classic Chart Patterns

When prices are plotted in various timeframes as bar charts, we can see many different patterns. These patterns are the mainstay of technical analysis, and a thorough knowledge of their shapes and implications for subsequent price behavior is essential for all traders.

Basically, there are five different types of patterns:

1. Up or down trends: Prices on the move, either up or down.
2. Tops and bottoms: Prices reversing their trends.
3. Consolidation patterns: Prices "resting" between moves.
4. Trading ranges or basing patterns: Prices fluctuating around perceived fair values.
5. Gaps: Prices "leaping away from the pack" at various price levels.

Recognizing these patterns is critical to a accurate analysis of price behavior. They can be seen in every market and period. On the next few pages, I'll show you sample chart patterns and give brief descriptions of each. However, a complete discussion of the price behaviors associated with these patterns would take up many chapters, so I'll cover that in a subsequent book.

1. Up or Down Trends

Prices that move more or less steadily up or down are said to be "trending." Straight lines, called *trendlines,* can be drawn across the tops or bottoms of the small cycles, literally underscoring the direction of the price movement. Frequently a "channel" can be constructed, and the tops and bottoms of the cycles touch the upper and lower confines of the channel (Figs. 5-1a and 5-1b). Special trendlines considered important by the famous trader W. D. Gann are the *1x1 line* (or 45 degree line), indicating an orderly market; the *1x2 line,* where the horizontal distance is twice that of the vertical, indicating a slow market; and the *2x1 line,* where the vertical distance is twice that of the horizontal, indicating an explosive market. Many markets seem to conform to those lines for long periods.

2. Tops and Bottoms

When a trend has been exhausted, and prices turn, a top or bottom is formed. Some markets form the same kind of tops or bottoms repeatedly. Tops are usually more volatile than bottoms, as there seems to be more interest in trading markets that show rising prices (Figs. 5-1c through 5-1h).

3. Consolidation Patterns

When prices have moved up or down for some time, the driving force begins to weaken, and the prices may enter a period during which a lot of trading occurs, but with no significant advance or decline. But, sooner or later, the original driving force is revived, and prices continue on their way again, usually in the same direction as before they entered the "resting" period. Such periods are known as "consolidation" periods. They act like compressing a spring and making it ready to expand again. The distance covered by prices immediately prior to entering the consolidation period is frequently repeated when they exit that period. This gives a rough estimate of the target zone that prices may head for (Figs. 5-2a through 5-2i and Figs. 5-4 through 5-6).

4. Trading Ranges

Sometimes prices will not resume their trend after a brief pause or consolidation. They might seem to "get stuck" in a *trading range,* meaning they will rise and fall within a relatively narrow range. At times such a range can be wide enough that profits can be made from buying at the bottom and selling at the top. The bottom of the trading range is called an *area of support,* while the top is an *area of resistance.* Prices seem to have difficulty breaking through resistance and may require several attempts at it before they succeed. Likewise, prices seem to find support from further falls after reaching a support level. Such areas or levels of support and resistance are levels where significant trading has taken place before, and prices are likely to pause there as if to "wrap up unfinished business." Price

Figures 5-1a-f

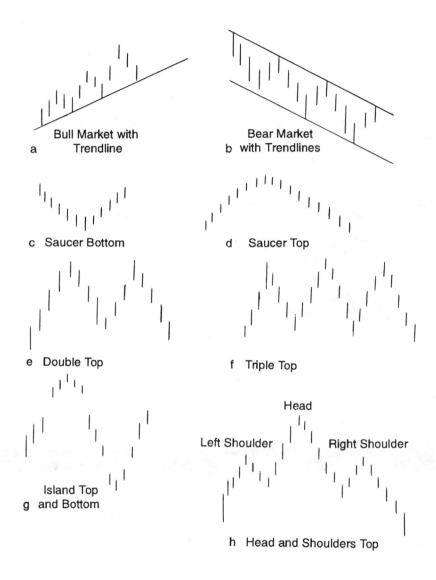

a   Bull Market with Trendline

b   Bear Market with Trendlines

c   Saucer Bottom

d   Saucer Top

e   Double Top

f   Triple Top

g   Island Top and Bottom

Head

Left Shoulder   Right Shoulder

h   Head and Shoulders Top

Figures 5-2a-k

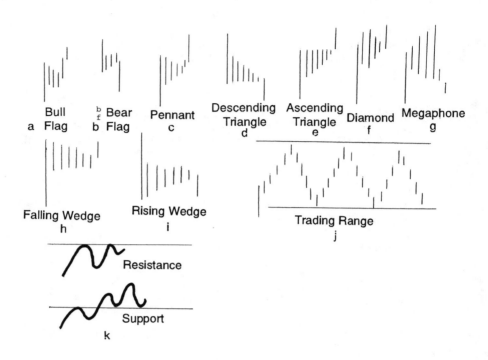

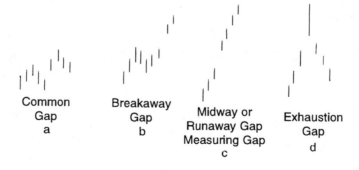

Figures 5-3a-d

Figure 5-4

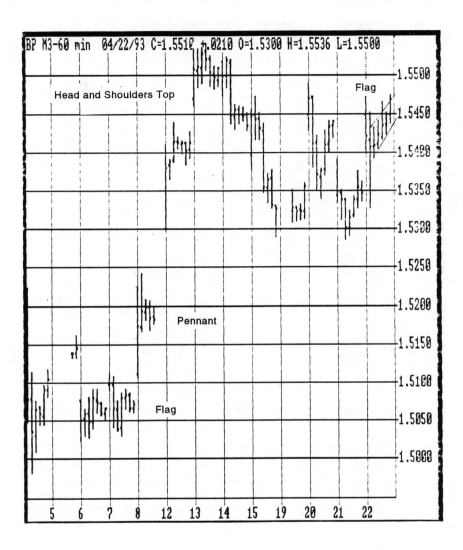

Figure 5-5

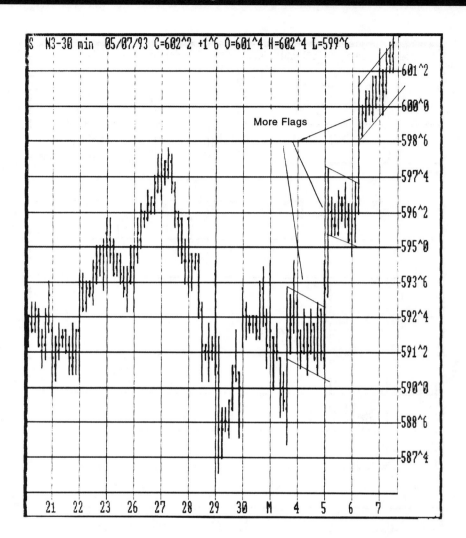

Figure 5-6

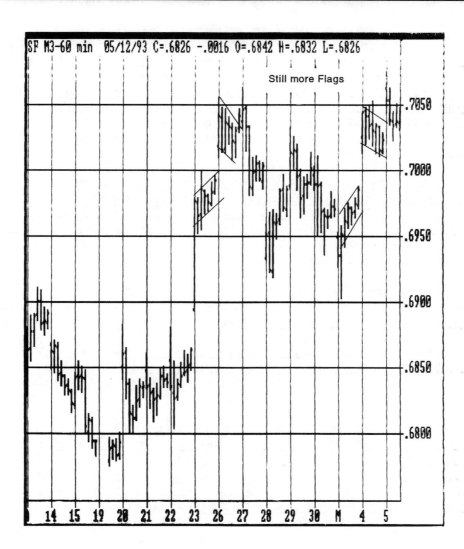

SF M3-60 min   05/12/93 C=.6826 -.0016 O=.6842 H=.6832 L=.6826

movement may be stopped there or even turned around. Previous tops and bottoms can become levels of both support and resistance. (Figs. 5-2j and 5-2k).

5. Gaps

Gaps represent an explosion of buying or selling pressure, during which prices are raised or lowered frantically in an effort to secure a second party for a transaction. Such excessive force may be very temporary, but it also could be an indication of a sudden new perception of what constitutes fair value for the commodity. There are essentially four different types of gaps, all of which are useful reflections of market sentiment with different but important implications for price movement.

Common Gap (Fig. 5-3a) A common gap occurs during orderly trading and represents just a momentary absence of matching numbers of buyers and sellers, which soon will be rectified. These gaps usually get filled in the subsequent course of trading. They have no real significance, but you need to recognize them for what they are, and not confuse them with other kinds of gaps that *do* have important implications.

Breakaway Gap (Fig. 5-3b) A breakaway gap occurs when prices come out of a consolidation period with a great deal of force in an explosive manner, which indicates that a strong movement may be getting under way.

Runaway Gap (Fig. 5-3c) A runaway gap (midway or measuring gap) occurs usually midway, or halfway, along a strong price movement. It signals that there is still a lot of "oomph" left in the move, and prices usually will move about as far after a runaway gap as they did before it.

Exhaustion Gap (Fig. 5-3d) An exhaustion gap occurs at the end of a long, frequently steep, price move. It represents the end of a speculator frenzy that has pushed prices to their limit. Here the experienced trader will liquidate his position into the hands of the novice speculator. Such gaps are accompanied by large increases in volume and are invariably followed by a turnaround in prices; they are most frequently seen at tops, but also can been seen at bottoms.

6

Monitoring the Market

No matter how inexperienced you are, I hope you know that any time you take a position in the market, you **must** keep it under close surveillance. Also, no one should take a position in any market without having studied and tracked that market for some time. In other words, before you can take a position in a market, you must have tracked that market and know what it is doing.

I promise this will be the last chapter on preparation, but just as a successful real estate purchase depends on only three things: location, location, location; successful trading in any market depends mainly on three things: preparation, preparation, preparation. So let's now add the final touch to your preparation: monitoring.

For day-trading and short-term trading it is essential to have real-time tick-by-tick data displayed on a computer screen. Real-time data vendors include Bonneville, Future Source, CQG, and Signal. Some provide analytical software to accompany their data, others leave that choice up to you. For use with Signal data, Omega Research, Inc., of Miami, has come up with several valuable programs. "System Writer" is one, and the company's latest, "TradeStation," has the unique and fascinating capability of allowing the trader to write his own formula and logic statements into the program. You can tell the program to analyze both present and past tick-by-tick data, as well as display the analyses in many different ways, all in real time.

Of course, the price action display is the essence of any monitoring. This is best represented by price ranges over fixed intervals, such as 1, 3, 5, 10, 15, 30, or 60 minutes; as well as daily, weekly, and monthly, each represented by a single bar on the screen. These bars, connecting the high and low of the day, should have opening and closing points displayed; they should all be updated tick by tick. That is exactly what we wish to see and follow. Where is the price *now*, and where has it been? From that display, we can speculate about where the price is headed. But remember, the predictions can only be speculation and can never become a certainty, whether based on price patterns, or anything else. We cannot ever be certain of the future, not even where a price will be 5, 10, or 15 minutes from now. We *can*, however, make our speculation more accurate than mere guesswork, or the flip of a coin, by using *two* observations of the market.

One is correlating the direction of subsequent price movement with the recurring price patterns we discussed in the previous chapter. Each pattern is composed of *many* price bars, and each pattern has its own statistically reproducible frequency of accuracy as an indicator of where prices are headed[15-18]—anywhere from 30–65 percent.

The *second* observation is an analysis of trader sentiment or psychology. There's that word again! We can make reliable correlations between certain displays of price behavior manifested by the pattern of each *individual* price bar. Two examples are when the cycle of buying pressure begins to loose its force as prices round a top, and selling pressure shows up as lower closing prices (Fig. 6-2); and when the prices spike up and fall back down as a failed attempt at advancement (Fig. 6-1). These are illustrations of sentiment as displayed by the configuration of the *individual* price bars.[19, 20]

We merely need to turn the price-bar display around 180 degrees to read the sentiment that has given rise to the action.

Japanese candlestick charting[21] is a good example of how these price actions have been given rather dramatic names to emphasize the underlying sentiment. The "Evening Star," "Hanging Man," "Hammer," and so on, all are meaningful and insightful names given to simple configurations of price bars, with the opening and closing points playing a key role (Fig. 6-3).

By combining these two observations (chart patterns and individual price bar configurations), we can speculate with a reasonable degree of accuracy about where prices are headed. However, in the commodity markets sentiment can change and change back very quickly, so these observations by themselves are not sufficient to trade with the degree of certainty I require. However, they are *very* important.

Since nothing ever is perfect, and since our market predictions are going to be dead wrong a number of times, our efforts at finding the best possible trading tool must be directed at analyzing those failures—our wrong predictions. The simple question: "What made them wrong?" will generate many hypotheses, and they will be the starting points for our market research, which is designed to find the answers and thus perfect our tools. We hope to find ways to confirm

Figure 6-1

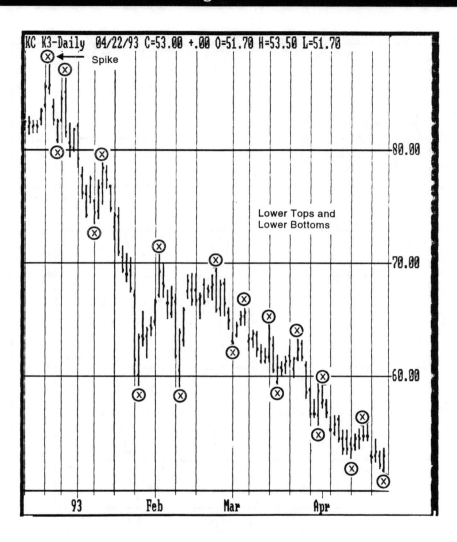

Figure 6-2

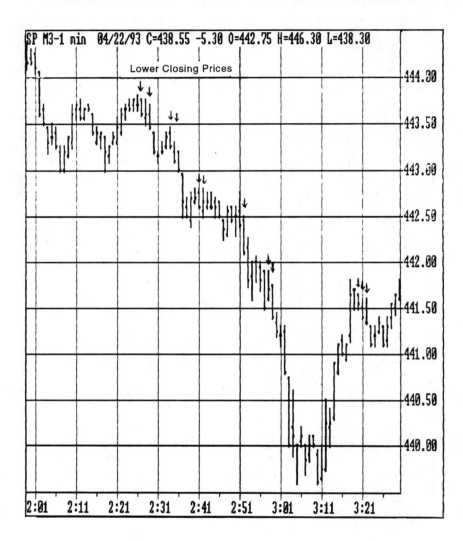

Figure 6-3

SP M3-1 min 04/22/93 C=438.55 -5.30 O=442.75 H=446.30 L=438.30

whether our proud predictions will be right or wrong. Of course, we can get that confirmation from subsequent price actions, or hindsight, but that's frequently too late, as some profits inevitably will have been lost by then.

We'd like confirmation by one or more additional tools, so we can enter the market as early as possible. At first it seems like a rather simple task: We only need to know whether prices will go up or down. It's that simple! They're going to go one way or the other. (Yes, they *could* go sideways for a while, but then we can either exit the market and evaluate again, or just stay in and evaluate again.)

We have at our disposal about 140 technical indicators! If we lined them all up and synchronized them all with the price action, would they not give us a splendid confirmation of price direction? You know as well as I do that they wouldn't; some would point up, some would point down, and some would refuse to point anywhere! Just as no one trading system has it all, likewise neither does any technical indicator. What is a poor trader to do?

"Oh, I can just stick my toe in the water and pull it out quickly if it's too hot!" I'm sure you've heard that one before! Do you still test the stove by touching the hot coil with your finger? As a little kid, you learned to pull your finger away very quickly if the coil was hot. That's a good reflex to have, and you'll need to have it when you are in the market and it gets "too hot." When the market turns against you, you must get out very quickly. However, the "toe or finger test" does not make a comfortable entry tool, even though many traders will say: "Yeah, we'll buy just one contract, and if it goes south, we'll just get out in a hurry!" It's another way of saying the same thing, and what does it sound like to you? Sounds like gambling doesn't it? That's *not* what we're here to do.

By now you may be saying to yourself that you have used several popular indicators, have gotten into the market nicely, and have done quite well for yourself. Yes, I know you may have, and that's fine. But I also know you've been handed losses by these same indicators, because they are *lagging indicators*. That is, they lag *behind* prices. They're determined *by* prices, not vice versa. You will sometimes see a nicely rising indicator following the price action, only to see the indicator suddenly turn back down because **prices** turned back down first! How can you rely on that? The truth is that, although each indicator has its own characteristics and rules of application, **no** lagging indicator has the degree of reliability that I require ... not even several taken together.

PART 2

TECHNICAL INDICATORS

In previous chapters we've discussed general concepts of preparation and monitoring. In this section we shall take a closer look at the tools called technical indicators. We'll look in greater detail at the importance of the net result of buying and selling on price action and develop that analysis into two types of useful indicators of where prices are headed. The first type is based on the change in the net difference between buying and selling, accessible to us in real time by tick data. The second type is based on identifying the earliest possible change in the trend of prices themselves.

I'll assume that you're familiar with at least some of the technical indicators known and available today. If you're just now entering the world of futures trading, you **must** study some of the books available on technical indicators.[15, 29, 34] I won't attempt to describe all 140 or more indicators, but will confine my discussion to those I use in my own trading.

As I've said, my primary focus will be on the development of two new types of real-time indicators of the type known as *leading* rather than *lagging*. The latter, used by nearly all traders, are not only based on prices themselves, usually closing prices for simplicity, but are so constructed that they cannot divorce themselves from those closing prices. As a result, those indicators turn up or down *after,* or *lag behind,* prices have made their turn; hence their classification as lagging indicators.

No one can forecast future prices from lagging indicators, but they can be of great help in defining, in a very general fashion, where prices find themselves at any one moment in the cycle of buying and selling. The study of cycles in the markets is a fascinating one and was responsible for my own entry into the markets in the very early 70s after reading the now-famous treatise on the subject by Hurst.[22] Basically, it is possible to detect a cyclical pattern in most markets (Fig. II-I), and that of course reflects the alternating waves of buying and selling.

Moving averages are excellent tools to define cycles in the markets (Fig. II-I), but lagging indicators can serve not only as cycle detectors, but also to highlight other aspects of price action (Fig. II-I). Complex analyses such as Fournier analysis represent the summit of scientific accuracy in that regard, but are seldom used by the ordinary trader. However, the ability of lagging indicators to define pertinent cycle tops and bottoms is an extremely important contribution, as we shall soon see. They all do this to a greater or lesser degree, but naturally some do it better than others. One called the Stochastic indicator does this very well. It is also quite a versatile indicator. For these reasons we'll use it as a reference indicator and also to do various other tasks for us. It will be discussed in detail in the next chapter.

Whatever they can do, the purpose of indicators is to point the way to the direction of price movement, both in the immediate and distant future. Obviously the perfect indicator has not yet been found, but we will attempt to close in on it in the coming chapters.

Figure II-1

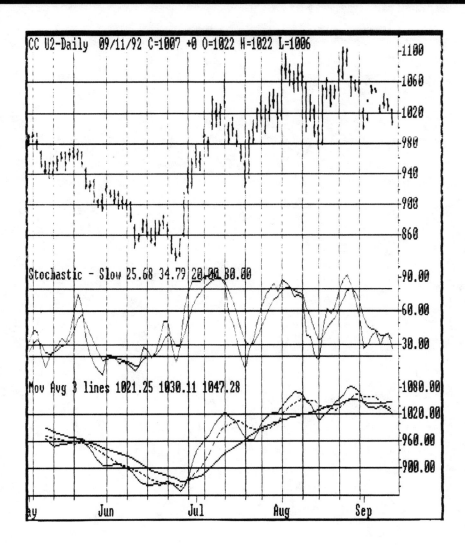

7

Classic Indicators

The indicators used today can be divided into two main groups: *mathematical functions*, limited in type and complexity only by the imagination; and *oscillators* that may or may not have preset limits or boundaries. The technical tools I use and recommend are limited to a few of each kind: such mathematical functions as *moving averages, summations*, and other *simple relationships*; and such oscillators as *momentum, Stochastics, relative strength index (RSI)*, and *average directional movement index (ADX)*. Volume and open interest are *data items* and do not constitute indicators; they will be discussed when needed in subsequent chapters.

Mathematical Functions

Moving averages The simplest indicator of all to construct, even without a computer, is a moving average. An average is just that, two or more prices (usually closing, but they could be opening, high, low, or median) added together and divided by the number of prices used. As a new day finishes, the value for that day is added and the value of the first day used is subtracted before division; this provides the movement to the average, as it moves along with the days (or bars on a graph). Any number of days or bars can be averaged, but the most popular are 4, 9, 18, 20, and 40. When prices go and stay above their average, it is considered bullish, when they move below their average, it is bearish.

Three useful variations are quite popular. *First,* two or more averages can be used on the same screen; for example, a 4- and 9-bar moving average would show two curves. When the curve for the shorter average crosses the one for the longer average, a signal is generated. Prices crossing these curves provide confirmation of those signals. *Second,* the averages can be fine-tuned to reflect more of the most current price action by "weighting" them, or simply giving more emphasis to more recent prices, either in a linear fashion (*weighted moving average*) or exponentially (*exponential moving average*). The *third* variation is the *displaced moving average,* in which a moving average is plotted a specified number of bars earlier or later than the one it refers to. Thus, a 10 by 5 displaced moving average would refer to a 10-bar simple average that is plotted five bars forward (Fig. 7-1).

Moving averages show excellent correlation with price movement, and every single change in direction will be recognized. However, there is one **big** catch; it's usually **too late!** They look great in hindsight, but they are slow to give signals. In other words, by the time the moving average has signaled a change in direction, a price move already is well on its way, and significant profits will have been lost. Nevertheless, moving averages are very useful in providing proper perspective to prices, and they are extremely useful both in defining cycles as well as smoothing all sorts of curves.

Summations A frequently-used mathematical function is the sum or *summation* of successive values. Instead of plotting each individual value each bar, the current value is added to the previous, with proper respect to sign, whether positive or negative. In itself this will serve to smoothen an otherwise jagged curve. A moving average can be taken of the resultant curve to smooth it further, a technique we shall use extensively in coming chapters (Fig. 7-2).

Simple functions Simple calculations such as median price, range, true range, average true range, and others are very simple to calculate and plot with each price bar. They all can be done by hand, but of course the computer makes it a breeze to do. We'll go into their construction on the computer in Part 5. *Median price* refers to the average of the high and low prices of a bar; a *range* refers to the difference between the high and the low prices of a bar; *true range* takes gaps into consideration; and *average true range* simply is an average of the true range of a specified number of bars, usually 10. Average true range is abbreviated ATR, and it's useful in gauging the volatility of a market and thereby assisting you in choosing a market for trading (Chapter 2), as well as placing stop-loss orders (Chapter 12).

Oscillators

Oscillators are slightly more complex mathematical relationships between prices; they compare the present price to one or more previous prices. Some

Figure 7-1

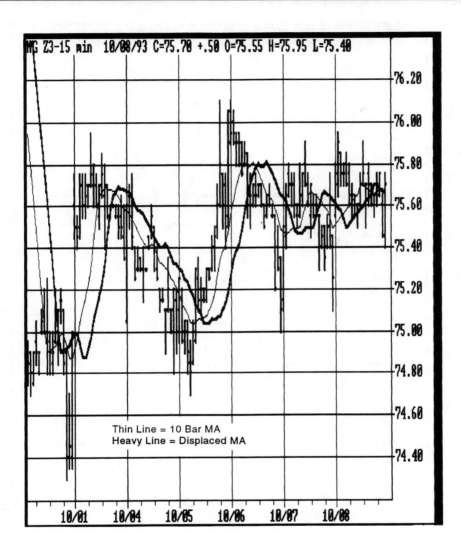

Thin Line = 10 Bar MA
Heavy Line = Displaced MA

Figure 7-2

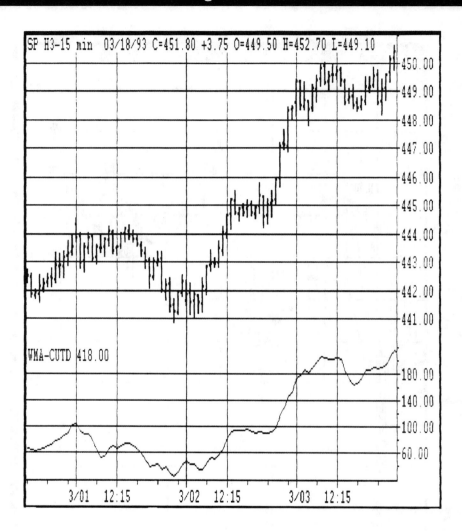

oscillators are so constructed that the resultant curves weave themselves under and over a midline (a zero line or reference line). Others employ upper and lower reference lines, set to highlight the curve's entrance into an *overbought zone* at the top or an *oversold zone* at the bottom. Midrange oscillators have no limits, but ones with upper and lower reference lines are designed to oscillate between 0 and 100. We'll briefly discuss four of the most widely used oscillators:

Momentum Momentum and rate-of-change indicators are very similar in that they both compare the closing (or other) value of the current price bar with the same value of a price bar a specified number of bars before. For example, today's closing price might be compared to the closing price 6 days ago (or 10 days ago, or 14, or any other number). Any mention of "rate" implies a division of numbers, such as miles per hour (miles ÷ hours), and the rate of change indicator compares prices by such division. Momentum does the comparison by subtraction or "differencing." The curves are almost identical, and we shall opt for the differencing and use momentum.

The most popular period is six bars, as that's fairly fast and gives good correlation with minor swings in prices. The desired period is usually set or adjusted to one-half the length of the cycle under study. The usual minor cycles might consist of 12 bars, and the 6-bar momentum would be chosen. A 60-bar momentum would not give much information about such a short cycle and should be applied only to much longer cycles.

If the current price is higher than the past price being compared, the difference is positive; if less, it's negative. As prices rise, the momentum curve will also rise, slow down, form a top, and descend as prices come to a peak. When the momentum crosses the zero line, prices will start down and acquire a negative momentum. Thus, momentum can serve as an early warning that a change in the course of prices is about to happen (Fig. 7-3). In the next chapter, we'll use momentum as a stepping stone to build a new indicator.

Stochastics The Stochastic indicator, developed by George Lane many years ago, is an overbought/oversold oscillator.[23] It is based on the premise that, as prices rise, the closing prices of the bars move closer to the top of the range and vice versa for falling prices. The formula determines where the closing price is in relation to the range of the period selected. Two lines are calculated and plotted as a percentage between 0 and 100. The first line is called %K, and the second, which is a 3-bar simple moving average of the first, is called %D. The formula is as follows:

$$\%K = 100(CL9)/(H9L9)$$

where C is the latest closing price, L9 the lowest low of the last 9 bars, and H9 the highest high of the same period.

Overbought readings are defined as above 80, and oversold as below 20, but all parameters can be changed according to your purposes. You could make the overbought/oversold areas 70/30 or 90/10 if you wish. Likewise the periods used can be varied. Signals are generated as the curves leave the overbought or oversold zones and when the fast %K crosses over the slower %D, preferably

Figure 7-3

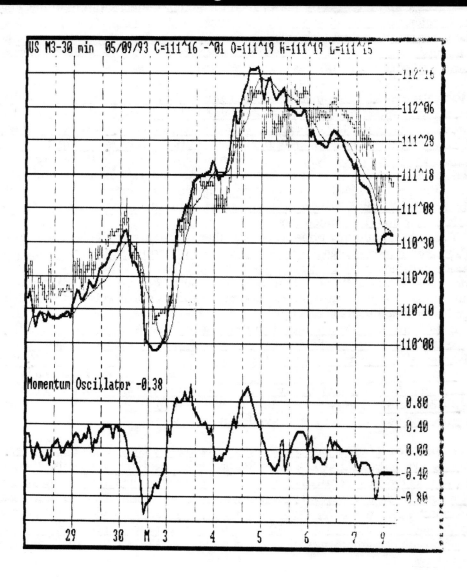

after the latter has peaked or bottomed (Fig. II-1). Divergence between prices and the %D line is a valuable signal that prices may soon follow the direction of the indicator.

We'll be discussing this application and others, but you also need to study some of the books available if you are not familiar with Stochastics. See *Technical Analysis of the Futures Market* by John J. Murphy; try page 304 for starters.[15]

As I mentioned, this indicator is most versatile because it can identify tops and bottoms of cycles and generate its own buy and sell signals. All these are based on the course of its two indicator lines: their locations; their behavior, such as the fast crossing over the slow; and their divergence from price direction. Many traders rely on this indicator alone or in combination with others and do quite well for themselves. My main criticism of this indicator is that it has limitations—but, then, what doesn't? Its main limitation is that it frequently will remain in the overbought or oversold zones for quite a while in a strongly trending market, thus being unable to compare the closing price and the selected range until prices turn around.

In our quest for a more secure approach to market entry, we must try to either eliminate or minimize its limitations, find a better independent indicator, or find one that will "fill in" where the Stochastic "leaves off." But, whatever we do, we shall always look to the Stochastic for what it *is* able to do, as long as we keep its limitations in mind. The Stochastic can be constructed for any time period you desire, but the most common choices are 5, 9, 14, and 21 periods. I prefer the 9-period timeframe, so keep in mind that we will be referring to a 9-bar slow Stochastic (Fig. II-1).

Relative Strength Index (RSI) The RSI also was developed many years ago, by Welles J. Wilder, Jr., and has since then been described in many places. His own description, in *New Concepts in Technical Trading Systems,*[29] is very worthwhile reading and I also recommend the descriptions found in *Technical Analysis of the Futures Markets*[15] and *Computer Analysis of the Futures Market.*[34] The way the RSI is commonly explained can be confusing, but if you refer to Wilder's book, page 65, it will become clear; he explains it all both clearly and thoroughly. The concept is that the ratio of net up-change to net down-change in prices over a selected interval will reflect the strength of the market. The greater the amount of gain to the upside as opposed to loss to the downside, the stronger the market, as reflected in a higher value of the RSI.

The RSI can easily be calculated by hand from a worksheet as shown by Wilder, but to have it on your computer is a blessing. The formula is:

$$RSI = 100 \ (100(1+RS))$$

where RS is the average of 14 days' closes-up divided by the average of 14 days' closes-down. The confusion comes in when you try to define "closes-up" and "closes-down." It does not mean the price of the commodity on an up day, it's only the **net** change. For example, if June gold closed at 356 yesterday and at 358 today, that would be a close-up and the net change would be **2**. There might then be several such up days, perhaps 4, during the past 14 days (or whatever period you have selected). Then the second point of confusion comes when you try to take the average. It is not the average of those four values, it is the sum of those four divided by 14—the number of days in your period! Since both halves of the equation are divided by the same number, no distortion of the relationship occurs. Now that all that has been clarified, you can go on and calculate the RSI without difficulty.

Most traders use the RSI as an overbought/oversold oscillator with the most popular settings at either 80/20 or 70/30 (Fig. 7-4). In addition, some traders feel that readings higher than 50 are indicative of a strong market and lower than 50 of a weak market. That's not always correct for commodities where swings can occur quite rapidly.

There are at least half a dozen good ways to use the RSI, which is why it's so popular.[34] However, a little-used concept actually has been more accurate than many of the others. I use the RSI as an oscillator around a reference line at 50, its midpoint. When the 6-bar RSI, a relatively fast time period, crosses the 50-line in a downward direction, it gives a sell signal; a buy signal is generated by crossing the 50-line in an upward direction (Fig. 7-5). Those signals are most reliable in all timeframes and in all markets; they could be used almost exclusively as your trading signals. This concept may be one of the best in this book!

Let's take a closer look at Figures 7-4 and 7-5. In Figure 7-4, you can see that a good buy signal was generated on 4/12, but no sell signal was seen around 4/15, nor any buy signal around 4/22. A sell signal did come on 4/28, but since no buy signal was seen on 4/29, the move up to 65 cents was missed! No sell signal was given at the top, thus causing great loss of profits if you were still long. However, if you watch the midpoint 50-line in Figure 7-5 and take the crossings of the RSI as signals, you will not miss any moves. There will be a few more trades generated, but the significant moves are caught, giving significantly more profits. The main buy signal on 4/22 was given by the crossing of the 50-line.

In all fairness, in Figure 7-4, although the crossing of the 20-line from the oversold zone did not occur, two other types of signals did. The first was the divergence between the falling lows of the prices and the rising lows of the RSI, always a very strong signal, and probably one of the best we have. The second was the "failed swing" sign, where a small peak is seen in the RSI, as it turns back down. When it turns up again and *passes* that previous, or "failed" peak, a buy signal is generated. The same sequence when inverted will generate a sell signal. These are also very strong signals. Figure 7-5 compares the standard RSI and its 80/20 reference lines with the RSI and the single reference line at 50. Perhaps using all possible signals of the RSI provides the best "coverage" of the markets, so that no turns or moves are missed.

Average Directional Movement Index (ADX) The ADX also was developed by Welles J. Wilder, Jr.,[29] and further studied by other traders, including LeBeau and Luca.[34] For a thorough discussion, see these two references. Briefly, the ADX is composed of two directional movement indices, one positive and one negative. The positive DMI measures the part of the true range, if any, that is higher each day; the negative DMI that part, if any, which is lower each day. The average of each then is taken over a selected period, originally 14 bars, but lately many use 18. Those two curves are then plotted on the same graph along with a third, the ADX, which is a composite of the two DMIs.

Figure 7-4

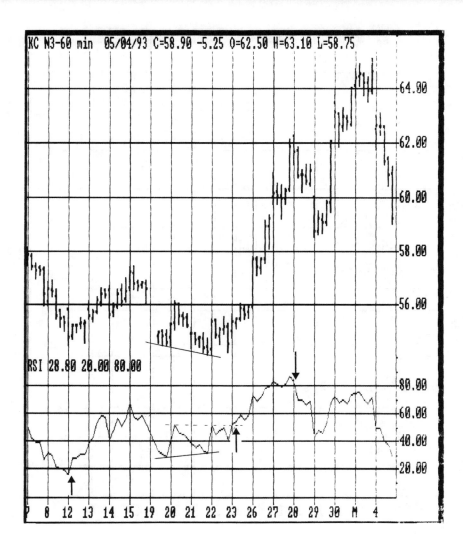

Figure 7-5

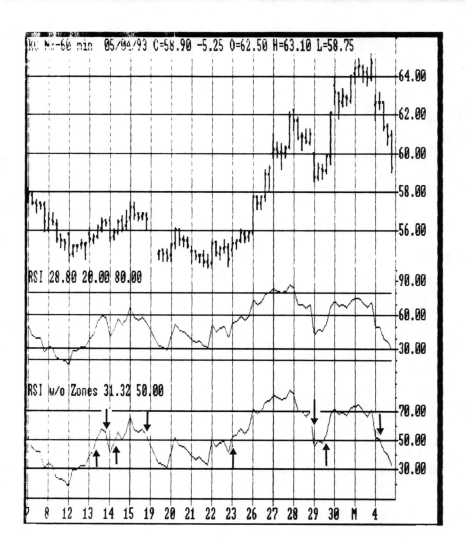

When the ADX is rising, the market is strengthening along its trend, whether up or down; when the ADX declines, the trend is changing either to the opposite direction or to a sideways market. If you have difficulty identifying a trend as opposed to a trading range, the ADX can be very valuable. The main weakness of the ADX is that it is slow to reveal its information. Figure 7-6 shows a rising ADX identifying the change in June treasury bonds from a sideways market to a strong downtrending market. When the ADX turns, or "hooks," it marks the end of the trend. When the value of the ADX exceeds 15, it is said to indicate that the market is trending, but some traders insist that a value above 25 is more reliable.

Figure 7-6

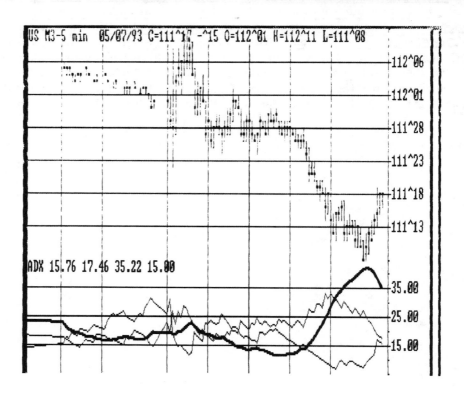

US M3-5 min 05/07/93 C=111^17 -^15 O=112^01 H=112^11 L=111^08

8

Market Sentiment Indicators

For prices to change, someone has to want that to happen. Prices can be bid up by a true supply-and-demand discrepancy, or they can be raised or lowered by floor traders in search of "fair value"—a level where trading can occur. The more trading that occurs (volume), the more floor traders earn. In either case, the sentiment of the participants (traders) determines what price level will generate "trade." Let's call that state of mind "market sentiment." Some studies have attempted to assess it by daily polling a large number of traders to determine whether they were bullish or bearish on certain commodities. When plotted, those results created an indicator that showed good correlation with price movements. The handicap with this method is that it's not available for most traders to do themselves, nor is it possible to do in real time. We'll attempt to approach market sentiment in real time, and in a manner that every trader can do on a minute-to-minute basis.

Let's try to correlate direction of price movement with both direction and magnitude of market sentiment. After all, traders' thinking steers the market, and that sentiment is reflected in price action. If only we could reverse that mirror and reveal the direction of the sentiment as well as its strength or magnitude. Can we really unmask the basic driving force behind the markets by analyzing the data available to us in real time today? We'll certainly give it a try!

Remember, we're trying to assess two things about traders' sentiment: direction and magnitude.

We can see the *direction* first and foremost from the individual price-bar patterns, combined with the chart patterns we discussed previously. Further confirmation is found by analyzing the trend of the net effect of buying vs. selling. This is available to us from the net up/down (U/D) tick figures. Thus, a decline in the net U/D tick figure indicates a trend from predominant buying toward less net buying and eventually more and more selling. Rising figures indicate more buying is taking place. We can get an even better idea of the changing sentiment by applying various technical studies to that primary curve of net up/down tick difference. Perhaps then we could get an early warning of a change in market sentiment—precisely what we've been searching for.

The second part of evaluating the traders' sentiment is measuring the magnitude. Although the sentiment of commodity traders can turn on a dime, the more widespread that sentiment, the longer it is likely to persist, and the longer it will take to fade or change direction. Obviously, if *all* the floor traders were in a selling mood, it would take quite a while before the majority were to change and become buyers, assuming no sudden fundamental news were to break and disrupt the trend. We could be more confident that the selling we were seeing would persist for a long period of time than if only a *slim majority* of the traders were sellers.

How can we assess magnitude of selling vs. buying? Let's go back and look at the display of the net up/down tick data. The reason we were able to see a change from one period to the next is that we can see a decrease or increase in the number of net up/down ticks. Thus, magnitude is already being shown in these figures; we only have to interpret them correctly. Again, if the net change is from 8 to 7, it is only a small change compared to, say, from 30 to 7. We could say that magnitude already is built in to the curve we're looking at. But, is it due to a small group of 50 traders doing the trading, or 5,000 of them? To answer that, we need the help of a second study. Ideally, we'd use *volume;* but since this data isn't available on a tick-by-tick basis, we'll use what is called *total ticks.* If we see a total tick figure in the high hundreds, does that mean that the direction of trader sentiment is going to remain for a while? How long? Will it be long enough for us to profit by it? To answer that, and to add the final touch to our magnitude assessment, we must do a third study.

We need to look at the price action and the previous studies in several other periods. Does that mean that we're going to be straddling several periods in our trading? No, we don't wish to trade in all those time periods, but we need to look at them to gain a better perspective.

Perspective is essential in any endeavor. A boy who sees a cute little bear cub in a forest clearing rushes in to play with it. However, if he had been 100 feet farther back, he would have noticed big Papa bear at the edge of the clearing, and, rather than rushing toward the cub, he would have run the other way! So it is in the markets. When you see a small group of traders making a cute little rally in the 5-minute bars, do you immediately rush in to join them? Or do you stand back and see on the 30- to 60-minute bars that dozens of big Papa bears are mounting a big sell-off, which would surely throw you for a loop a couple of 5-minute bars later? If you saw that, you obviously would wait, and that's using your sense of perspective.

For success in the markets, you *must* develop a sense of perspective. To do that, simply look at the 30- and 60-minute bars. Yes, weekly and monthly charts are also important, but much less so to the day trader than to the position trader.

Tick Difference Indicator (TDI)

Now let's get back to the market where new buying and selling is the prime determinant of where prices will go. If we take the net difference between buying and selling—all upticks minus all downticks—we get a curve that looks like Figure 8-1. You can see that it's very irregular and difficult to correlate with price action. If we apply momentum to this curve (Fig. 8-2), we get only a minimal smoothing effect, and contrary to our expectation, it doesn't correlate well with price action, either. However, if we first smooth the curve of Figure 8-1 by taking a moving average, we get an indicator that shows more promise (Fig. 8-3).

This curve represents a *3-bar weighted moving average of the up/down tick difference*. If we also construct a *6-bar weighted moving average* of the tick difference curve, we see that it correlates even better with price action (Fig. 8-4). We can see an even better correlation when we plot both averages together. The crossing of the fast line over the slow generates a signal and crossing over the 0 line serves to confirm that signal slightly later (Fig. 8-5). We'll call this indicator the TD-3, short for 3-bar weighted moving average of the up/down tick difference. The computer formula is:

TD-3 INDICATOR: WAVERAGE ((UPTICKS-DOWNTICKS),3);

That's what you'd write into your computer program, provided that it gives you access to tick-by-tick data and allows you to enter your own formulas. I use TradeStation by Omega Research, Inc. It's exceptionally user friendly in this regard, but other available software should be able to accommodate your formulas. If not, get in touch with the company's support people so they can do it for you. All the formulas in this book were written for TradeStation.

If we now compare the TD-3 indicator with the Stochastic (Fig. 8-6), we can make two very useful observations. First, the TD-3 gives a very good prediction of the direction of price movement in *real time* and *ahead* of any signal given by the Stochastic. However, only *some* of the signals given by the TD-3 are useful to our trading. We're not interested in going in and out of the market every other bar. We see too many buy and sell signals for our purpose, but we can filter out the very minor signals by taking only those that coincide with the Stochastic.

In other words, if prices are climbing up toward the top of a cycle of buying, we should not take any sell signals, as they represent only very minor swings. The same goes for prices falling in the downward part of the cycle: no buy signals should be taken. Figure 8-6 shows all the buy and sell signals generated by the TD-3, as it reflects buying and selling. These are all quite accurate reflections of what is happening, but since so far we have no measurement of magnitude,

Figure 8-1

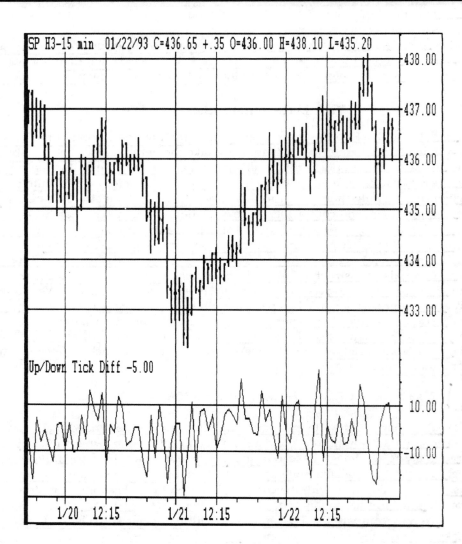

Figure 8-2

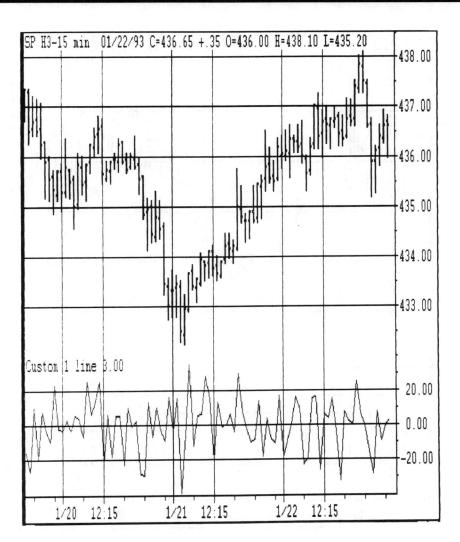

Figure 8-3

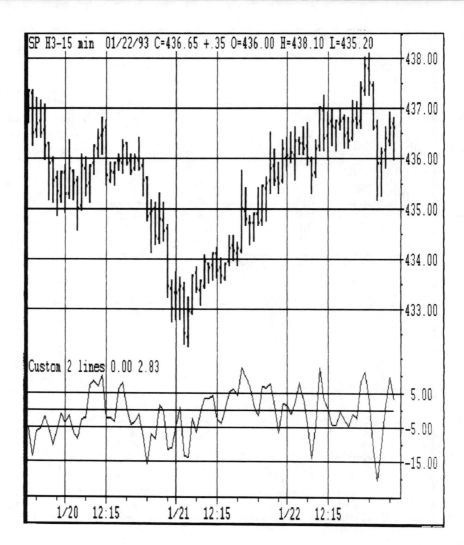

Figure 8-4

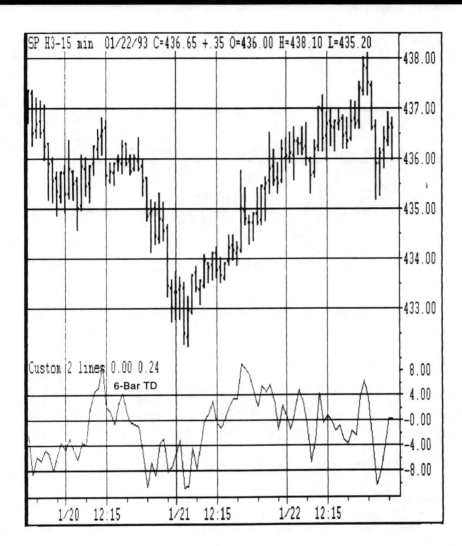

Figure 8-5

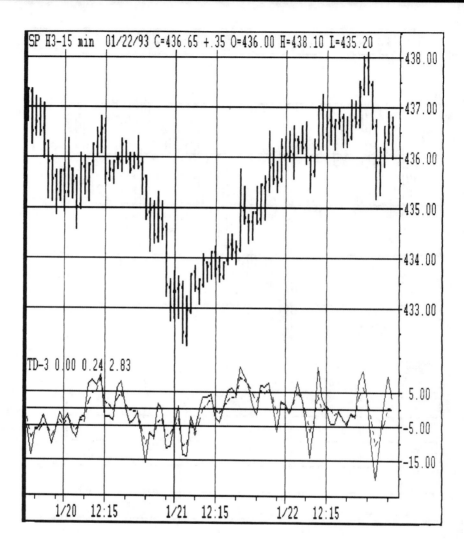

Figure 8-6

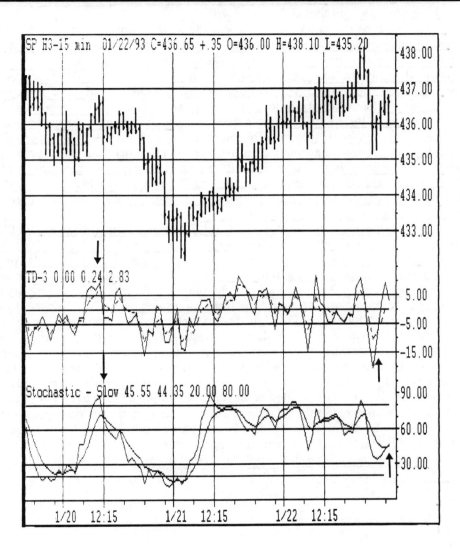

we cannot differentiate between minor and major swings, or useless and useful tops and bottoms. But remember, the Stochastic indicator is able to define the cycles quite well, and that ability now will assist us.

   If we combine the TD-3 and the Stochastic on the same plot or graph, we can immediately orient prices to the part of the cycle where they belong. That will give us the necessary perspective to take the proper signals and gives us the proper direction to take. Since we don't wish to sell on very minor swings, we won't follow such signals if prices are headed upward as indicated by a *rising* Stochastic. In fact, since the Stochastic indicator can remain in the overbought (or oversold) zone for a while (its main limitation), we should not consider any sell signal until the SlowK (actually the faster half of the indicator) has crossed the %D line **and** is crossing downward over the 80 reference line, since prices still can be rising until that time. In this fashion, we can see an excellent joint venture between these two indicators. By adding the TD-3, we can achieve an entry signal that many times will occur earlier than that given by the Stochastic. Figure 8-6 shows these two indicators in action.

   So, using logic, we've developed a fast leading real-time indicator, capable of producing buy and sell signals before the Stochastic indicator, but which does depend on a cycle-defining indicator such as the Stochastic to eliminate excessive and undesirable signals. Now let's try to carry our logic further and see if we can develop our TD-3 into a fully independent indicator. We simply need to distinguish the major turning points from the minor ones. Couldn't we do this by considering the magnitude of the trading taking place? Perhaps. One difficulty with that premise is that volume of trading represented by total ticks can either dry up near a top or a bottom, or it can explode as in a blow-off top or blow-off bottom, so either extreme could be seen (Fig. 8-7). We see that decreasing volume eventually leads to a change in prices, usually down, but that increasing volume is associated with continuation of price movement, whether up or down, and extremes of volume often occur at major turning points. This seems to contradict our theory of a large volume indicating a large move. We must look for additional data and analyze it further.

   If we compare volume to the point move of the price we can establish a new relationship as follows:

$$\text{Point Volume} = \frac{\text{Volume}}{H - L}$$

   Here we shall define point volume as total ticks divided by the total points in the range of the price bar considered. This relationship can be defined in a more meaningful way by taking only the real price range—the closing price minus the opening price—rather than the entire range of the high minus the low. Letting TT stand for total ticks, we get the following formula, a plot of which is shown in Figure 8-8:

$$\text{Point Volume} = \frac{TT}{C - O}$$

Figure 8-7

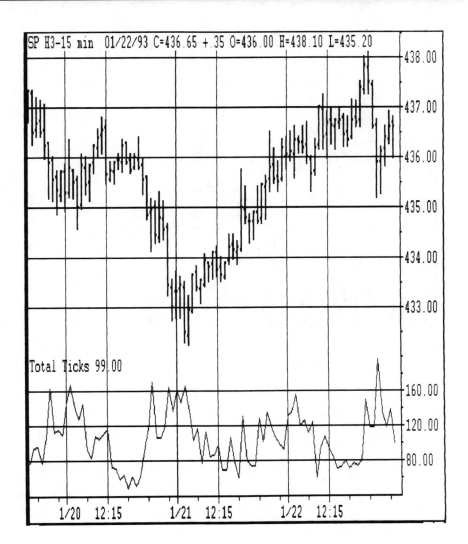

Figure 8-8

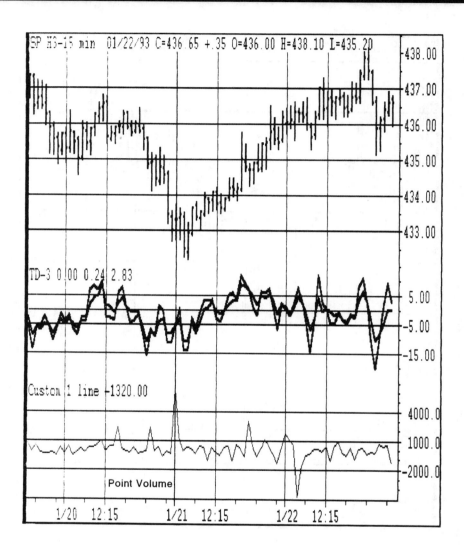

Although some investigators suggest that point volume is a factor in the buying and selling equation, I have not found this to be true for intra-day trading. Neither of the two ways of calculating point volume (volume/high-low or volume/close-open), nor a moving average of those figures, shows any correlation with price movement. Many other possible correlations also are negative, so we won't use point volume for anything.

There is, however, an interesting pattern in the tick volume, if we plot total ticks—upticks + downticks—then take a weighted 6-bar moving average. We see that the plot shows a cyclical pattern. It is also possible to see a vague correlation with prices (Fig. 8-9). It seems that upward price movements are preceded by a rising wave of volume. When the volume wave is receding, and half over, prices begin to consolidate, move sideways, or even down, but never up; they only rise again *after* a new rising volume wave appears.

What can we make of this correlation? It seems to support the premise that volume is helpful to price movement. However, it would be wrong to say that "volume moves prices," because we know that *people* move prices, and volume then follows. (If it doesn't, *people* move prices back again in search for better volume!) We also could say that volume *follows* prices, but that isn't quite right, either. More likely both movements occur together, actually depending on each other. If prices are raised and more interest is generated, more trading occurs. If the bias is upward—that is if there are more buyers than sellers—the increased volume tends to support that movement as more and more buyers come forth, always outnumbering the sellers. After a while, this interest will fade, and soon prices no longer will advance.

How can we benefit from this insight? Let's look at the plot in Figure 8-9. We can gain confidence that prices have a favorable environment for advancing if they are on the rising half of the volume curve, but if they are approaching the lower half of the falling part of that curve, be cautious; prices will not likely advance and may well decline. Take your profits and do not enter the market at that point. Wait until the volume curve rises again. Although this observation does not constitute a razor-sharp indicator that gives us an exact entry point, it's a new and unique correlation that gives significant assistance in entering the market before prices head higher! The formula for this indicator, which we shall call MATT for "moving average of total ticks" is:

MATT = Waverage ((Upticks + Downticks),6);

Another mathematical concept that will express relationships is the cumulative sum, which we discussed in the previous chapter. Here, each new value, whether positive or negative, is added to the sum of all the previous values, forming a never-ending cumulative sum. When plotted, the curve will go up and down, all according to the sign and value of the new value. In computer language, the formula for this type of function is called a simple "counter," and it's written basically as: $X=X+Y$, where X is the starting value and Y is each new value. You can see that X changes as each new value of Y is added on.

In TradeStation language, the word "VALUE" is used to represent a variable such as X or Y; each variable is distinguished from all the others by a number, such as VALUE1, VALUE2, and so on. The above formula thus becomes:

Figure 8-9

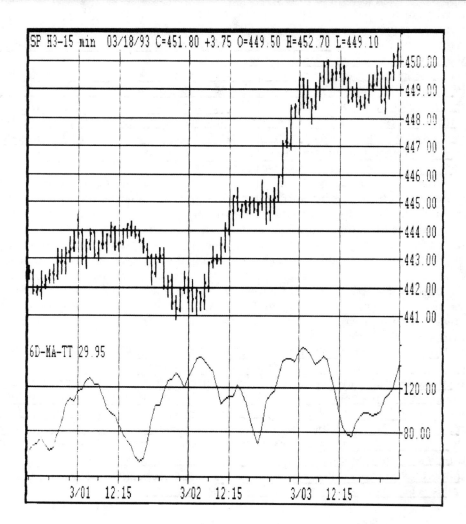

VALUE1 = VALUE1 + VALUE2. Here VALUE1 is the ever-changing cumulative sum and VALUE2 is each new value of the function plotted.

We can express the market sentiment, as shown by the trend of the difference between up and down ticks (buying and selling), by means of a cumulative sum. This plot is seen in Figure 8-10. The curve, as usual, is quite jagged and needs to be smoothed. For this purpose we'll use an average. First we try a 3-bar weighted moving average. Now you can see that the curve closely corresponds to price movements (Fig. 7-2). If we now take an 11-bar weighted moving average of that function, we have a reference curve for the shorter 3-bar weighted moving average (Fig. 8-11). Can you see that both curves resemble simple moving averages in the way they "hug" prices (Fig. 8-12)? However, this particular combination of weighted moving averages produces reasonably early signals when the shorter average crosses the longer (the arrows in Fig. 8-12). We also see that this indicator works well in *all* markets and timeframes, which makes it a truly versatile indicator, based on the concept of buying and selling as the driving force behind market action (Figs. 8-13 and 8-14). We'll call this indicator TDAC for "tick difference accumulation," and we'll return to it many times in later chapters.

Kurtosis Indicator

Now let's develop a second type of indicator, one that still reflects market sentiment, but is one step further removed from it than tick difference, since it's directly based on price movements. But didn't we decide that's a self-limiting concept, which can only be taken so far? How much can we do with prices alone? More than you might think. The problem is that the presently used indicators based on price alone examine prices only in one step. For example, momentum and rate of change compare the present price with that of a certain number of price bars ago (6, 9, 18, or whatever: Fig. 7-3). Stochastics compares the present price to a range for a group of bars going back a certain number of bars (5, 9, 14, 21, etc.: Fig. 8-4), but does add a second step, comparing that plot to a moving average of itself. Keep in mind this second step and the additional value it gives that indicator. What if we took the initial comparison one step further before we compared it to a moving average of itself?

To see that clearly, and to see how it can be of value in looking "behind the scenes" of the market, let's use an example from general physics.

Think of a tennis ball. Most of you either have played tennis or at least have thrown a tennis ball a few times, so you can imagine throwing a tennis ball straight up into the air and watching it come down again. You throw it straight up, perhaps 20 feet, watch it rise, slow down, come to a stop, then descend. Compare that action to price action. The ball receives a force in an upward direction that makes it accelerate upward, which means that for a short time (while it's in your hand) its speed (velocity) is increasing. Then the ball begins to slow down (but it's still heading up), and finally comes to a stop (for only a fraction of a second). Next it begins to be pulled downward by the force of gravity) and it accelerates downward until it hits the ground. Only the first part of that tennis ball's journey interests us (Fig. 8-15a).

If we plot the speed or velocity of the ball, we get a curve as seen in Figure 8-15b. The upward speed increases, levels off, then decreases before the ball reach-

Figure 8-10

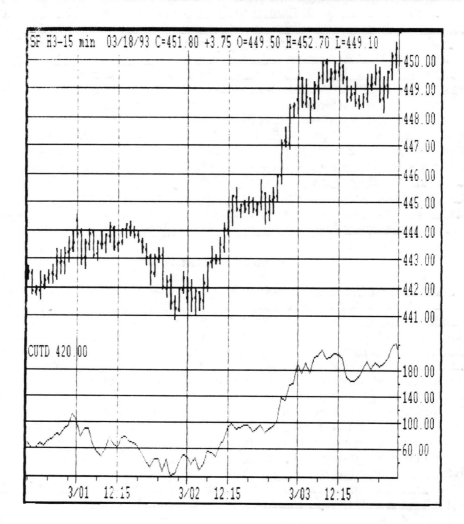

Figure 8-11

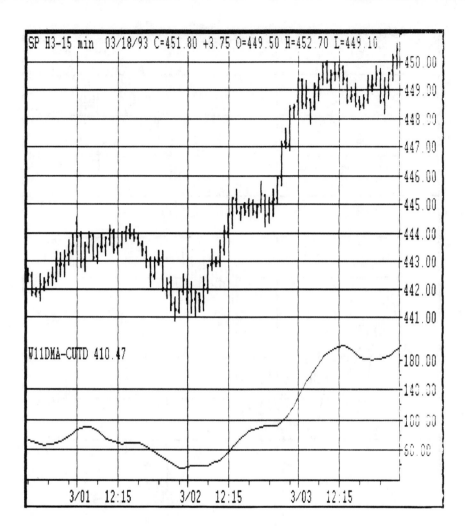

Figure 8-12

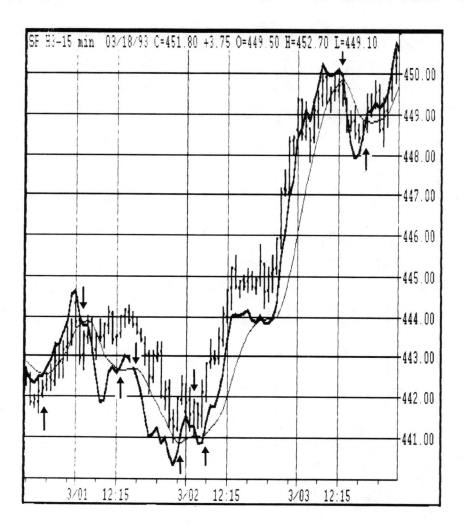

Figure 8-13

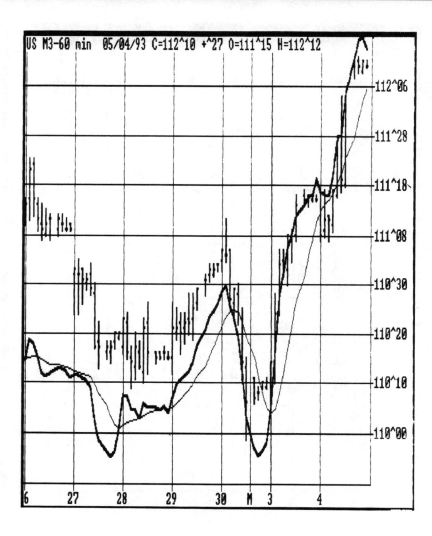

Figure 8-14

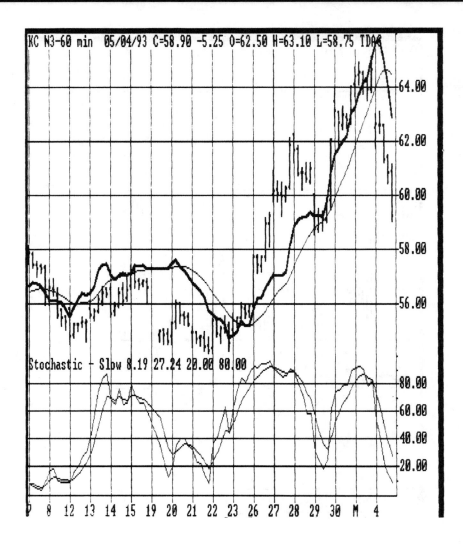

Figure 8-15a-d

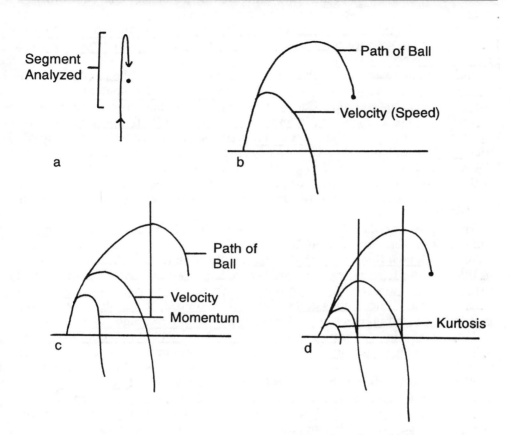

Segment
Analyzed

a

Path of Ball

Velocity (Speed)

b

Path of
Ball

Velocity

Momentum

c

Kurtosis

d

es its maximum height above the ground. At that instant, downward speed begins, increases slowly at first, then more rapidly as the ball falls back down. If we plot the change in speed, or take the momentum, we get the curve seen in Figure 8-15c. Here's the interesting thing: The momentum curve begins to turn down *before* the velocity curve, and actually returns all the way back to zero as the velocity reaches its peak.

Although momentum can give us an early warning, we'd like to take this concept one step further. What if we took the momentum of the momentum itself to get an even earlier warning? Could we not go on like that forever and get ever-earlier warnings, perhaps one before we even started? Well, not quite. Yes, we *could* go on forever, but the yield in terms of useful information would rapidly diminish beyond any value. The place to stop is after the second time around, or the second determination of momentum. This is called *Kurtosis*, a Greek word, which simply means a "bulge" or prominence to a curve. This concept was discussed very briefly by Robert M. Barnes in his 1983 book, *Megaprofit Commodity Methods.*[24]

The concept of subjecting your data to continued smoothing, averaging, or differencing, is not uncommon, but up to now has involved very laborious calculations. Omega Research's TradeStation software has made it possible for the ordinary trader to enter any mathematical or logic formula into the program and subject his idea to analysis, also in *real time*. Therefore, we can easily subject our data to repeated calculations of the same type and produce very fine curves. The plot of the second momentum, or Kurtosis, would look like Figure 8-15d.

You can see that continuing in this maneuver, we would paint ourselves into a corner to little advantage. Notice that the Kurtosis curve has reached its peak even *before* the momentum has reached its peak, which is *before the velocity* has reached its peak, which is *before the ball* has reached its peak. We cannot take this maneuver any further without losing practical value, but with an early warning four steps ahead of the actual event ... should we not be able to take advantage of that? You bet we can! We can also make small fine-tuning adjustments to the curve to make it more sensitive. Remember also that taking a moving average of the plot itself will give us a further advantage, as we shall soon see.

Now let's make the Kurtosis plot as sensitive as possible by applying some mathematical fine tuning (Fig. 8-16). As I mentioned before, we can get more advantage by comparing this plot to a moving average of itself (Fig. 8-17). Next, check the correlation with prices and Stochastics (Fig. 8-18). We again can see a beautiful correlation between our indicator and the price action. However, because of its great sensitivity, we again have more than the desired number of swings and signals. Again, we must use the Stochastic to help us filter out the unwanted signals.

We note again that the Kurtosis gives a signal *before* the Stochastic, because it anticipated the change in price movement, rather than responding to it. It's still dependent on price, but it senses a change coming long before it happens. The earliest signal is given by a turn in the curve, the next when it crosses its moving average, and the last of three signals comes when it crosses its zero line. We shall call this indicator FSK for "fast and slow Kurtosis." We've plotted a 3-bar Kurtosis and a 3-bar weighted moving average of that. A slower 6-bar Kurtosis and a 6-bar weighted moving average of that also can be plotted (Fig. 8-19), with

Figure 8-16

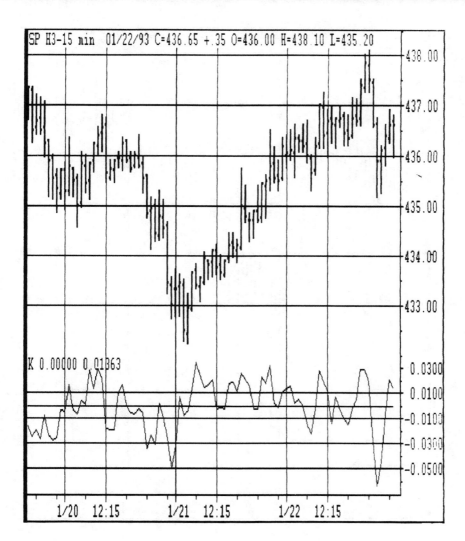

Figure 8-17

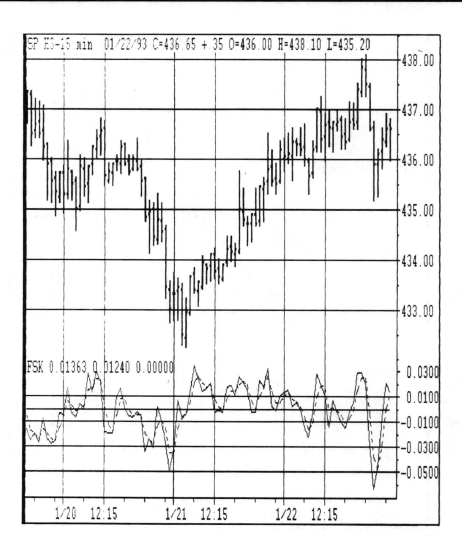

Figure 8-18

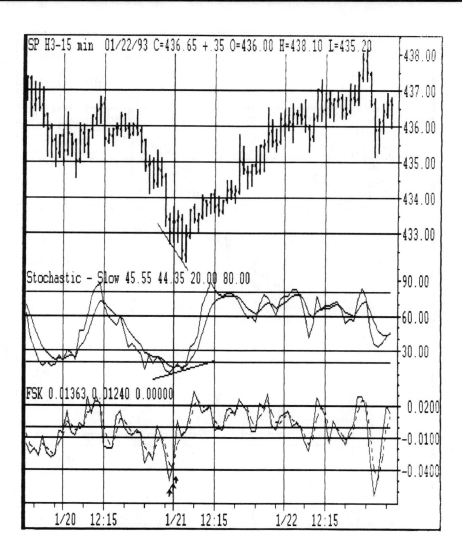

Figure 8-19

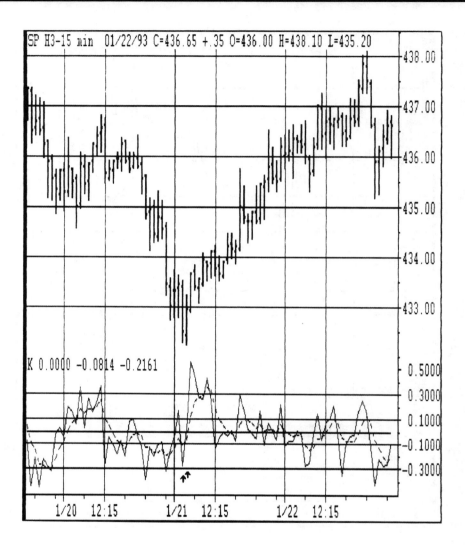

equally fine results. The only difference is that the 6-bar Kurtosis generates signals a little later.

You may ask, "Why is it necessary to get an indicator that gives such very early signals?" The answer is that they all present a certain number of unwanted signals. The more sensitive the indicator is, the more unwanted signals. These can be removed only by a smoothing process, usually averaging, and that "slows down" the signals. If you need three bars to get your signal, the process obviously is slower than if you needed just one bar. Therefore, if we can get a signal as early as four bars before an event happens, then smooth it over three bars, we'll have a signal that can be seen at the close of that third bar, in time for us to take action on the opening of the fourth bar! The computer formula for this is:

```
VALUE1 = @MOMENTUM(C,3);
VALUE2 = @MOMENTUM(C,3)[1];
VALUE3 = .03*(VALUE1-VALUE2)+(1-.03)*VALUE3;
VALUE4 = WAVERAGE((VALUE3),3);
INPUT:BUYZONE(0);
PLOT1(VALUE3,"FK");
PLOT2(VALUE4,"FSK");
PLOT3(BUYZONE,"BZ");
```

I hope you can see that these indicators can be used to generate precise entry and exit points in real time. The fact that they are based on the present market sentiment and a very early warning of a change in price movement make them truly fascinating tools for real time. However, I must give you one word of caution: Since these indicators are so sensitive and immediately responsive, **do not** act on them until the current price bar has closed! You'll see these indicators wiggle and squirm with each price tick, but until the price bar has closed you can't know where that indicator is going. You also don't know the closing price of the bar until the period comes to an end and that bar actually closes. The indicators will do all the anticipation you need; don't try to anticipate the anticipator!

This is as far as we can take the concept of market sentiment (buying and selling) in real time as independent functions. However, as I've already mentioned, we can combine these concepts with other indicators. The number of such possible combinations is infinite, so I shall limit my discussion to the three most logical choices. But, before I begin combining our newly developed indicators with classic indicators, let me take the logic one step further. Could we not start our combinations by combining two of what we already have? For example, the TD-3 is an oscillator, based directly on buying and selling; the FSK also is an oscillator, based on early changes in price movement. Would it not be logical to see if the FSK could detect an early change in the net effect of buying and selling without having to detect such a change in the price movement? Couldn't we go directly to the force behind the price movement and apply our FSK indicator? Let's see what happens.

First we must smooth the U/D tick difference with at least a 3-bar average, if not longer. Otherwise a very jagged curve results (Fig. 8-1). Having tried several averages, we find that a 7-bar weighted moving average works quite well. We get a reasonable curve that we already know will predict price movement (Fig.

8-20). Applying the FSK to this curve should be able to give us an early warning of any change, or tell us at what point the market sentiment is beginning to change. Again, we need to smooth the curve (Fig. 8-21), which is not yet acceptable. We find that a 3-bar weighted moving average is very satisfactory (Fig. 8-22). We can see that very early and true signals are generated; in fact, this indicator will pinpoint tops and bottoms one bar *before* they occur! (See the arrows in Fig. 8-22.)

This combination of our new indicators (the TD-3 and the FSK) we shall call "KTD-7," short for "Kurtosis of the tick difference; 7-bar weighted moving average." We'll also include a 3-bar weighted moving average of that function itself. This indicator will work well in markets that are in a good trading range, or have good cycles in a bull or bear market. It does not give much help in congestion or consolidation phases, when the cyclical nature of the market is temporarily suppressed. In those situations simply go to shorter periods to find cyclical activity to which you can apply the indicator. For example, we see excellent signals on a 60-minute bar chart during a bull market full of cycles, but once the move changed to a consolidation of 30 bars or so, those signals became less helpful. Switching to 5-minute bars immediately revealed the cyclical behavior, and the indicator once again became very helpful (Figs. 8-22 and 8-23).

When you're testing ideas and concepts, and developing indicators, it's important to use the largest possible markets, such as the S&P 500, treasury bonds, and foreign currencies. Those markets are so huge that various sporadic influences "get lost" in the big picture, making price movements more regular and a more accurate reflection of the market. However, we must not forget the smaller markets, since all the markets, large or small, will be of interest to some traders. The KTD-7 works extremely well in the large markets, as you might expect. But what happens in a smaller market, a less volatile market, such as one of the grain markets?

If we apply the KTD-7 indicator to the July wheat market, we see the pattern in Figure 8-24. If you look closely, you can see that both peaks, as well as the crossovers of the KTD-7 over its 3-bar weighted moving average, occur at the very peak in prices. This is great, and as expected, but it would be so nice to have a warning just one bar earlier. We're getting very demanding! But you must realize, even though the FSK signals an event four bars ahead, the 7-bar average brings us two bars behind that event. We'd like to make up for that. Can we get an even earlier signal?

I know I said earlier, when I first described Kurtosis, that we would "paint ourselves into a corner" if we continued with that process. However, for the benefit of the grains, let's try just one more time. Instead of taking the Kurtosis of the tick difference, we'll take the Kurtosis of the KTD-7; then we'll smooth that curve by taking a 3-bar weighted moving average and get the curve shown in Figure 8-25. **Bingo!** We now have the signals coming one bar earlier, that is one bar *before* the peaks! If you can't make money with that, no indicator in the world will help you! We'll call this indicator KKTD-7, the extra "K" reflecting the fact that we have taken a second Kurtosis.

There will be many possibilities for research with this concept, and many possible indicators are just waiting to be displayed. This indicator alone made the profits from the wheat market mushroom. You might ask, "Why was it neces-

Figure 8-20

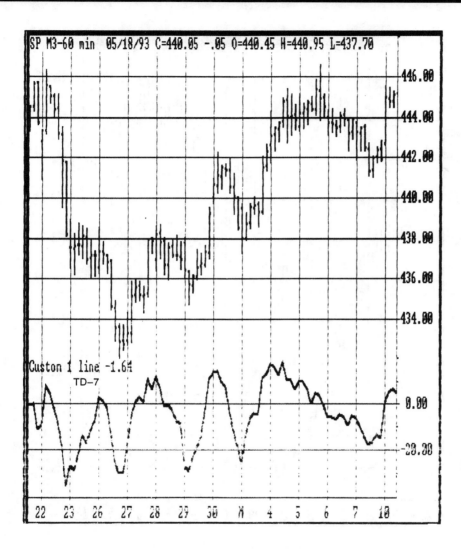

SP M3-60 min   05/18/93 C=440.05 -.05 O=440.45 H=440.95 L=437.70

Figure 8-21

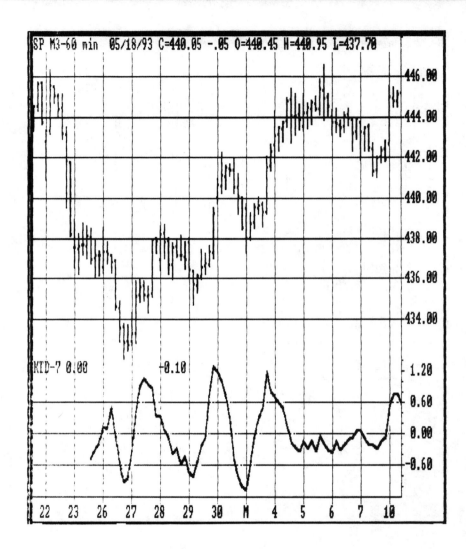

Figure 8-22

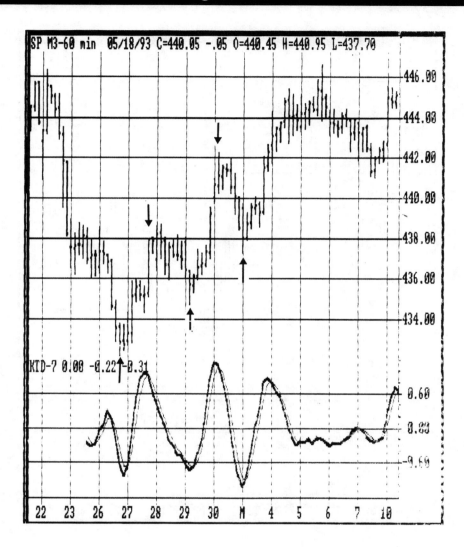

Figure 8-23

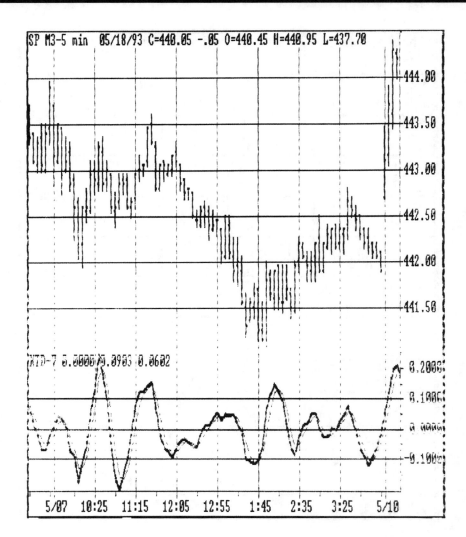

Figure 8-24

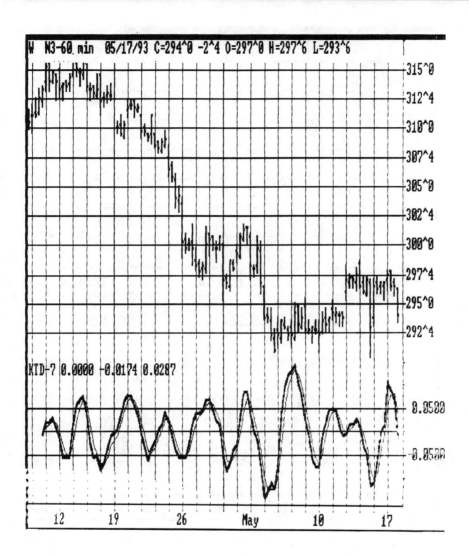

Figure 8-25

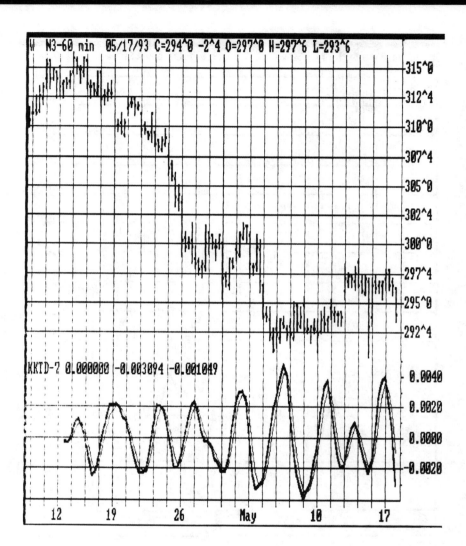

sary to get the warning a bar earlier?" It has to do with writing systems. If a computer has to wait for the closing of the current price bar before it can act on a signal, it can act only at the *close* of the bar *following* the bar that generated the signal. In small markets, such as the grains, with low volatility of price bars, a good part of the move may be consumed by those two price bars; hence the need for a signal one bar earlier in those markets. Figure 8-26 shows a comparison of those two indicators to point out the critical difference in timing, the KKTD-7 gives signals one to three bars earlier than the KTD-7. (Also see Figures 10-40 and 10-41.)

Figure 8-26

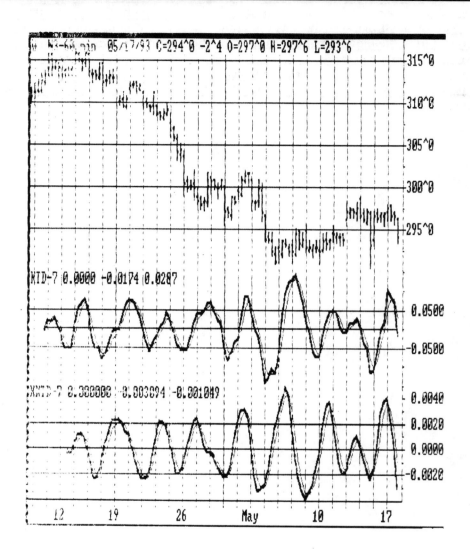

9

Combination Indicators

We come now to another path toward finding a better indicator. In this chapter we will examine the results of combining our newly developed indicators with three of the classic indicators: momentum, Stochastics, and relative strength index (RSI).

Combining TD-3 with Momentum: "MTD-6" We'll begin by using a 6-bar weighted moving average of the U/D tick difference. If we apply a 6-bar momentum to that curve, we shall see what we had expected to see in Figure 8-2, back in the previous chapter. We just needed to smooth the tick difference curve a little more by using a moving average before we applied the momentum function. We shall call this new indicator the "MTD-6" for "momentum of tick difference." Figure 9-1 shows excellent correlation of the MTD-6 with price movement, as signals are being generated by the curve crossing the zero line. Figure 9-2 shows how the added 6-bar weighted moving average of itself adds crossover signals, which generally will occur slightly earlier than the signals from crossing the zero line. Much like the KTD-7 we discussed in the last chap-

Figure 9-1

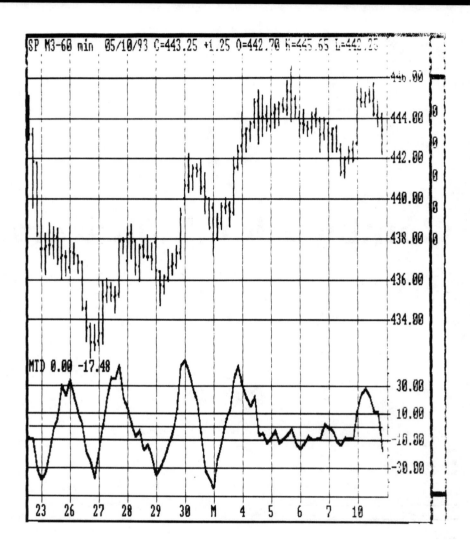

Figure 9-2

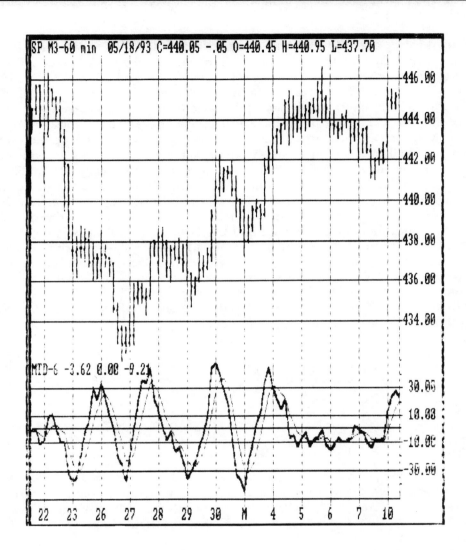

ter, the MTD-6 will give early warning of a change in the trend of buying and selling, and will have similar limitations—it will work better the more cyclical activity there is.

Combining the TD-3 with Stochastics: "TDST" The Stochastic indicator is one of the most logical choices to combine with the TD-3. You might ask: "Why would anyone even think of combining two such indicators? Will you get the best of both, or the worst of both? Exactly how can they be combined? Addition? Multiplication? Division? What kind of indicator will result—a price-hugging curve like a moving average or an oscillator?" Any more questions?

It would be a contradiction in logic to combine a trend following indicator with an oscillator; such an attempt would result in a useless squiggle. So when you combine mathematical functions, be sure they are generically similar. Since our TD-3 oscillates around a zero line and is itself an oscillator, it can be combined with any of the other oscillators. I previously mentioned that the Stochastic is one of the most versatile indicators, so we shall use it again. We wish to add the more active nature of the TD-3 to the filtering action of the Stochastic. The Stochastic can identify that part of the cycle in which prices are located, and the TD-3 can pinpoint the turns in market sentiment within that cycle. The TD-3 also should be able to "activate" the often useless portion of the Stochastic in the overbought and oversold zones. We shall call this new combination indicator the "TDST" for "tick difference and Stochastic," and it is constructed from the following computer formula:

```
VALUE1=UPTICKS-DOWNTICKS;
VALUE2=WAVERAGE((VALUE1),3);
VALUE3=@SLOWK(9);
VALUE4=VALUE2+VALUE3;
INPUT:BUYZONE(50);
PLOT1(BUYZONE,"BZ");
PLOT2(VALUE4,"TDST");
```

The resulting curve is seen in Figure 9-3. Signals are produced whenever the indicator crosses the 50 reference line. Compared with the standard Stochastics, these signals occur just a little later, but are quite reliable. Earlier signals can be seen when the indicator crosses the extreme zones of 0 and 100, and those signals are almost as reliable as the ones from crossing the 50 line. It is noteworthy that between 4/13 and 4/22, the Stochastic was quite useless, and in fact it gave a false signal, marked by an "x," on 4/20. The TDST indicator did not cross in a definite manner and thus did not give a clear buy signal.

We're on the right track in pursuit of our goal, but this combination still leaves something to be desired. For example, the turning points do not show reliable signals, and the other signals occur later than the standard Stochastic's. Let's see how another indicator might help.

Combining the TD-3 with Relative Strength Index: "TDRS" Since the RSI is also an oscillator, it can be combined with the TD-3 in a similar manner as the Stochastic. Here is the computer formula:

Figure 9-3

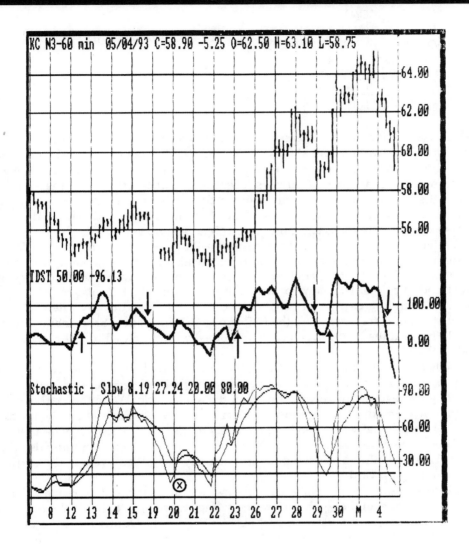

```
VALUE1=UPTICKS-DOWNTICKS;
VALUE2=WAVERAGE((VALUE1),3);
VALUE3=@RSI(6);
VALUE4=2*VALUE2+VALUE3;
VALUE5=WAVERAGE((VALUE4),6);
INPUT:BUYZONE(50);
PLOT1(BUYZONE,"BZ");
PLOT2(VALUE4,"TDRS");
PLOT3(VALUE5,"MATD");
```

As usual, I like to see a longer weighted moving average of a function to generate an early warning signal from the crossing of the indicator curve over that of its longer average (Fig. 9-4). You can easily see the crossover signals at the 50 reference line marked with arrows, preceded by the earlier warning signals when the TDRS crosses its moving average. Still earlier warnings are given when the TDRS turns around, or "hooks," as it's sometimes called. This indicator works well in all markets and timeframes (Figs. 9-5 and 9-6).

We've concentrated on the buying and selling concept as the driving force behind price movement, but you will recall we also developed an effective indicator called the FSK using another concept—that of early warning of a change in the trend of prices. That concept was called Kurtosis. The FSK also is an oscillator and therefore easily can be combined with either of our favorite classical oscillators, the Stochastics and the RSI. Figure 9-7 shows the FSK combined with the RSI, called the FSRS, and the FSK combined with the SlowK of the Stochastic, called the FSST.

Notice that both the FSST and the FSRS give the earliest possible warning—a buy signal—on Feb. 15, when they cross over their respective 9-bar weighted moving averages at the turning points of the major cycle. When the market subsequently entered a trading range, such crossings were a little late to be useful, and a better signal was given by the *turning points of the indicators*. Note that all such peaks or turning points were excellent signals and there were **no** false signals. This reliability is outstanding and actually continued even as the market began a long upward trend.

Since we cannot predict how large the swings inside the trading range will be, it is best to take all the signals. Here the swings turned out to be on the order of 300 points or so, and could give very substantial profits. During the uptrend you could take all the signals offered, but that is not necessary. Once the 9-bar weighted moving average (WMA) has crossed the 50 reference line, and you are of course long, you need not take any more signals until that 9-bar WMA returns and crosses downward over the 50 line. So the 9-bar WMA of either indicator constitutes a trend identifier and timer, serving to keep us in the market until it signals the end of the trend.

There is not a whole lot of difference between the FSST and the FSRS in these respects, but I am partial to the FSRS, since it seems to be a little more reliable in reflecting the strength of the market. For example, the 3rd and 4th lows in the trading range are progressively higher than the 2nd low. This is nicely reflected in the FSRS, but not in the FSST, which actually makes a *lower* low at the 4th low; the 9-bar WMAs display the same picture. My conclusion is that the FSRS is a

Figure 9-4

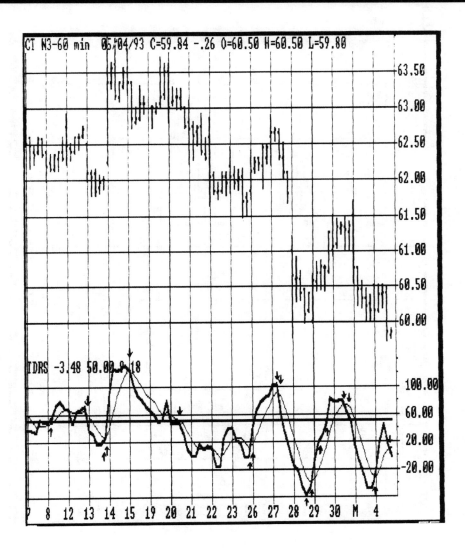

Figure 9-5

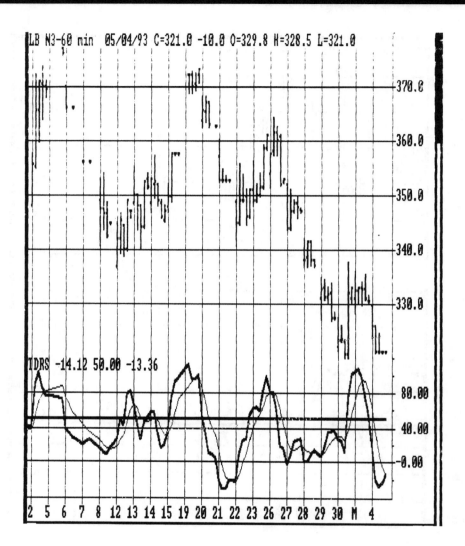

Figure 9-6

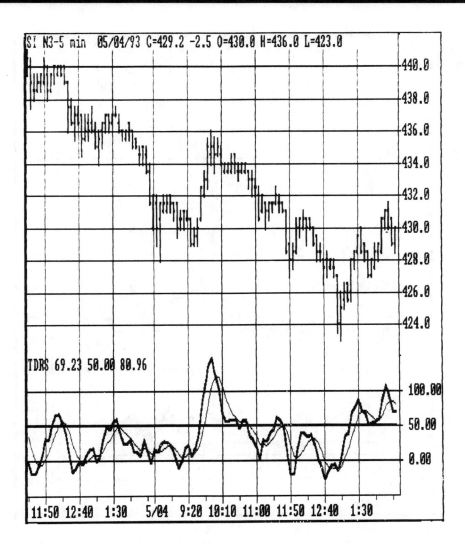

Figure 9-7

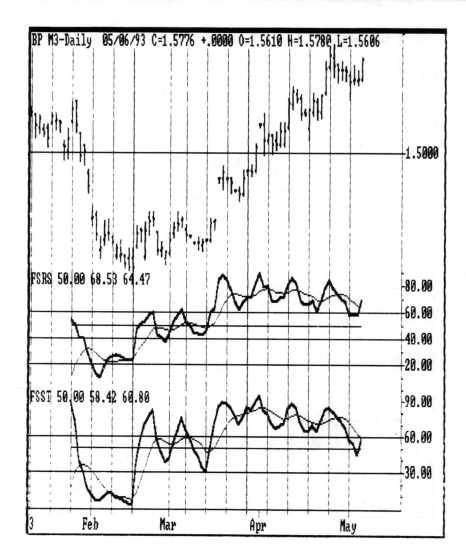

superior combination. It gives us excellent, 100 percent reliable signals at its sharp peaks and valleys, and its 9-bar WMA is an excellent trend identifier and timer. The formulas for these two combination indicators as written in Easy Language for TradeStation programming are:

1) FSST

```
VALUE1=@MOMENTUM(C,3);
VALUE2=@MOMENTUM(C,3)[1];
VALUE3=.03*(VALUE1-VALUE2)+(1-.03)*VALUE3;
VALUE4=WAVERAGE((VALUE3),6);
VALUE5=500*VALUE4+@SLOWK(9);
VALUE6=WAVERAGE((VALUE5),9);
INPUT:BUYZONE(50);
PLOT1(BUYZONE,"BZ");
PLOT2(VALUE5,"FSST");
PLOT3(VALUE6,"WMAFSST");
```

2) FSRS

```
VALUE1=@MOMENTUM(C,3);
VALUE2=@MOMENTUM(C,3)[1];
VALUE3=.03*(VALUE1-VALUE2)+(1-.03)*VALUE3;
VALUE4=WAVERAGE((VALUE3),6);
VALUE5=10000*VALUE4+@RSI(C,9);
VALUE6=WAVERAGE((VALUE5),6);
INPUT:BUYZONE(50);
PLOT1(BUYZONE,"BZ");
PLOT2(VALUE5,"FSRS");
PLOT3(VALUE6,"WMAFSRS");
```

Now let's go back and compare two previously developed indicators, the FSK and the TDRS, and see how they stand up to the FSRS. Figure 9-8 shows the FSK and the FSRS. It can be seen that they are very similar. That's to be expected, since the FSK is one-half of the FSRS. A few observations stand out.

1. Without being combined with the RSI, the FSK remains flatter, as it is not buoyed up by the rising RSI.
2. The crossings are very early and give good signals as opposed to the later ones in the FSRS.
3. Again the turning points are reliable and quite early.
4. The signal for the turnaround of the intermediate cycle, one of the most elusive signals we've been searching for, is again, as in the FSRS, given by the longer WMA of the indicator itself.
5. The amplitude of the swings of the FSK are more dramatic because we have added a line to the formula that produces accentuation of the swings, i.e. increases their amplitude (see Chapter 17: "Constructing Mathematical Functions"). This characteristic makes the crossings more definite, so you will see fewer ambiguous signals. We could also do that to the FSRS if we wanted. Clearly these two indicators are very comparable, and further study is needed to discover areas where one might be

Figure 9-8

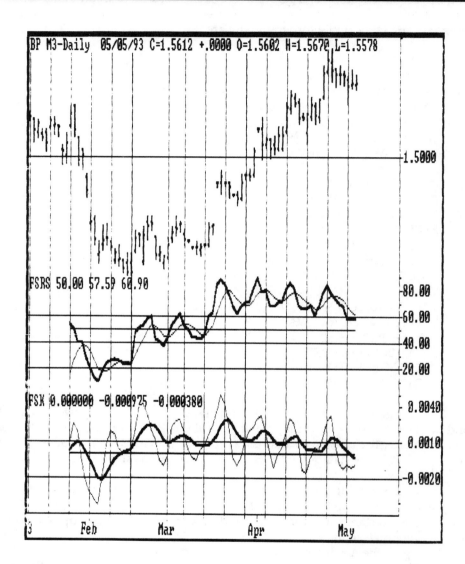

superior to the other. They both handle all markets, all timeframes, and all types of data, making them extremely versatile and independent.

If we now also look at the Stochastic (Fig. 9-9), we see that the first buy signal was given two bars after that of the FSK. After that, the Stochastic was essentially useless, giving several false sell signals in the up-trending market. It does show interesting swings, but, "Don't Diddle in the Middle!" as the saying goes; those signals are not reliable. Trending markets point out the weakness of the Stochastic indicator.

The TDRS already is a combination indicator, resulting from the combination of the TD-3 and the RSI. Since the TD-3 and therefore also the TDRS are based on the concept of buying and selling, they are dependent on tick data and won't work with the daily data, provided after the markets close. You might conclude that their use is limited to intra-day trading, and only important for long-term trading as timing devices for better and earlier entry and exit signals on 15- , 30- , and 60-minute bar charts. Fortunately, that's not true. Although they are indeed valuable for the purposes just mentioned, they can do more.

As we do many times, we can outfox the computer. We merely construct a tick data chart, not with 30- or 60-minute bars, but with bars having as many minutes as constitutes a daily trading session! For the currencies, starting at 8:20 a.m. New York time and finishing at 3 p.m., that amounts to 6 hours and 40 minutes, or *400 minutes*. Thus, a 400-minute bar chart will represent a daily bar chart, but it will be made up of tick data, allowing us to use our tick-data-based indicators.

Let's see how the FSRS compares with the TDRS and TDAC, thus comparing indicators based on two different concepts. Figure 9-10 shows a 60-minute chart of July coffee, which is of course an intra-day real time or tick data chart. The TDAC is overlaid on the price bars, as it becomes more dramatic with more "room to play."

We first notice that the TDAC gives excellent buy and sell signals, catching all the moves as well as keeping us in the market during the significant retracement halfway up the long bull move. The TDAC did not cross its 11-bar WMA and thus refused to give a sell signal! It succeeded in keeping us in the market! We also see that, as alluded to earlier, the TDAC tends to "hug" the price action much like a moving average. However, don't use it in that manner. In other words, when prices cross the TDAC, it may not mean the same thing as when prices cross a moving average, which is based on price itself. Here we see an unusually close resemblance to that type of pattern, but it doesn't always work that way.

We also see that the excellent signals are a little bit on the late side. The sell signal just past the top of 65 cents is seen first as the TDAC "hooks," then we see another, the more reliable one, as it crosses its WMA. The first is given at 62.60, the second at 61.60; we'd like to have a signal somewhere above 64.00. For that, we must look to our early warning curve, the FSRS. There we see a signal already at the peak, prior to the very top; but should it be acted on? With its WMA having just crossed over the 50 line, it may be too early to take that signal. We will wait for the crossing, which occurs at 64.40, inside the top. We should either sell at that price bar on the close, or at the high of the next bar if possible, either one a perfect spot.

Figure 9-9

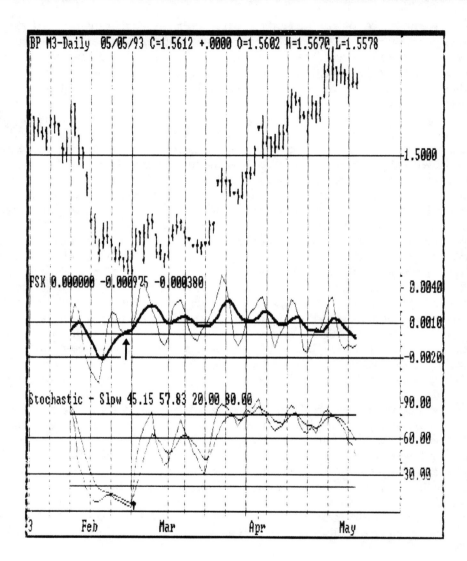

Figure 9-10

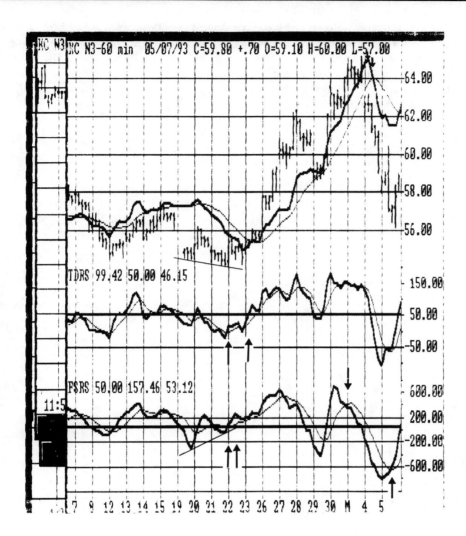

The TDRS is rather vague at this broad top, hence the advantage of using several indicators. There may be an unusual time when your favorite indicator is "outfoxed" by the market and gives no readable signal. Then ignore it and use one of the other good ones, as we have done here. We can also see both a failed swing and a divergence in the FSRS. It is also of interest that the TDRS gave an early buy signal by crossing its WMA on 4/22 and another when crossing the 50 line on 4/23, but the FSRS had *already* crossed its 50 line at the *first* of those two buy signals. The FSRS remains the best early warning indicator of them all, and in this case its signals are clearer.

10
Testing the Indicators

To do elaborate testing of all these indicators would be beyond the scope of this book and would consume a huge amount of paper. Therefore I've selected the markets and time periods in which these indicators have shown their best performance. For more details of construction, testing, and application see the relevant chapters elsewhere in this book.

Of the many necessary criteria for a good indicator, the last mentioned was the ability of an indicator to be incorporated into a profitable system. In other words, if it's as good as you think it is, it should be able to lead the way to profits. We'll also mention in Chapter 18: "Constructing Indicators," that an indicator might still be quite good, even if it could *not* meet that last strict criterion. You will see that *all* these indicators *do* meet that strict criterion in the markets and time periods selected here. Therefore, for each indicator shown, I also show an analysis of a very profitable system based on that indicator.

Although the oscillators TD-3, TD-7, FSK, KTD-7, KKTD-7, and FSRS are fascinating, other market sentiment indicators such as TDAC and MATT give the most insight into that ever changing engine.

On the 15-minute bars, the TDAC kept us short from 119^24 all the way down to 118^04 when it hooked and began to turn upward, signaling the first sign of a change in market sentiment. It was ready to cross its longer average just before the market closed, and we covered our short at 118^14. The afternoon session saw a huge upward gap and further upward action the following day. The TDAC got us our profit of $1,313 at just the right time. A most valuable signal (Fig. 10-1)!

In the T-bonds, the 60-minute bars show excellent correlation with the MATT. A rising MATT is associated with rising prices; when the MATT hooks or begins to turn down, prices cease to rise. If the MATT is in negative territory, prices will begin to drop, sometimes rapidly. That correlation is repeated half a dozen times (Fig. 10-2)!

Some of these indicators are very active and will indicate a great many turning points. The illustrations given here were chosen to show that, as well as to serve as tests. Most traders wouldn't think of acting on all those signals, correct though they may be. To reduce the number of signals, increase the length of the indicator. For example, compare the TD-3 and the TD-7. Any length is possible, and I encourage you to experiment further.

The very early signals given by the KKTD-7 make quite a difference in the wheat market, but may be much too early in other markets. But note the comparison between the KTD-7 and the KKTD-7 *systems*, based on their respective indicators, when applied to the wheat market. The very early signals of the KKTD-7 are crucial for the computer to be able to catch the small price movements at the optimum levels to be profitable.

Finally, I remind you that no indicator, whether classic or newly developed, will ever give 100 percent accurate and reliable signals. If one could, everyone would buy and sell at the same time, according to this Holy Grail. Thus, don't expect *too* much from indicators. As I said elsewhere in this book, "There is more to trading than following indicators!" but they *can* give you a decided edge in improving your timing, and many times they will be able to go far beyond that. Now study Figures 10-3 through 10-41.

Figure 10-1

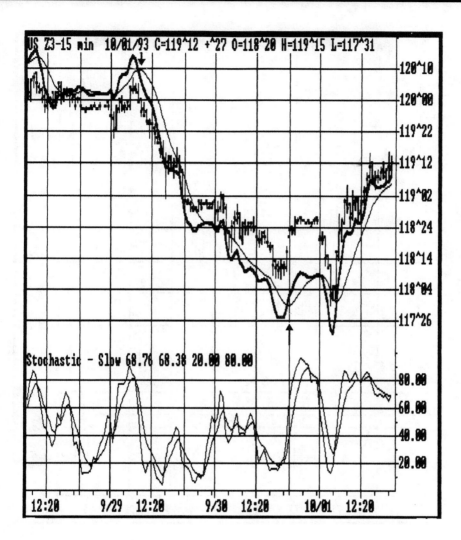

Figure 10-2

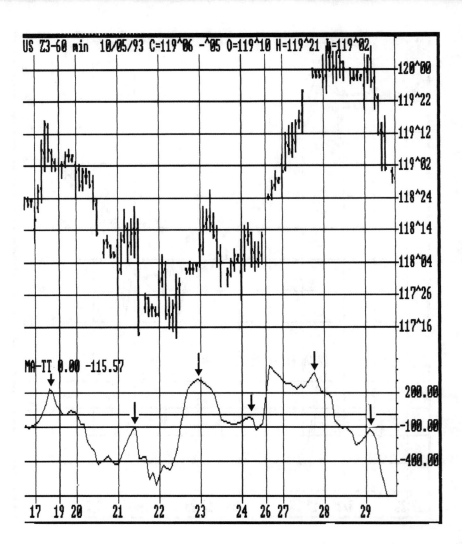

Figure 10-3

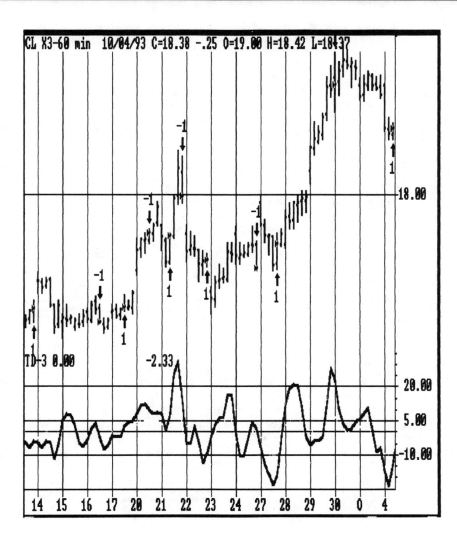

Figure 10-4

TD-3 CL X3-60 min   09/07/93 - 10/04/93

Performance Summary: All Trades

Total net profit	$	2470.00	Open position P/L	$	0.00
Gross profit	$	2930.00	Gross loss	$	-460.00
Total # of trades		13	Percent profitable		62%
Number winning trades		8	Number losing trades		5
Largest winning trade	$	1000.00	Largest losing trade	$	-150.00
Average winning trade	$	366.25	Average losing trade	$	-92.00
Ratio avg win/avg loss		3.98	Avg trade(win & loss)	$	190.00
Max consec. winners		4	Max consec. losers		3
Avg # bars in winners		7	Avg # bars in losers		8
Max intraday drawdown	$	-490.00		
Profit factor		6.37	Max # contracts held		1
Account size required	$	490.00	Return on account		504%

Performance Summary: Long Trades

Total net profit	$	1780.00	Open position P/L	$	0.00
Gross profit	$	1920.00	Gross loss	$	-140.00
Total # of trades		6	Percent profitable		67%
Number winning trades		4	Number losing trades		2
Largest winning trade	$	1000.00	Largest losing trade	$	-90.00
Average winning trade	$	480.00	Average losing trade	$	-70.00
Ratio avg win/avg loss		6.86	Avg trade(win & loss)	$	296.67
Max consec. winners		2	Max consec. losers		1
Avg # bars in winners		7	Avg # bars in losers		14
Max intraday drawdown	$	-340.00		
Profit factor		13.71	Max # contracts held		1
Account size required	$	340.00	Return on account		524%

Performance Summary: Short Trades

Total net profit	$	690.00	Open position P/L	$	0.00
Gross profit	$	1010.00	Gross loss	$	-320.00
Total # of trades		7	Percent profitable		57%
Number winning trades		4	Number losing trades		3
Largest winning trade	$	400.00	Largest losing trade	$	-150.00
Average winning trade	$	252.50	Average losing trade	$	-106.67
Ratio avg win/avg loss		2.37	Avg trade(win & loss)	$	98.57
Max consec. winners		2	Max consec. losers		2
Avg # bars in winners		7	Avg # bars in losers		5
Max intraday drawdown	$	-440.00		
Profit factor		3.16	Max # contracts held		1
Account size required	$	440.00	Return on account		157%

Figure 10-5

```
TD-3  CL X3-60 min    09/07/93 - 10/04/93
Date      Time     Type  Cnts    Price  Signal Name      Entry P/L  Cumulative
09/09/93  2:45pm  Sell  1        17.32
09/10/93 12:45pm  SExit 1        17.01               $     310.00 $     310.00
09/10/93 12:45pm  Buy   1        17.01
09/13/93 12:45pm  LExit 1        17.21               $     200.00 $     510.00
09/13/93 12:45pm  Sell  1        17.21
09/13/93  3:10pm  SExit 1        17.28               $     -70.00 $     440.00
09/13/93  3:10pm  Buy   1        17.28
09/16/93  1:45pm  LExit 1        17.19               $     -90.00 $     350.00
09/16/93  1:45pm  Sell  1        17.19
09/17/93  1:45pm  SExit 1        17.29               $    -100.00 $     250.00
09/17/93  1:45pm  Buy   1        17.29
09/20/93  1:45pm  LExit 1        17.76               $     470.00 $     720.00
09/20/93  1:45pm  Sell  1        17.76
09/21/93 12:45pm  SExit 1        17.74               $      20.00 $     740.00
09/21/93 12:45pm  Buy   1        17.74
09/21/93  3:10pm  LExit 1        17.99               $     250.00 $     990.00
09/21/93  3:10pm  Sell  1        17.99
09/22/93  3:10pm  SExit 1        17.59               $     400.00 $    1390.00
09/22/93  3:10pm  Buy   1        17.59
09/24/93  3:10pm  LExit 1        17.54               $     -50.00 $    1340.00
09/24/93  3:10pm  Sell  1        17.54
09/27/93  2:45pm  SExit 1        17.69               $    -150.00 $    1190.00
09/27/93  2:45pm  Buy   1        17.69
09/30/93 10:45am  LExit 1        18.69               $    1000.00 $    2190.00
09/30/93 10:45am  Sell  1        18.69
10/04/93 12:45pm  SExit 1        18.41               $     280.00 $    2470.00
10/04/93 12:45pm  Buy   1        18.41
```

Figure 10-6

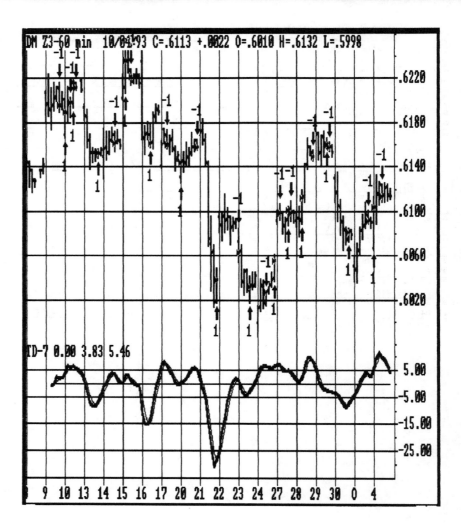

Figure 10-7

```
ID-7  DM Z3-60 min    09/07/93 - 10/04/93
                  Performance Summary:  All Trades

Total net profit        $    4150.00   Open position P/L     $       0.00
Gross profit            $    6537.50   Gross loss            $   -2387.50

Total # of trades             28       Percent profitable            54%
Number winning trades         15       Number losing trades          13

Largest winning trade   $    1487.50   Largest losing trade  $    -937.50
Average winning trade   $     435.83   Average losing trade  $    -183.65
Ratio avg win/avg loss        2.37     Avg trade(win & loss) $     148.21

Max consec. winners           5        Max consec. losers            3
Avg # bars in winners         5        Avg # bars in losers          3

Max intraday drawdown   $   -1412.50
Profit factor                 2.74     Max # contracts held          1
Account size required   $    1412.50   Return on account           294%
```

```
                  Performance Summary:  Long Trades

Total net profit        $    1562.50   Open position P/L     $       0.00
Gross profit            $    1937.50   Gross loss            $    -375.00

Total # of trades             14       Percent profitable            57%
Number winning trades          8       Number losing trades           6

Largest winning trade   $     537.50   Largest losing trade  $    -187.50
Average winning trade   $     242.19   Average losing trade  $     -62.50
Ratio avg win/avg loss        3.88     Avg trade(win & loss) $     111.61

Max consec. winners           2        Max consec. losers            2
Avg # bars in winners         5        Avg # bars in losers          3

Max intraday drawdown   $    -587.50
Profit factor                 5.17     Max # contracts held          1
Account size required   $     587.50   Return on account           266%
```

```
                  Performance Summary:  Short Trades

Total net profit        $    2587.50   Open position P/L     $       0.00
Gross profit            $    4600.00   Gross loss            $   -2012.50

Total # of trades             14       Percent profitable            50%
Number winning trades          7       Number losing trades           7

Largest winning trade   $    1487.50   Largest losing trade  $    -937.50
Average winning trade   $     657.14   Average losing trade  $    -287.50
Ratio avg win/avg loss        2.29     Avg trade(win & loss) $     184.82

Max consec. winners           4        Max consec. losers            4
Avg # bars in winners         6        Avg # bars in losers          3

Max intraday drawdown   $   -1225.00
Profit factor                 2.29     Max # contracts held          1
Account size required   $    1225.00   Return on account           211%
```

Figure 10-8

```
TD-7  DM Z3-60 min   09/07/93 - 10/04/93
```

Date	Time	Type	Cnts	Price	Signal Name		Entry P/L		Cumulative
09/09/93	2:20pm	Sell	1	.6195					
09/10/93	9:20am	SExit	1	.6189		$	75.00	$	75.00
09/10/93	9:20am	Buy	1	.6189					
09/10/93	11:20am	LExit	1	.6198		$	112.50	$	187.50
09/10/93	11:20am	Sell	1	.6198					
09/10/93	12:20pm	SExit	1	.6216		$	-225.00	$	-37.50
09/10/93	12:20pm	Buy	1	.6216					
09/10/93	1:20pm	LExit	1	.6212		$	-50.00	$	-87.50
09/10/93	1:20pm	Sell	1	.6212					
09/13/93	2:20pm	SExit	1	.6152		$	750.00	$	662.50
09/13/93	2:20pm	Buy	1	.6152					
09/14/93	1:20pm	LExit	1	.6161		$	112.50	$	775.00
09/14/93	1:20pm	Sell	1	.6161					
09/15/93	10:20am	SExit	1	.6236		$	-937.50	$	-162.50
09/15/93	10:20am	Buy	1	.6236					
09/15/93	12:20pm	LExit	1	.6221		$	-187.50	$	-350.00
09/15/93	12:20pm	Sell	1	.6221					
09/16/93	12:20pm	SExit	1	.6161		$	750.00	$	400.00
09/16/93	12:20pm	Buy	1	.6161					
09/17/93	11:20am	LExit	1	.6160		$	-12.50	$	387.50
09/17/93	11:20am	Sell	1	.6160					
09/20/93	9:20am	SExit	1	.6144		$	200.00	$	587.50
09/20/93	9:20am	Buy	1	.6144					
09/20/93	3:00pm	LExit	1	.6157		$	162.50	$	750.00
09/20/93	3:00pm	Sell	1	.6157					
09/21/93	3:00pm	SExit	1	.6038		$	1487.50	$	2237.50
09/21/93	3:00pm	Buy	1	.6038					
09/23/93	9:20am	LExit	1	.6063		$	312.50	$	2550.00
09/23/93	9:20am	Sell	1	.6063					
09/23/93	1:20pm	SExit	1	.6032		$	387.50	$	2937.50
09/23/93	1:20pm	Buy	1	.6032					
09/24/93	12:20pm	LExit	1	.6027		$	-62.50	$	2875.00
09/24/93	12:20pm	Sell	1	.6027					
09/24/93	3:00pm	SExit	1	.6056		$	-362.50	$	2512.50
09/24/93	3:00pm	Buy	1	.6056					
09/27/93	10:20am	LExit	1	.6099		$	537.50	$	3050.00
09/27/93	10:20am	Sell	1	.6099					
09/27/93	1:20pm	SExit	1	.6101		$	-25.00	$	3025.00
09/27/93	1:20pm	Buy	1	.6101					
09/27/93	2:20pm	LExit	1	.6099		$	-25.00	$	3000.00
09/27/93	2:20pm	Sell	1	.6099					
09/28/93	11:20am	SExit	1	.6112		$	-162.50	$	2837.50
09/28/93	11:20am	Buy	1	.6112					
09/28/93	3:00pm	LExit	1	.6149		$	462.50	$	3300.00
09/28/93	3:00pm	Sell	1	.6149					
09/29/93	1:20pm	SExit	1	.6160		$	-137.50	$	3162.50
09/29/93	1:20pm	Buy	1	.6160					
09/29/93	2:20pm	LExit	1	.6157		$	-37.50	$	3125.00
09/29/93	2:20pm	Sell	1	.6157					
09/30/93	2:20pm	SExit	1	.6081		$	950.00	$	**4075.00**
09/30/93	2:20pm	Buy	1	.6081					
10/01/93	2:20pm	LExit	1	.6091		$	125.00	$	**4200.00**

Figure 10-9

```
TD-7  DM  Z3-60 min   09/07/93 - 10/04/93
Date       Time     Type   Cnts    Price  Signal Name      Entry P/L   Cumulative
10/01/93   2:20pm   Sell   1       .6091
10/04/93   9:20am   SExit  1       .6104               $   -162.50 $   4037.50
10/04/93   9:20am   Buy    1       .6104
10/04/93  12:20pm   LExit  1       .6113               $    112.50 $   4150.00
10/04/93  12:20pm   Sell   1       .6113
```

Figure 10-10

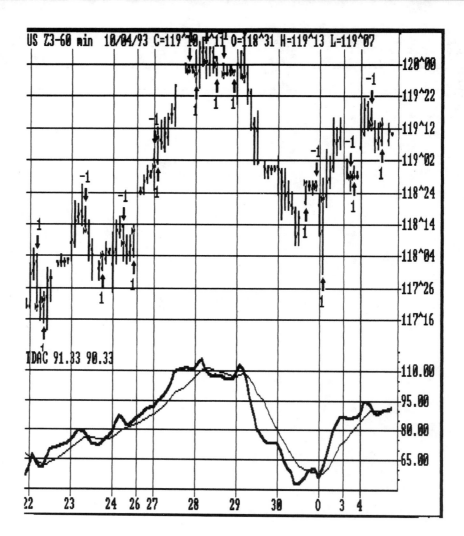

Figure 10-11

```
TDAC TURNING PTS   US Z3-60 min   08/31/93 - 10/04/93

                    Performance Summary:  All Trades

Total net profit       $    9906.25   Open position P/L      $     -62.50
Gross profit           $   12906.25   Gross loss             $   -3000.00

Total # of trades            50       Percent profitable            54%
Number winning trades        27       Number losing trades          23

Largest winning trade  $    1437.50   Largest losing trade   $    -718.75
Average winning trade  $     478.01   Average losing trade   $    -130.43
Ratio avg win/avg loss       3.66     Avg trade(win & loss)  $     198.13

Max consec. winners           5       Max consec. losers             4
Avg # bars in winners         7       Avg # bars in losers           3

Max intraday drawdown  $   -1062.50
Profit factor                4.30     Max # contracts held           1
Account size required  $    1062.50   Return on account            932%
```

```
                    Performance Summary:  Long Trades

Total net profit       $    5500.00   Open position P/L      $     -62.50
Gross profit           $    6906.25   Gross loss             $   -1406.25

Total # of trades            25       Percent profitable            60%
Number winning trades        15       Number losing trades          10

Largest winning trade  $    1031.25   Largest losing trade   $    -718.75
Average winning trade  $     460.42   Average losing trade   $    -140.63
Ratio avg win/avg loss       3.27     Avg trade(win & loss)  $     220.00

Max consec. winners           5       Max consec. losers             3
Avg # bars in winners         7       Avg # bars in losers           4

Max intraday drawdown  $   -1156.25
Profit factor                4.91     Max # contracts held           1
Account size required  $    1156.25   Return on account            476%
```

```
                    Performance Summary:  Short Trades

Total net profit       $    4406.25   Open position P/L      $       0.00
Gross profit           $    6000.00   Gross loss             $   -1593.75

Total # of trades            25       Percent profitable            48%
Number winning trades        12       Number losing trades          13

Largest winning trade  $    1437.50   Largest losing trade   $    -281.25
Average winning trade  $     500.00   Average losing trade   $    -122.60
Ratio avg win/avg loss       4.08     Avg trade(win & loss)  $     176.25

Max consec. winners           4       Max consec. losers             5
Avg # bars in winners         7       Avg # bars in losers           2

Max intraday drawdown  $    -593.75
Profit factor                3.76     Max # contracts held           1
Account size required  $     593.75   Return on account            742%
```

Figure 10-12

```
TDAC TURNING PTS   US Z3-60 min    08/31/93 - 10/04/93
```

Date	Time	Type	Cnts	Price	Signal Name		Entry P/L		Cumulative
09/01/93	10:20am	Buy	1	118^10					
09/01/93	1:20pm	LExit	1	118^09		$	-31.25	$	-31.25
09/01/93	1:20pm	Sell	1	118^09					
09/01/93	2:20pm	SExit	1	118^12		$	-93.75	$	-125.00
09/01/93	2:20pm	Buy	1	118^12					
09/01/93	3:00pm	LExit	1	118^08		$	-125.00	$	-250.00
09/01/93	3:00pm	Sell	1	118^08					
09/01/93	8:00pm	SExit	1	118^09		$	-31.25	$	-281.25
09/01/93	8:00pm	Buy	1	118^09					
09/02/93	2:20pm	LExit	1	118^27		$	562.50	$	281.25
09/02/93	2:20pm	Sell	1	118^27					
09/02/93	3:00pm	SExit	1	118^31		$	-125.00	$	156.25
09/02/93	3:00pm	Buy	1	118^31					
09/06/93	8:00pm	LExit	1	119^27		$	875.00	$	1031.25
09/06/93	8:00pm	Sell	1	119^27					
09/07/93	9:20am	SExit	1	120^00		$	-156.25	$	875.00
09/07/93	9:20am	Buy	1	120^00					
09/07/93	8:00pm	LExit	1	120^14		$	437.50	$	1312.50
09/07/93	8:00pm	Sell	1	120^14					
09/07/93	9:00pm	SExit	1	120^17		$	-93.75	$	1218.75
09/07/93	9:00pm	Buy	1	120^17					
09/08/93	3:00pm	LExit	1	120^16		$	-31.25	$	1187.50
09/08/93	3:00pm	Sell	1	120^16					
09/09/93	10:00pm	SExit	1	119^02		$	1437.50	$	2625.00
09/09/93	10:00pm	Buy	1	119^02					
09/12/93	8:00pm	LExit	1	120^03		$	1031.25	$	3656.25
09/12/93	8:00pm	Sell	1	120^03					
09/12/93	9:00pm	SExit	1	120^10		$	-218.75	$	3437.50
09/12/93	9:00pm	Buy	1	120^10					
09/13/93	12:20pm	LExit	1	120^12		$	62.50	$	3500.00
09/13/93	12:20pm	Sell	1	120^12					
09/13/93	1:20pm	SExit	1	120^16		$	-125.00	$	3375.00
09/13/93	1:20pm	Buy	1	120^16					
09/13/93	3:00pm	LExit	1	120^12		$	-125.00	$	3250.00
09/13/93	3:00pm	Sell	1	120^12					
09/14/93	2:20pm	SExit	1	119^01		$	1343.75	$	4593.75
09/14/93	2:20pm	Buy	1	119^01					
09/14/93	3:00pm	LExit	1	119^00		$	-31.25	$	4562.50
09/14/93	3:00pm	Sell	1	119^00					
09/15/93	12:20pm	SExit	1	118^07		$	781.25	$	5343.75
09/15/93	12:20pm	Buy	1	118^07					
09/16/93	10:20am	LExit	1	118^17		$	312.50	$	5656.25
09/16/93	10:20am	Sell	1	118^17					
09/16/93	11:20am	SExit	1	118^24		$	-218.75	$	5437.50
09/16/93	11:20am	Buy	1	118^24					
09/16/93	3:00pm	LExit	1	119^01		$	281.25	$	5718.75
09/16/93	3:00pm	Sell	1	119^01					
09/16/93	10:30pm	SExit	1	118^23		$	312.50	$	6031.25
09/16/93	10:30pm	Buy	1	118^23					
09/17/93	2:20pm	LExit	1	119^04		$	406.25	$	6437.50

Figure 10-13

```
TDAC TURNING PTS   US Z3-60 min    08/31/93 - 10/04/93
```

Date	Time	Type	Cnts	Price	Signal Name	Entry P/L	Cumulative
09/17/93	2:20pm	Sell	1	119^04			
09/19/93	9:00pm	SExit	1	119^05		$ -31.25	$ 6406.25
09/19/93	9:00pm	Buy	1	119^05			
09/20/93	9:20am	LExit	1	119^00		$ -156.25	$ 6250.00
09/20/93	9:20am	Sell	1	119^00			
09/21/93	10:20am	SExit	1	118^11		$ 656.25	$ 6906.25
09/21/93	10:20am	Buy	1	118^11			
09/22/93	11:20am	LExit	1	117^20		$ -718.75	$ 6187.50
09/22/93	11:20am	Sell	1	117^20			
09/22/93	1:20pm	SExit	1	117^22		$ -62.50	$ 6125.00
09/22/93	1:20pm	Buy	1	117^22			
09/23/93	1:20pm	LExit	1	118^12		$ 687.50	$ 6812.50
09/23/93	1:20pm	Sell	1	118^12			
09/23/93	9:00pm	SExit	1	118^04		$ 250.00	$ 7062.50
09/23/93	9:00pm	Buy	1	118^04			
09/24/93	12:20pm	LExit	1	118^08		$ 125.00	$ 7187.50
09/24/93	12:20pm	Sell	1	118^08			
09/24/93	3:00pm	SExit	1	118^12		$ -125.00	$ 7062.50
09/24/93	3:00pm	Buy	1	118^12			
09/27/93	9:20am	LExit	1	119^00		$ 625.00	$ 7687.50
09/27/93	9:20am	Sell	1	119^00			
09/27/93	10:20am	SExit	1	119^09		$ -281.25	$ 7406.25
09/27/93	10:20am	Buy	1	119^09			
09/27/93	10:00pm	LExit	1	119^30		$ 656.25	$ 8062.50
09/27/93	10:00pm	Sell	1	119^30			
09/28/93	9:20am	SExit	1	119^29		$ 31.25	$ 8093.75
09/28/93	9:20am	Buy	1	119^29			
09/28/93	12:20pm	LExit	1	120^01		$ 125.00	$ 8218.75
09/28/93	12:20pm	Sell	1	120^01			
09/28/93	3:00pm	SExit	1	120^00		$ 31.25	$ 8250.00
09/28/93	3:00pm	Buy	1	120^00			
09/28/93	8:00pm	LExit	1	119^29		$ -93.75	$ 8156.25
09/28/93	8:00pm	Sell	1	119^29			
09/28/93	10:30pm	SExit	1	119^30		$ -31.25	$ 8125.00
09/28/93	10:30pm	Buy	1	119^30			
09/29/93	11:20am	LExit	1	119^28		$ -62.50	$ 8062.50
09/29/93	11:20am	Sell	1	119^28			
09/30/93	8:00pm	SExit	1	118^27		$ 1031.25	$ 9093.75
09/30/93	8:00pm	Buy	1	118^27			
09/30/93	10:30pm	LExit	1	118^26		$ -31.25	$ 9062.50
09/30/93	10:30pm	Sell	1	118^26			
10/01/93	10:20am	SExit	1	118^22		$ 125.00	$ 9187.50
10/01/93	10:20am	Buy	1	118^22			
10/03/93	9:00pm	LExit	1	118^29		$ 218.75	$ 9406.25
10/03/93	9:00pm	Sell	1	118^29			
10/03/93	10:00pm	SExit	1	118^29		$ 0.00	$ 9406.25
10/03/93	10:00pm	Buy	1	118^29			
10/04/93	12:20pm	LExit	1	119^13		$ 500.00	$ 9906.25
10/04/93	12:20pm	Sell	1	119^13			
10/04/93	3:00pm	SExit	1	119^13		$ 0.00	$ 9906.25

Figure 10-14

```
TDAC TURNING PTS   US Z3-60 min    08/31/93 - 10/04/93
Date       Time     Type  Cnts    Price  Signal Name       Entry P/L  Cumulative
10/04/93  3:00pm Buy    1          119^13
```

Figure 10-15

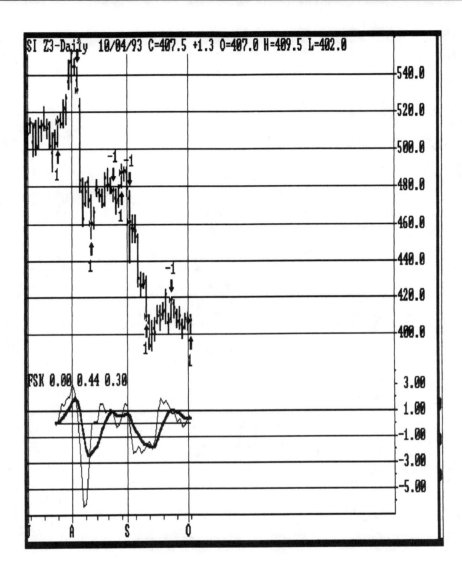

Figure 10-16

FSK-XOVER SI Z3-Daily   07/09/93 - 10/04/93

Figure 74   Performance Summary: All Trades

Total net profit	$ 6990.00	Open position P/L	$	0.00
Gross profit	$ 8820.00	Gross loss	$	-1830.00
Total # of trades	8	Percent profitable		75%
Number winning trades	6	Number losing trades		2
Largest winning trade	$ 3575.00	Largest losing trade	$	-1340.00
Average winning trade	$ 1470.00	Average losing trade	$	-915.00
Ratio avg win/avg loss	1.61	Avg trade(win & loss)	$	873.75
Max consec. winners	3	Max consec. losers		2
Avg # bars in winners	7	Avg # bars in losers		3
Max intraday drawdown	$ -2880.00			
Profit factor	4.82	Max # contracts held		1
Account size required	$ 2880.00	Return on account		243%

                            Performance Summary: Long Trades

Total net profit	$ 805.00	Open position P/L	$	0.00
Gross profit	$ 2145.00	Gross loss	$	-1340.00
Total # of trades	4	Percent profitable		75%
Number winning trades	3	Number losing trades		1
Largest winning trade	$ 875.00	Largest losing trade	$	-1340.00
Average winning trade	$ 715.00	Average losing trade	$	-1340.00
Ratio avg win/avg loss	0.53	Avg trade(win & loss)	$	201.25
Max consec. winners	2	Max consec. losers		1
Avg # bars in winners	8	Avg # bars in losers		3
Max intraday drawdown	$ -2390.00			
Profit factor	1.60	Max # contracts held		1
Account size required	$ 2390.00	Return on account		34%

                            Performance Summary: Short Trades

Total net profit	$ 6185.00	Open position P/L	$	0.00
Gross profit	$ 6675.00	Gross loss	$	-490.00
Total # of trades	4	Percent profitable		75%
Number winning trades	3	Number losing trades		1
Largest winning trade	$ 3575.00	Largest losing trade	$	-490.00
Average winning trade	$ 2225.00	Average losing trade	$	-490.00
Ratio avg win/avg loss	4.54	Avg trade(win & loss)	$	1546.25
Max consec. winners	2	Max consec. losers		1
Avg # bars in winners	6	Avg # bars in losers		3
Max intraday drawdown	$ -675.00			
Profit factor	13.62	Max # contracts held		1
Account size required	$ 675.00	Return on account		916%

Figure 10-17

```
FSK-XOVER  SI Z3-Daily   07/09/93 - 10/04/93
Date       Time    Type  Cnts   Price  Signal Name     Entry P/L   Cumulative
07/26/93   2:25pm  Buy    1     515.1
08/04/93   2:25pm  LExit  1     532.0              $     845.00 $     845.00
08/04/93   2:25pm  Sell   1     532.0
08/12/93   2:25pm  SExit  1     460.5              $    3575.00 $    4420.00
08/12/93   2:25pm  Buy    1     460.5
08/25/93   2:25pm  LExit  1     478.0              $     875.00 $    5295.00
08/25/93   2:25pm  Sell   1     478.0
08/30/93   2:25pm  SExit  1     487.8              $    -490.00 $    4805.00
08/30/93   2:25pm  Buy    1     487.8
09/02/93   2:25pm  LExit  1     461.0              $   -1340.00 $    3465.00
09/02/93   2:25pm  Sell   1     461.0
09/10/93   2:25pm  SExit  1     410.0              $    2550.00 $    6015.00
09/10/93   2:25pm  Buy    1     410.0
09/23/93   2:25pm  LExit  1     418.5              $     425.00 $    6440.00
09/23/93   2:25pm  Sell   1     418.5
10/04/93   2:25pm  SExit  1     407.5              $     550.00 $    6990.00
10/04/93   2:25pm  Buy    1     407.5
```

Figure 10-18

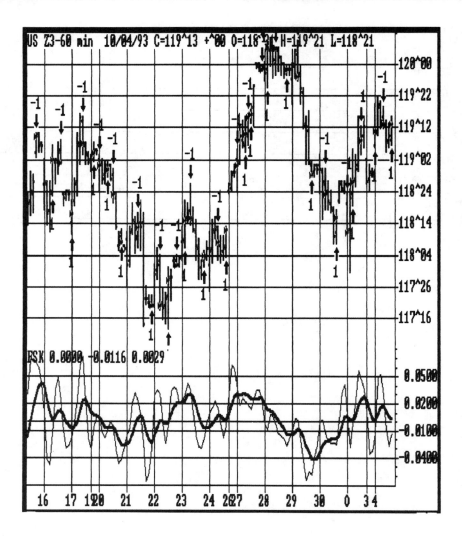

Figure 10-19

FSK US Z3-60 min   08/31/93 - 10/04/93

Figure 77   Performance Summary: All Trades

Total net profit	$	7375.00	Open position P/L	$	0.00
Gross profit	$	13156.25	Gross loss	$	-5781.25
Total # of trades		67	Percent profitable		61%
Number winning trades		41	Number losing trades		26
Largest winning trade	$	1250.00	Largest losing trade	$	-968.75
Average winning trade	$	320.88	Average losing trade	$	-222.36
Ratio avg win/avg loss		1.44	Avg trade(win & loss)	$	110.07
Max consec. winners		6	Max consec. losers		4
Avg # bars in winners		4	Avg # bars in losers		3
Max intraday drawdown	$	-1562.50			
Profit factor		2.28	Max # contracts held		1
Account size required	$	1562.50	Return on account		472%

Performance Summary: Long Trades

Total net profit	$	4250.00	Open position P/L	$	0.00
Gross profit	$	6906.25	Gross loss	$	-2656.25
Total # of trades		33	Percent profitable		61%
Number winning trades		20	Number losing trades		13
Largest winning trade	$	1062.50	Largest losing trade	$	-968.75
Average winning trade	$	345.31	Average losing trade	$	-204.33
Ratio avg win/avg loss		1.69	Avg trade(win & loss)	$	128.79
Max consec. winners		9	Max consec. losers		4
Avg # bars in winners		4	Avg # bars in losers		2
Max intraday drawdown	$	-1656.25			
Profit factor		2.60	Max # contracts held		1
Account size required	$	1656.25	Return on account		257%

Performance Summary: Short Trades

Total net profit	$	3125.00	Open position P/L	$	0.00
Gross profit	$	6250.00	Gross loss	$	-3125.00
Total # of trades		34	Percent profitable		62%
Number winning trades		21	Number losing trades		13
Largest winning trade	$	1250.00	Largest losing trade	$	-562.50
Average winning trade	$	297.62	Average losing trade	$	-240.38
Ratio avg win/avg loss		1.24	Avg trade(win & loss)	$	91.91
Max consec. winners		9	Max consec. losers		4
Avg # bars in winners		4	Avg # bars in losers		3
Max intraday drawdown	$	-1062.50			
Profit factor		2.00	Max # contracts held		1
Account size required	$	1062.50	Return on account		294%

Figure 10-20

```
FSK   US Z3-60 min   08/31/93 - 10/04/93
Date       Time    Type   Cnts   Price  Signal Name      Entry P/L   Cumulative
09/01/93   1:20pm  Sell   1      118^09
09/01/93   8:20pm  SExit  1      118^10                 $  -31.25 $    -31.25
09/01/93   8:20pm  Buy    1      118^10
09/01/93   9:20pm  LExit  1      118^12                 $   62.50 $     31.25
09/01/93   9:20pm  Sell   1      118^12
09/01/93  10:05pm  SExit  1      118^12                 $    0.00 $     31.25
09/01/93  10:05pm  Buy    1      118^12
09/02/93   9:20am  LExit  1      118^11                 $  -31.25 $      0.00
09/02/93   9:20am  Sell   1      118^11
09/02/93  10:20am  SExit  1      118^19                 $ -250.00 $   -250.00
09/02/93  10:20am  Buy    1      118^19
09/02/93   1:20pm  LExit  1      118^31                 $  375.00 $    125.00
09/02/93   1:20pm  Sell   1      118^31
09/02/93   9:20pm  SExit  1      118^30                 $   31.25 $    156.25
09/02/93   9:20pm  Buy    1      118^30
09/02/93  10:05pm  LExit  1      118^31                 $   31.25 $    187.50
09/02/93  10:05pm  Sell   1      118^31
09/03/93   9:20am  SExit  1      119^08                 $ -281.25 $    -93.75
09/03/93   9:20am  Buy    1      119^08
09/03/93   1:20pm  LExit  1      120^00                 $  750.00 $    656.25
09/03/93   1:20pm  Sell   1      120^00
09/07/93   9:20am  SExit  1      120^00                 $    0.00 $    656.25
09/07/93   9:20am  Buy    1      120^00
09/07/93   3:00pm  LExit  1      120^19                 $  593.75 $   1250.00
09/07/93   3:00pm  Sell   1      120^19
09/08/93   9:20am  SExit  1      120^14                 $  156.25 $   1406.25
09/08/93   9:20am  Buy    1      120^14
09/08/93   2:20pm  LExit  1      120^22                 $  250.00 $   1656.25
09/08/93   2:20pm  Sell   1      120^22
09/08/93  10:05pm  SExit  1      120^15                 $  218.75 $   1875.00
09/08/93  10:05pm  Buy    1      120^15
09/09/93   9:20am  LExit  1      119^16                 $ -968.75 $    906.25
09/09/93   9:20am  Sell   1      119^16
09/09/93  12:20pm  SExit  1      119^13                 $   93.75 $   1000.00
09/09/93  12:20pm  Buy    1      119^13
09/09/93   2:20pm  LExit  1      119^04                 $ -281.25 $    718.75
09/09/93   2:20pm  Sell   1      119^04
09/09/93   8:20pm  SExit  1      119^04                 $    0.00 $    718.75
09/09/93   8:20pm  Buy    1      119^04
09/10/93  12:20pm  LExit  1      120^02                 $  937.50 $   1656.25
09/10/93  12:20pm  Sell   1      120^02
09/13/93   9:20am  SExit  1      120^20                 $ -562.50 $   1093.75
09/13/93   9:20am  Buy    1      120^20
09/13/93  10:20am  LExit  1      120^15                 $ -156.25 $    937.50
09/13/93  10:20am  Sell   1      120^15
09/13/93   1:20pm  SExit  1      120^16                 $  -31.25 $    906.25
09/13/93   1:20pm  Buy    1      120^16
09/13/93   2:20pm  LExit  1      120^15                 $  -31.25 $    875.00
09/13/93   2:20pm  Sell   1      120^15
09/13/93   3:00pm  SExit  1      120^12                 $   93.75 $    968.75
```

Figure 10-21

```
FSK  US Z3-60 min   08/31/93 - 10/04/93
```

Date	Time	Type	Cnts	Price	Signal Name	Entry P/L	Cumulative
09/13/93	3:00pm	Buy	1	120^12			
09/13/93	8:20pm	LExit	1	120^08		$ -125.00	$ 843.75
09/13/93	8:20pm	Sell	1	120^08			
09/14/93	12:20pm	SExit	1	119^00		$ 1250.00	$ 2093.75
09/14/93	12:20pm	Buy	1	119^00			
09/14/93	8:20pm	LExit	1	118^24		$ -250.00	$ 1843.75
09/14/93	8:20pm	Sell	1	118^24			
09/15/93	12:20pm	SExit	1	118^07		$ 531.25	$ 2375.00
09/15/93	12:20pm	Buy	1	118^07			
09/15/93	8:20pm	LExit	1	119^09		$ 1062.50	$ 3437.50
09/15/93	8:20pm	Sell	1	119^09			
09/16/93	12:20pm	SExit	1	119^02		$ 218.75	$ 3656.25
09/16/93	12:20pm	Buy	1	119^02			
09/16/93	3:00pm	LExit	1	119^01		$ -31.25	$ 3625.00
09/16/93	3:00pm	Sell	1	119^01			
09/17/93	9:20am	SExit	1	118^17		$ 500.00	$ 4125.00
09/17/93	9:20am	Buy	1	118^17			
09/17/93	1:20pm	LExit	1	119^07		$ 687.50	$ 4812.50
09/17/93	1:20pm	Sell	1	119^07			
09/19/93	9:20pm	SExit	1	119^04		$ 93.75	$ 4906.25
09/19/93	9:20pm	Buy	1	119^04			
09/20/93	9:20am	LExit	1	119^00		$ -125.00	$ 4781.25
09/20/93	9:20am	Sell	1	119^00			
09/20/93	12:20pm	SExit	1	118^31		$ 31.25	$ 4812.50
09/20/93	12:20pm	Buy	1	118^31			
09/20/93	2:20pm	LExit	1	118^23		$ -250.00	$ 4562.50
09/20/93	2:20pm	Sell	1	118^23			
09/20/93	9:20pm	SExit	1	118^08		$ 468.75	$ 5031.25
09/20/93	9:20pm	Buy	1	118^08			
09/21/93	1:20pm	LExit	1	118^13		$ 156.25	$ 5187.50
09/21/93	1:20pm	Sell	1	118^13			
09/21/93	10:05pm	SExit	1	117^20		$ 781.25	$ 5968.75
09/21/93	10:05pm	Buy	1	117^20			
09/22/93	11:20am	LExit	1	117^20		$ 0.00	$ 5968.75
09/22/93	11:20am	Sell	1	117^20			
09/22/93	2:20pm	SExit	1	117^28		$ -250.00	$ 5718.75
09/22/93	2:20pm	Buy	1	117^28			
09/22/93	9:20pm	LExit	1	118^01		$ 156.25	$ 5875.00
09/22/93	9:20pm	Sell	1	118^01			
09/23/93	10:20am	SExit	1	118^15		$ -437.50	$ 5437.50
09/23/93	10:20am	Buy	1	118^15			
09/23/93	12:20pm	LExit	1	118^16		$ 31.25	$ 5468.75
09/23/93	12:20pm	Sell	1	118^16			
09/23/93	9:20pm	SExit	1	118^04		$ 375.00	$ 5843.75
09/23/93	9:20pm	Buy	1	118^04			
09/24/93	12:20pm	LExit	1	118^08		$ 125.00	$ 5968.75
09/24/93	12:20pm	Sell	1	118^08			
09/24/93	3:00pm	SExit	1	118^12		$ -125.00	$ 5843.75
09/24/93	3:00pm	Buy	1	118^12			
09/27/93	9:20am	LExit	1	119^00		$ 625.00	$ 6468.75

Figure 10-22

```
FSK   US Z3-60 min    08/31/93 - 10/04/93
Date      Time    Type   Cnts    Price  Signal Name    Entry P/L   Cumulative
09/27/93  9:20am  Sell   1       119^00
09/27/93  12:20pm SExit  1       119^10                    $  -312.50 $  6156.25
09/27/93  12:20pm Buy    1       119^10
09/27/93  1:20pm  LExit  1       119^15                    $   156.25 $  6312.50
09/27/93  1:20pm  Sell   1       119^15
09/27/93  2:20pm  SExit  1       119^16                    $   -31.25 $  6281.25
09/27/93  2:20pm  Buy    1       119^16
09/27/93  10:05pm LExit  1       119^30                    $   437.50 $  6718.75
09/27/93  10:05pm Sell   1       119^30
09/28/93  10:20am SExit  1       120^05                    $  -218.75 $  6500.00
09/28/93  10:20am Buy    1       120^05
09/28/93  1:20pm  LExit  1       120^05                    $     0.00 $  6500.00
09/28/93  1:20pm  Sell   1       120^05
09/28/93  9:20pm  SExit  1       119^30                    $   218.75 $  6718.75
09/28/93  9:20pm  Buy    1       119^30
09/29/93  11:20am LExit  1       119^28                    $   -62.50 $  6656.25
09/29/93  11:20am Sell   1       119^28
09/29/93  8:20pm  SExit  1       118^29                    $   968.75 $  7625.00
09/29/93  8:20pm  Buy    1       118^29
09/30/93  11:20am LExit  1       118^23                    $  -187.50 $  7437.50
09/30/93  11:20am Sell   1       118^23
09/30/93  3:00pm  SExit  1       118^16                    $   218.75 $  7656.25
09/30/93  3:00pm  Buy    1       118^16
10/01/93  9:20am  LExit  1       118^11                    $  -156.25 $  7500.00
10/01/93  9:20am  Sell   1       118^11
10/01/93  11:20am SExit  1       118^27                    $  -500.00 $  7000.00
10/01/93  11:20am Buy    1       118^27
10/01/93  2:20pm  LExit  1       119^08                    $   406.25 $  7406.25
10/01/93  2:20pm  Sell   1       119^08
10/04/93  9:20am  SExit  1       119^11                    $   -93.75 $  7312.50
10/04/93  9:20am  Buy    1       119^11
10/04/93  12:20pm LExit  1       119^13                    $    62.50 $  7375.00
10/04/93  12:20pm Sell   1       119^13
10/04/93  3:00pm  SExit  1       119^13                    $     0.00 $  7375.00
10/04/93  3:00pm  Buy    1       119^13
```

Figure 10-23

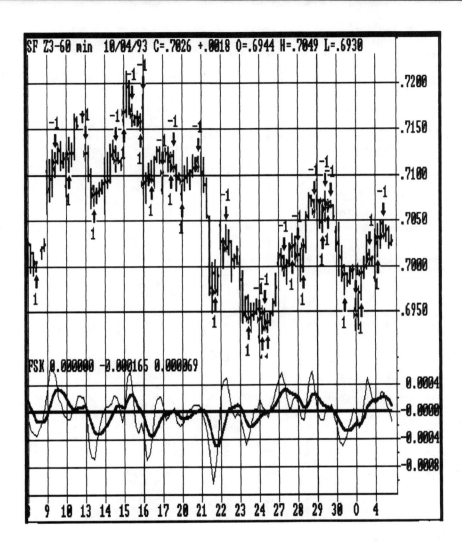

Figure 10-24

FSK   SF Z3-60 min   08/24/93 - 10/04/93

Figure 82   Performance Summary: All Trades

Total net profit	$	5237.50	Open position P/L	$	87.50
Gross profit	$	12587.50	Gross loss	$	-7350.00
Total # of trades		52	Percent profitable		46%
Number winning trades		24	Number losing trades		28
Largest winning trade	$	1712.50	Largest losing trade	$	-850.00
Average winning trade	$	524.48	Average losing trade	$	-262.50
Ratio avg win/avg loss		2.00	Avg trade(win & loss)	$	100.72
Max consec. winners		5	Max consec. losers		4
Avg # bars in winners		4	Avg # bars in losers		3
Max intraday drawdown	$	-1862.50			
Profit factor		1.71	Max # contracts held		1
Account size required	$	1862.50	Return on account		281%

Performance Summary: Long Trades

Total net profit	$	4087.50	Open position P/L	$	0.00
Gross profit	$	6550.00	Gross loss	$	-2462.50
Total # of trades		26	Percent profitable		58%
Number winning trades		15	Number losing trades		11
Largest winning trade	$	1375.00	Largest losing trade	$	-850.00
Average winning trade	$	436.67	Average losing trade	$	-223.86
Ratio avg win/avg loss		1.95	Avg trade(win & loss)	$	157.21
Max consec. winners		6	Max consec. losers		3
Avg # bars in winners		4	Avg # bars in losers		2
Max intraday drawdown	$	-1062.50			
Profit factor		2.66	Max # contracts held		1
Account size required	$	1062.50	Return on account		385%

Performance Summary: Short Trades

Total net profit	$	1150.00	Open position P/L	$	87.50
Gross profit	$	6037.50	Gross loss	$	-4887.50
Total # of trades		26	Percent profitable		35%
Number winning trades		9	Number losing trades		17
Largest winning trade	$	1712.50	Largest losing trade	$	-662.50
Average winning trade	$	670.83	Average losing trade	$	-287.50
Ratio avg win/avg loss		2.33	Avg trade(win & loss)	$	44.23
Max consec. winners		3	Max consec. losers		6
Avg # bars in winners		5	Avg # bars in losers		3
Max intraday drawdown	$	-2350.00			
Profit factor		1.24	Max # contracts held		1
Account size required	$	2350.00	Return on account		49%

Figure 10-25

```
FSK  SF  Z3-60 min   08/24/93 - 10/04/93
Date     Time     Type  Cnts    Price  Signal Name      Entry P/L  Cumulative
08/26/93 12:20pm Sell  1        .6798
08/27/93 11:20am SExit 1        .6751                 $    587.50 $    587.50
08/27/93 11:20am Buy   1        .6751
08/27/93  3:00pm LExit 1        .6793                 $    525.00 $   1112.50
08/27/93  3:00pm Sell  1        .6793
08/30/93 12:20pm SExit 1        .6756                 $    462.50 $   1575.00
08/30/93 12:20pm Buy   1        .6756
08/31/93  9:20am LExit 1        .6727                 $   -362.50 $   1212.50
08/31/93  9:20am Sell  1        .6727
08/31/93 12:20pm SExit 1        .6733                 $    -75.00 $   1137.50
08/31/93 12:20pm Buy   1        .6733
08/31/93  3:00pm LExit 1        .6742                 $    112.50 $   1250.00
08/31/93  3:00pm Sell  1        .6742
09/01/93  9:20am SExit 1        .6793                 $   -637.50 $    612.50
09/01/93  9:20am Buy   1        .6793
09/01/93 12:20pm LExit 1        .6823                 $    375.00 $    987.50
09/01/93 12:20pm Sell  1        .6823
09/02/93 11:20am SExit 1        .6872                 $   -612.50 $    375.00
09/02/93 11:20am Buy   1        .6872
09/02/93  2:20pm LExit 1        .6893                 $    262.50 $    637.50
09/02/93  2:20pm Sell  1        .6893
09/03/93 10:20am SExit 1        .6930                 $   -462.50 $    175.00
09/03/93 10:20am Buy   1        .6930
09/03/93  1:20pm LExit 1        .6990                 $    750.00 $    925.00
09/03/93  1:20pm Sell  1        .6990
09/07/93 10:20am SExit 1        .7016                 $   -325.00 $    600.00
09/07/93 10:20am Buy   1        .7016
09/07/93  1:20pm LExit 1        .7047                 $    387.50 $    987.50
09/07/93  1:20pm Sell  1        .7047
09/08/93 12:20pm SExit 1        .7004                 $    537.50 $   1525.00
09/08/93 12:20pm Buy   1        .7004
09/09/93 12:20pm LExit 1        .7114                 $   1375.00 $   2900.00
09/09/93 12:20pm Sell  1        .7114
09/10/93 10:20am SExit 1        .7124                 $   -125.00 $   2775.00
09/10/93 10:20am Buy   1        .7124
09/13/93  9:20am LExit 1        .7123                 $    -12.50 $   2762.50
09/13/93  9:20am Sell  1        .7123
09/13/93 12:20pm SExit 1        .7079                 $    550.00 $   3312.50
09/13/93 12:20pm Buy   1        .7079
09/14/93  1:20pm LExit 1        .7116                 $    462.50 $   3775.00
09/14/93  1:20pm Sell  1        .7116
09/15/93  9:20am SExit 1        .7169                 $   -662.50 $   3112.50
09/15/93  9:20am Buy   1        .7169
09/15/93 12:20pm LExit 1        .7166                 $    -37.50 $   3075.00
09/15/93 12:20pm Sell  1        .7166
09/15/93  3:00pm SExit 1        .7158                 $    100.00 $   3175.00
09/15/93  3:00pm Buy   1        .7158
09/16/93  9:20am LExit 1        .7090                 $   -850.00 $   2325.00
09/16/93  9:20am Sell  1        .7090
09/16/93 12:20pm SExit 1        .7095                 $    -62.50 $   2262.50
```

Figure 10-26

```
FSK   SF Z3-60 min    08/24/93 - 10/04/93
Date      Time     Type    Cnts    Price   Signal Name        Entry P/L   Cumulative
09/16/93 12:20pm Buy     1         .7095
09/17/93  9:20am LExit 1          .7102                    $     87.50 $    2350.00
09/17/93  9:20am Sell  1          .7102
09/17/93 12:20pm SExit 1          .7121                    $   -237.50 $    2112.50
09/17/93 12:20pm Buy   1          .7121
09/17/93  1:20pm LExit 1          .7108                    $   -162.50 $    1950.00
09/17/93  1:20pm Sell  1          .7108
09/20/93  9:20am SExit 1          .7093                    $    187.50 $    2137.50
09/20/93  9:20am Buy   1          .7093
09/20/93  3:00pm LExit 1          .7108                    $    187.50 $    2325.00
09/20/93  3:00pm Sell  1          .7108
09/21/93  2:20pm SExit 1          .6971                    $   1712.50 $    4037.50
09/21/93  2:20pm Buy   1          .6971
09/22/93 11:20am LExit 1          .7019                    $    600.00 $    4637.50
09/22/93 11:20am Sell  1          .7019
09/23/93 12:20pm SExit 1          .6943                    $    950.00 $    5587.50
09/23/93 12:20pm Buy   1          .6943
09/24/93  9:20am LExit 1          .6941                    $    -25.00 $    5562.50
09/24/93  9:20am Sell  1          .6941
09/24/93 10:20am SExit 1          .6948                    $    -87.50 $    5475.00
09/24/93 10:20am Buy   1          .6948
09/24/93 11:20am LExit 1          .6932                    $   -200.00 $    5275.00
09/24/93 11:20am Sell  1          .6932
09/24/93 12:20pm SExit 1          .6938                    $    -75.00 $    5200.00
09/24/93 12:20pm Buy   1          .6938
09/27/93 11:20am LExit 1          .6998                    $    750.00 $    5950.00
09/27/93 11:20am Sell  1          .6998
09/27/93  2:20pm SExit 1          .7021                    $   -287.50 $    5662.50
09/27/93  2:20pm Buy   1          .7021
09/28/93  9:20am LExit 1          .7012                    $   -112.50 $    5550.00
09/28/93  9:20am Sell  1          .7012
09/28/93 11:20am SExit 1          .7022                    $   -125.00 $    5425.00
09/28/93 11:20am Buy   1          .7022
09/28/93  3:00pm LExit 1          .7059                    $    462.50 $    5887.50
09/28/93  3:00pm Sell  1          .7059
09/29/93 11:20am SExit 1          .7071                    $   -150.00 $    5737.50
09/29/93 11:20am Buy   1          .7071
09/29/93 12:20pm LExit 1          .7063                    $   -100.00 $    5637.50
09/29/93 12:20pm Sell  1          .7063
09/29/93  1:20pm SExit 1          .7069                    $    -75.00 $    5562.50
09/29/93  1:20pm Buy   1          .7069
09/29/93  2:20pm LExit 1          .7066                    $    -37.50 $    5525.00
09/29/93  2:20pm Sell  1          .7066
09/30/93 12:20pm SExit 1          .6990                    $    950.00 $    6475.00
09/30/93 12:20pm Buy   1          .6990
10/01/93  9:20am LExit 1          .6945                    $   -562.50 $    5912.50
10/01/93  9:20am Sell  1          .6945
10/01/93 11:20am SExit 1          .6992                    $   -587.50 $    5325.00
10/01/93 11:20am Buy   1          .6992
10/01/93  2:20pm LExit 1          .7007                    $    187.50 $    5512.50
```

Figure 10-27

10/01/93	2:20pm	Sell	1	.7007				
10/04/93	10:20am	SExit	1	.7031	$	-300.00	$	5212.50
10/04/93	10:20am	Buy	1	.7031				
10/04/93	12:20pm	LExit	1	.7033	$	25.00	$	5237.50
10/04/93	12:20pm	Sell	1	.7033				

Figure 10-28

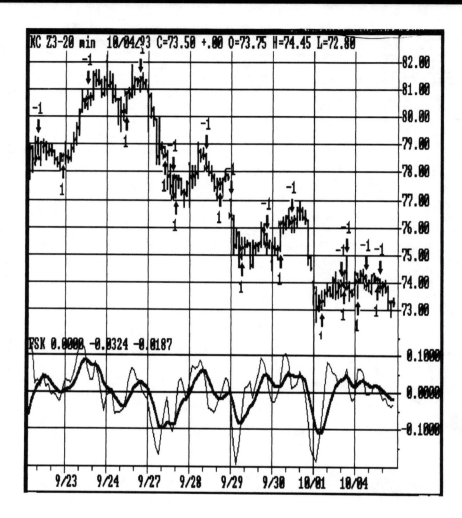

Figure 10-29

```
FSK-XOVER   KC Z3-20 min    09/07/93 - 10/04/93

   Figure 87              Performance Summary:  All Trades

Total net profit       $    2493.75  Open position P/L      $     225.00
Gross profit           $    7968.75  Gross loss             $   -5475.00

Total # of trades              52    Percent profitable            44%
Number winning trades          23    Number losing trades          29

Largest winning trade  $    1087.50  Largest losing trade   $    -543.75
Average winning trade  $     346.47  Average losing trade   $    -188.79
Ratio avg win/avg loss        1.84   Avg trade(win & loss)  $      47.96

Max consec. winners            3     Max consec. losers             6
Avg # bars in winners          7     Avg # bars in losers           4

Max intraday drawdown  $   -1181.25
Profit factor                 1.46   Max # contracts held           1
Account size required  $    1181.25  Return on account            211%
---------------------------------------------------------------------------
                       Performance Summary:  Long Trades

Total net profit       $     543.75  Open position P/L      $       0.00
Gross profit           $    3037.50  Gross loss             $   -2493.75

Total # of trades              26    Percent profitable            50%
Number winning trades          13    Number losing trades          13

Largest winning trade  $     787.50  Largest losing trade   $    -543.75
Average winning trade  $     233.65  Average losing trade   $    -191.83
Ratio avg win/avg loss        1.22   Avg trade(win & loss)  $      20.91

Max consec. winners            3     Max consec. losers             3
Avg # bars in winners          6     Avg # bars in losers           3

Max intraday drawdown  $   -1106.25
Profit factor                 1.22   Max # contracts held           1
Account size required  $    1106.25  Return on account             49%
---------------------------------------------------------------------------
                       Performance Summary:  Short Trades

Total net profit       $    1950.00  Open position P/L      $     225.00
Gross profit           $    4931.25  Gross loss             $   -2981.25

Total # of trades              26    Percent profitable            38%
Number winning trades          10    Number losing trades          16

Largest winning trade  $    1087.50  Largest losing trade   $    -487.50
Average winning trade  $     493.13  Average losing trade   $    -186.33
Ratio avg win/avg loss        2.65   Avg trade(win & loss)  $      75.00

Max consec. winners            2     Max consec. losers             4
Avg # bars in winners          7     Avg # bars in losers           4

Max intraday drawdown  $   -1200.00
Profit factor                 1.65   Max # contracts held           1
Account size required  $    1200.00  Return on account            163%
```

Figure 10-30

```
FSK-XOVER  KC Z3-20 min  09/07/93 - 10/04/93
Date      Time     Type   Cnts   Price  Signal Name      Entry P/L   Cumulative
09/07/93  1:35pm Sell   1    77.60                      /
09/08/93  9:35am SExit  1    78.80               $   -450.00 $   -450.00
09/08/93  9:35am Buy    1    78.80
09/08/93 10:55am LExit  1    78.90               $     37.50 $   -412.50
09/08/93 10:55am Sell   1    78.90
09/09/93  9:55am SExit  1    79.50               $   -225.00 $   -637.50
09/09/93  9:55am Buy    1    79.50
09/09/93 11:15am LExit  1    80.70               $    450.00 $   -187.50
09/09/93 11:15am Sell   1    80.70
09/09/93  1:55pm SExit  1    82.00               $   -487.50 $   -675.00
09/09/93  1:55pm Buy    1    82.00
09/10/93  9:55am LExit  1    81.75               $    -93.75 $   -768.75
09/10/93  9:55am Sell   1    81.75
09/10/93 11:55am SExit  1    81.15               $    225.00 $   -543.75
09/10/93 11:55am Buy    1    81.15
09/13/93 10:35am LExit  1    82.30               $    431.25 $   -112.50
09/13/93 10:35am Sell   1    82.30
09/13/93 12:55pm SExit  1    81.60               $    262.50 $    150.00
09/13/93 12:55pm Buy    1    81.60
09/13/93  1:55pm LExit  1    81.20               $   -150.00 $      0.00
09/13/93  1:55pm Sell   1    81.20
09/14/93  9:35am SExit  1    81.90               $   -262.50 $   -262.50
09/14/93  9:35am Buy    1    81.90
09/14/93 11:35am LExit  1    83.00               $    412.50 $    150.00
09/14/93 11:35am Sell   1    83.00
09/15/93 10:35am SExit  1    82.05               $    356.25 $    506.25
09/15/93 10:35am Buy    1    82.05
09/15/93  1:35pm LExit  1    81.95               $    -37.50 $    468.75
09/15/93  1:35pm Sell   1    81.95
09/16/93  9:55am SExit  1    82.10               $    -56.25 $    412.50
09/16/93  9:55am Buy    1    82.10
09/16/93 10:55am LExit  1    81.50               $   -225.00 $    187.50
09/16/93 10:55am Sell   1    81.50
09/16/93 11:15am SExit  1    81.60               $    -37.50 $    150.00
09/16/93 11:15am Buy    1    81.60
09/16/93  1:15pm LExit  1    81.95               $    131.25 $    281.25
09/16/93  1:15pm Sell   1    81.95
09/17/93 10:55am SExit  1    82.10               $    -56.25 $    225.00
09/17/93 10:55am Buy    1    82.10
09/17/93 12:35pm LExit  1    82.25               $     56.25 $    281.25
09/17/93 12:35pm Sell   1    82.25
09/17/93  1:35pm SExit  1    82.65               $   -150.00 $    131.25
09/17/93  1:35pm Buy    1    82.65
09/20/93  9:35am LExit  1    82.25               $   -150.00 $    -18.75
09/20/93  9:35am Sell   1    82.25
09/20/93 12:35pm SExit  1    81.35               $    337.50 $    318.75
09/20/93 12:35pm Buy    1    81.35
09/20/93  1:58pm LExit  1    81.25               $    -37.50 $    281.25
09/20/93  1:58pm Sell   1    81.25
09/21/93  9:35am SExit  1    81.90               $   -243.75 $     37.50
```

Figure 10-31

```
FSK-XOVER   KC Z3-20 min    09/07/93 - 10/04/93
Date       Time     Type  Cnts    Price  Signal Name      Entry P/L   Cumulative
09/21/93  9:35am Buy    1        81.90
09/21/93 10:15am LExit  1        80.80                  $   -412.50 $   -375.00
09/21/93 10:15am Sell   1        80.80
09/21/93 11:15am SExit  1        80.75                  $     18.75 $   -356.25
09/21/93 11:15am Buy    1        80.75
09/21/93 12:35pm LExit  1        81.15                  $    150.00 $   -206.25
09/21/93 12:35pm Sell   1        81.15
09/22/93  9:35am SExit  1        78.60                  $    956.25 $    750.00
09/22/93  9:35am Buy    1        78.60
09/22/93 11:15am LExit  1        78.45                  $    -56.25 $    693.75
09/22/93 11:15am Sell   1        78.45
09/22/93  1:58pm SExit  1        78.55                  $    -37.50 $    656.25
09/22/93  1:58pm Buy    1        78.55
09/23/93 12:15pm LExit  1        80.65                  $    787.50 $   1443.75
09/23/93 12:15pm Sell   1        80.65
09/24/93 11:55am SExit  1        80.85                  $    -75.00 $   1368.75
09/24/93 11:55am Buy    1        80.85
09/24/93  1:35pm LExit  1        81.30                  $    168.75 $   1537.50
09/24/93  1:35pm Sell   1        81.30
09/27/93 11:35am SExit  1        78.55                  $   1031.25 $   2568.75
09/27/93 11:35am Buy    1        78.55
09/27/93 12:35pm LExit  1        77.10                  $   -543.75 $   2025.00
09/27/93 12:35pm Sell   1        77.10
09/27/93 12:55pm SExit  1        77.80                  $   -262.50 $   1762.50
09/27/93 12:55pm Buy    1        77.80
09/28/93 11:35am LExit  1        78.10                  $    112.50 $   1875.00
09/28/93 11:35am Sell   1        78.10
09/28/93  1:15pm SExit  1        77.55                  $    206.25 $   2081.25
09/28/93  1:15pm Buy    1        77.55
09/29/93  9:35am LExit  1        76.45                  $   -412.50 $   1668.75
09/29/93  9:35am Sell   1        76.45
09/29/93 10:55am SExit  1        75.25                  $    450.00 $   2118.75
09/29/93 10:55am Buy    1        75.25
09/29/93  1:55pm LExit  1        75.40                  $     56.25 $   2175.00
09/29/93  1:55pm Sell   1        75.40
09/30/93 10:35am SExit  1        76.15                  $   -281.25 $   1893.75
09/30/93 10:35am Buy    1        76.15
09/30/93 11:55am LExit  1        76.20                  $     18.75 $   1912.50
09/30/93 11:55am Sell   1        76.20
10/01/93 10:35am SExit  1        73.30                  $   1087.50 $   3000.00
10/01/93 10:35am Buy    1        73.30
10/01/93 12:55pm LExit  1        73.90                  $    225.00 $   3225.00
10/01/93 12:55pm Sell   1        73.90
10/01/93  1:15pm SExit  1        74.35                  $   -168.75 $   3056.25
10/01/93  1:15pm Buy    1        74.35
10/01/93  1:35pm LExit  1        73.80                  $   -206.25 $   2850.00
10/01/93  1:35pm Sell   1        73.80
10/04/93  9:55am SExit  1        74.05                  $    -93.75 $   2756.25
10/04/93  9:55am Buy    1        74.05
10/04/93 10:55am LExit  1        73.90                  $    -56.25 $   2700.00
```

Figure 10-32

10/04/93	10:55am	Sell	1	73.90				
10/04/93	12:15pm	SExit	1	74.15	$	-93.75	$	2606.25
10/04/93	12:15pm	Buy	1	74.15				
10/04/93	12:35pm	LExit	1	73.85	$	-112.50	$	2493.75
10/04/93	12:35pm	Sell	1	73.85				

Figure 10-33

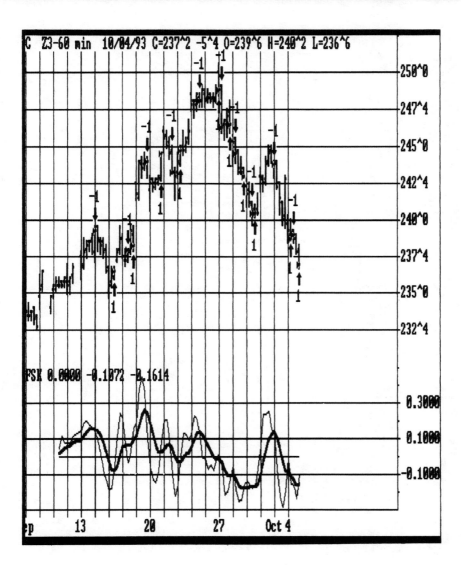

Figure 10-34

```
FSK-XOVER   C   Z3-60 min    09/07/93 - 10/04/93
```

Figure 92

Performance Summary: All Trades

Total net profit	$	687.50	Open position P/L	$	0.00
Gross profit	$	1262.50	Gross loss	$	-575.00
Total # of trades		19	Percent profitable		53%
Number winning trades		10	Number losing trades		9
Largest winning trade	$	287.50	Largest losing trade	$	-125.00
Average winning trade	$	126.25	Average losing trade	$	-63.89
Ratio avg win/avg loss		1.98	Avg trade(win & loss)	$	36.18
Max consec. winners		5	Max consec. losers		4
Avg # bars in winners		4	Avg # bars in losers		3
Max intraday drawdown	$	-362.50		
Profit factor		2.20	Max # contracts held		1
Account size required	$	362.50	Return on account		190%

Performance Summary: Long Trades

Total net profit	$	287.50	Open position P/L	$	0.00
Gross profit	$	700.00	Gross loss	$	-412.50
Total # of trades		9	Percent profitable		56%
Number winning trades		5	Number losing trades		4
Largest winning trade	$	287.50	Largest losing trade	$	-125.00
Average winning trade	$	140.00	Average losing trade	$	-103.13
Ratio avg win/avg loss		1.36	Avg trade(win & loss)	$	31.94
Max consec. winners		2	Max consec. losers		3
Avg # bars in winners		5	Avg # bars in losers		3
Max intraday drawdown	$	-387.50		
Profit factor		1.70	Max # contracts held		1
Account size required	$	387.50	Return on account		74%

Performance Summary: Short Trades

Total net profit	$	400.00	Open position P/L	$	0.00
Gross profit	$	562.50	Gross loss	$	-162.50
Total # of trades		10	Percent profitable		50%
Number winning trades		5	Number losing trades		5
Largest winning trade	$	250.00	Largest losing trade	$	-75.00
Average winning trade	$	112.50	Average losing trade	$	-32.50
Ratio avg win/avg loss		3.46	Avg trade(win & loss)	$	40.00
Max consec. winners		4	Max consec. losers		5
Avg # bars in winners		4	Avg # bars in losers		4
Max intraday drawdown	$	-237.50		
Profit factor		3.46	Max # contracts held		1
Account size required	$	237.50	Return on account		168%

Figure 10-35

```
FSK-XOVER  C  Z3-60 min   09/07/93 - 10/04/93
Date      Time     Type  Cnts    Price  Signal Name      Entry P/L   Cumulative
09/14/93 10:30am Sell  1        239^2
09/15/93 12:30pm SExit 1        236^4               $    137.50 $    137.50
09/15/93 12:30pm Buy   1        236^4
09/16/93 12:30pm LExit 1        238^0               $     75.00 $    212.50
09/16/93 12:30pm Sell  1        238^0
09/16/93  2:15pm SExit 1        238^2               $    -12.50 $    200.00
09/16/93  2:15pm Buy   1        238^2
09/17/93  2:15pm LExit 1        244^0               $    287.50 $    487.50
09/17/93  2:15pm Sell  1        244^0
09/20/93  2:15pm SExit 1        244^4               $    -25.00 $    462.50
09/20/93  2:15pm Buy   1        244^4
09/21/93  1:30pm LExit 1        243^2               $    -62.50 $    400.00
09/21/93  1:30pm Sell  1        243^2
09/22/93 11:30am SExit 1        244^6               $    -75.00 $    325.00
09/22/93 11:30am Buy   1        244^6
09/23/93  1:30pm LExit 1        248^0               $    162.50 $    487.50
09/23/93  1:30pm Sell  1        248^0
09/27/93 10:30am SExit 1        248^6               $    -37.50 $    450.00
09/27/93 10:30am Buy   1        248^6
09/27/93 11:30am LExit 1        246^2               $   -125.00 $    325.00
09/27/93 11:30am Sell  1        246^2
09/27/93  2:15pm SExit 1        246^4               $    -12.50 $    312.50
09/27/93  2:15pm Buy   1        246^4
09/28/93 11:30am LExit 1        244^4               $   -100.00 $    212.50
09/28/93 11:30am Sell  1        244^4
09/28/93  2:15pm SExit 1        243^0               $     75.00 $    287.50
09/28/93  2:15pm Buy   1        243^0
09/29/93 12:30pm LExit 1        240^4               $   -125.00 $    162.50
09/29/93 12:30pm Sell  1        240^4
09/29/93  1:30pm SExit 1        240^4               $      0.00 $    162.50
09/29/93  1:30pm Buy   1        240^4
10/01/93 10:30am LExit 1        243^6               $    162.50 $    325.00
10/01/93 10:30am Sell  1        243^6
10/04/93 11:30am SExit 1        238^6               $    250.00 $    575.00
10/04/93 11:30am Buy   1        238^6
10/04/93 12:30pm LExit 1        239^0               $     12.50 $    587.50
10/04/93 12:30pm Sell  1        239^0
10/04/93  2:15pm SExit 1        237^0               $    100.00 $    687.50
10/04/93  2:15pm Buy   1        237^0
```

Figure 10-36

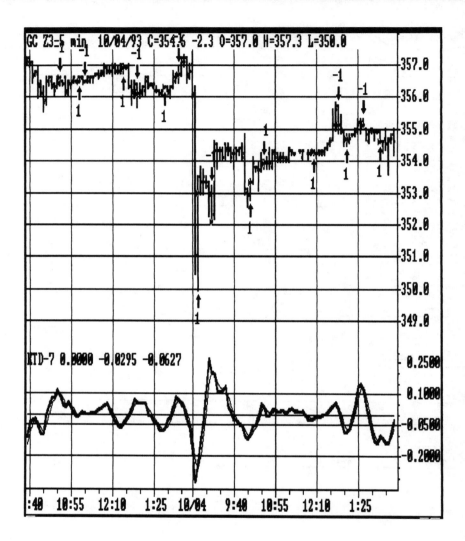

Figure 10-37

```
KTD-7-T   GC Z3-5 min    09/28/93 - 10/04/93

Figure 95                    Performance Summary:  All Trades

Total net profit       $      1010.00   Open position P/L      $          0.00
Gross profit           $      2030.00   Gross loss             $      -1020.00

Total # of trades              47       Percent profitable               60%
Number winning trades          28       Number losing trades             19

Largest winning trade  $       370.00   Largest losing trade   $       -120.00
Average winning trade  $        72.50   Average losing trade   $        -53.68
Ratio avg win/avg loss           1.35   Avg trade(win & loss)  $         21.49

Max consec. winners             6       Max consec. losers                4
Avg # bars in winners           6       Avg # bars in losers              9

Max intraday drawdown  $      -390.00
Profit factor                    1.99   Max # contracts held              1
Account size required  $       390.00   Return on account              259%

------------------------------------------------------------------------------

                             Performance Summary:  Long Trades

Total net profit       $       360.00   Open position P/L      $          0.00
Gross profit           $       860.00   Gross loss             $       -500.00

Total # of trades              23       Percent profitable               65%
Number winning trades          15       Number losing trades              8

Largest winning trade  $       220.00   Largest losing trade   $       -120.00
Average winning trade  $        57.33   Average losing trade   $        -62.50
Ratio avg win/avg loss           0.92   Avg trade(win & loss)  $         15.65

Max consec. winners             4       Max consec. losers                2
Avg # bars in winners           6       Avg # bars in losers              8

Max intraday drawdown  $      -270.00
Profit factor                    1.72   Max # contracts held              1
Account size required  $       270.00   Return on account              133%

------------------------------------------------------------------------------

                             Performance Summary:  Short Trades

Total net profit       $       650.00   Open position P/L      $          0.00
Gross profit           $      1170.00   Gross loss             $       -520.00

Total # of trades              24       Percent profitable               54%
Number winning trades          13       Number losing trades             11

Largest winning trade  $       370.00   Largest losing trade   $       -120.00
Average winning trade  $        90.00   Average losing trade   $        -47.27
Ratio avg win/avg loss           1.90   Avg trade(win & loss)  $         27.08

Max consec. winners             4       Max consec. losers                4
Avg # bars in winners           7       Avg # bars in losers             10

Max intraday drawdown  $      -270.00
Profit factor                    2.25   Max # contracts held              1
Account size required  $       270.00   Return on account              241%
```

Figure 10-38

```
KTD-7-T   GC Z3-5 min    09/28/93 - 10/04/93
Date      Time     Type  Cnts    Price  Signal Name      Entry P/L   Cumulative
09/28/93  9:45am  Sell   1       357.5
09/28/93  10:10am SExit  1       357.5                 $     0.00 $      0.00
09/28/93  10:10am Buy    1       357.5
09/28/93  10:40am LExit  1       357.9                 $    40.00 $     40.00
09/28/93  10:40am Sell   1       357.9
09/28/93  11:30am SExit  1       357.8                 $    10.00 $     50.00
09/28/93  11:30am Buy    1       357.8
09/28/93  12:00pm LExit  1       357.3                 $   -50.00 $      0.00
09/28/93  12:00pm Sell   1       357.3
09/28/93  12:40pm SExit  1       358.0                 $   -70.00 $    -70.00
09/28/93  12:40pm Buy    1       358.0
09/28/93  1:00pm  LExit  1       358.2                 $    20.00 $    -50.00
09/28/93  1:00pm  Sell   1       358.2
09/28/93  1:35pm  SExit  1       357.5                 $    70.00 $     20.00
09/28/93  1:35pm  Buy    1       357.5
09/28/93  2:05pm  LExit  1       357.8                 $    30.00 $     50.00
09/28/93  2:05pm  Sell   1       357.8
09/29/93  8:30am  SExit  1       355.8                 $   200.00 $    250.00
09/29/93  8:30am  Buy    1       355.8
09/29/93  9:00am  LExit  1       356.6                 $    80.00 $    330.00
09/29/93  9:00am  Sell   1       356.6
09/29/93  10:05am SExit  1       355.5                 $   110.00 $    440.00
09/29/93  10:05am Buy    1       355.5
09/29/93  10:40am LExit  1       354.3                 $  -120.00 $    320.00
09/29/93  10:40am Sell   1       354.3
09/29/93  11:15am SExit  1       352.5                 $   180.00 $    500.00
09/29/93  11:15am Buy    1       352.5
09/29/93  11:40am LExit  1       353.6                 $   110.00 $    610.00
09/29/93  11:40am Sell   1       353.6
09/29/93  12:30pm SExit  1       353.8                 $   -20.00 $    590.00
09/29/93  12:30pm Buy    1       353.8
09/29/93  12:40pm LExit  1       353.7                 $   -10.00 $    580.00
09/29/93  12:40pm Sell   1       353.7
09/29/93  1:15pm  SExit  1       353.6                 $    10.00 $    590.00
09/29/93  1:15pm  Buy    1       353.6
09/29/93  1:40pm  LExit  1       353.6                 $     0.00 $    590.00
09/29/93  1:40pm  Sell   1       353.6
09/29/93  2:20pm  SExit  1       354.5                 $   -90.00 $    500.00
09/29/93  2:20pm  Buy    1       354.5
09/30/93  8:45am  LExit  1       356.7                 $   220.00 $    720.00
09/30/93  8:45am  Sell   1       356.7
09/30/93  9:10am  SExit  1       356.5                 $    20.00 $    740.00
09/30/93  9:10am  Buy    1       356.5
09/30/93  9:45am  LExit  1       356.9                 $    40.00 $    780.00
09/30/93  9:45am  Sell   1       356.9
09/30/93  10:35am SExit  1       355.9                 $   100.00 $    880.00
09/30/93  10:35am Buy    1       355.9
09/30/93  11:05am LExit  1       356.5                 $    60.00 $    940.00
09/30/93  11:05am Sell   1       356.5
09/30/93  11:25am SExit  1       356.8                 $   -30.00 $    910.00
```

Figure 10-39

```
KTD-7-T   GC Z3-5 min   09/28/93 - 10/04/93
Date       Time    Type  Cnts   Price  Signal Name      Entry P/L   Cumulative
09/30/93  11:25am Buy   1      356.8
09/30/93  12:15pm LExit 1      356.5            $    -30.00 $    880.00
09/30/93  12:15pm Sell  1      356.5
09/30/93  12:35pm SExit 1      357.0            $    -50.00 $    830.00
09/30/93  12:35pm Buy   1      357.0
09/30/93   1:00pm LExit 1      357.4            $     40.00 $    870.00
09/30/93   1:00pm Sell  1      357.4
09/30/93   1:25pm SExit 1      357.6            $    -20.00 $    850.00
09/30/93   1:25pm Buy   1      357.6
09/30/93   2:30pm LExit 1      357.0            $    -60.00 $    790.00
09/30/93   2:30pm Sell  1      357.0
10/01/93   9:30am SExit 1      357.2            $    -20.00 $    770.00
10/01/93   9:30am Buy   1      357.2
10/01/93  10:35am LExit 1      356.6            $    -60.00 $    710.00
10/01/93  10:35am Sell  1      356.6
10/01/93  11:10am SExit 1      356.5            $     10.00 $    720.00
10/01/93  11:10am Buy   1      356.5
10/01/93  11:20am LExit 1      356.5            $      0.00 $    720.00
10/01/93  11:20am Sell  1      356.5
10/01/93  12:30pm SExit 1      356.9            $    -40.00 $    680.00
10/01/93  12:30pm Buy   1      356.9
10/01/93  12:55pm LExit 1      356.1            $    -80.00 $    600.00
10/01/93  12:55pm Sell  1      356.1
10/01/93   1:45pm SExit 1      356.3            $    -20.00 $    580.00
10/01/93   1:45pm Buy   1      356.3
10/01/93   2:10pm LExit 1      356.7            $     40.00 $    620.00
10/01/93   2:10pm Sell  1      356.7
10/04/93   8:35am SExit 1      353.0            $    370.00 $    990.00
10/04/93   8:35am Buy   1      353.0
10/04/93   9:00am LExit 1      352.1            $    -90.00 $    900.00
10/04/93   9:00am Sell  1      352.1
10/04/93  10:10am SExit 1      353.3            $   -120.00 $    780.00
10/04/93  10:10am Buy   1      353.3
10/04/93  10:35am LExit 1      353.9            $     60.00 $    840.00
10/04/93  10:35am Sell  1      353.9
10/04/93  12:05pm SExit 1      354.3            $    -40.00 $    800.00
10/04/93  12:05pm Buy   1      354.3
10/04/93  12:50pm LExit 1      355.1            $     80.00 $    880.00
10/04/93  12:50pm Sell  1      355.1
10/04/93   1:05pm SExit 1      354.7            $     40.00 $    920.00
10/04/93   1:05pm Buy   1      354.7
10/04/93   1:35pm LExit 1      355.1            $     40.00 $    960.00
10/04/93   1:35pm Sell  1      355.1
10/04/93   2:05pm SExit 1      354.6            $     50.00 $   1010.00
10/04/93   2:05pm Buy   1      354.6
```

Figure 10-40

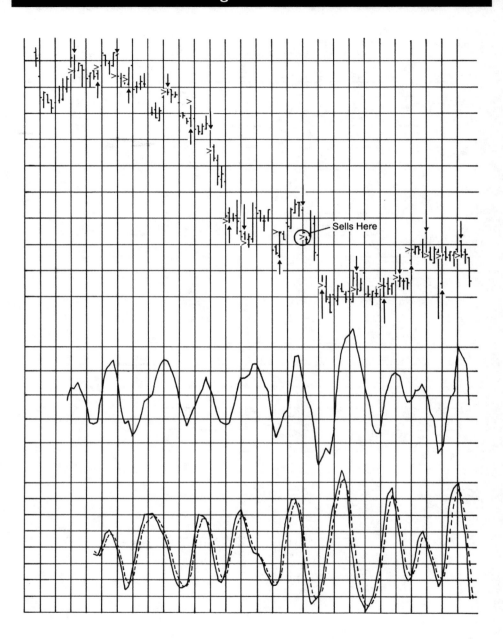

Figure 10-41

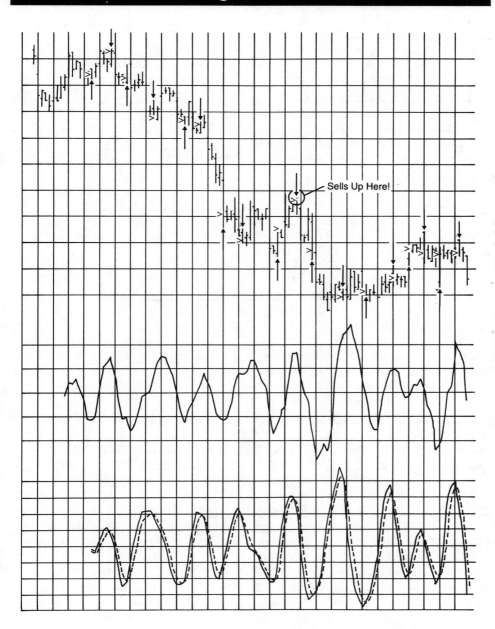

Summary

We've discussed no less than 15 indicators. Now you know why I didn't discuss the 140 others! It's simply mind boggling what the manipulation of figures can do. Even with computers to do the calculations and displays for us, we're left with the still-enormous task of trying to make sense out of this mass of information. I'll attempt to make sense out of the "few" indicators I have presented here.

We looked at four of the classics: momentum, Stochastics, RSI, and ADX. We developed four new indicators: TD-3, MATT, TDAC, and FSK. We then combined the TD-3 and FSK to produce two more new indicators: KTD-7 and KKTD-7. Finally, we combined the TD-3 and the FSK with the three most popular oscillators to produce the last five indicators: MTD-6, TDST, TDRS, FSST, and the FSRS.

We need not say more about the four classics. With the exception of the ADX, they primarily are used in non-trending markets—markets in a trading range. The ADX is of course in a class by itself, as it monitors the market for signs of trending. My favorite is the RSI with its signals of crossing the 50 line, the failed swings, and divergence from prices.

Two basic concepts developed by using logic served to produce two different oscillators, the TD-3 and FSK, as well as the cumulative indices, MATT and TDAC. Three out of those four can be used only with tick data, but we have described a way by which to adapt such tick data to construct daily bars. Of those four indicators, the FSK and the TDAC have become my favorites.

The combination of the TD-3 and the FSK produced the most exciting early warning indicator of them all: the KKTD-7. It can produce signals that identify tops and bottoms one to three bars *before* they occur! For short-term signals, that ability is unsurpassed. Further research on this indicator will focus on the development of long-term signals.

Of the five combinations with classic indicators, I believe the TDRS and the FSRS, both of which use the RSI as the second component, are superior to the other two, which use the Stochastic as the second component; and superior to the MTD-6. However, the last three all are excellent confirmatory indicators. Both the TDRS and FSRS are trend identifiers, and also are capable of producing reliable entry and exit signals, so they definitely are my two favorites from this group. We have narrowed the field down to eight. We have cut the field in half. You may still be confused as to how they are best applied, so you definitely will need to read Chapter 21: "Putting It All Together." Figure 10-42 gives a tabular listing of the properties of all these indicators.

I know some of you will rave about your favorite indicators that I didn't discuss here, and that's fine. Certainly, there are other good indicators, such as MACD, Williams %R, Bollinger bands, parabolic, volatility, and many more. Even if you've used these and liked them, now you have a few more at your disposal, and, more important, *these work well.* I use them to generate and take profits, and so will you after you finish this book, provided you adhere to its principles. I promised to show you my favorite indicators, and I have. The finer points of their use for entry and exit will be discussed in "Putting It All Together." But, since there's far more to trading than just following indicators, don't leave and trade quite yet. **Stay tuned!**

Figure 10-42

INDICATOR	TYPE	DATA NEEDED	RELATION TO PRICE	TYPE OF SIGNALS GIVEN	TYPE OF MARKETS	BEST SIGNAL
1. Stochastic	Oscillator	Any	Lagging	X-over reference lines and its MA, Divergence	Trading range	X-over reference lines
2. RSI	Oscillator	Any	Lagging	X-over reference lines and 50 line, Divergence and failed swing	Trading range	Failed Swing
3. Momentum	Oscillator	Any	Lagging	X-over zero line, Turning points and Divergence	Any	X-over zero line
4. ADX	Oscillator	Any	Lagging	Rising curve and "hook"	Any	Rising line
5. TD-3	Oscillator	Tick Data	Lagging	X-over zero line and its MA, Turning points	Any	Turning points
6. MATT	Cummul.Sum	Tick Data	Leading	Rising and falling curve	Trading range	Rising and falling line
7. TDAC	Cummul.Sum	Tick Data	Lagging	Turning points, rising curve, X-over its MA, "hook"	Any	X-over its MA
8. FSK	Oscillator	Any	Leading	X-over zero line and its MA, Turning points	Any	Turning points
9. KTD-7	Oscillator	Tick Data	Leading	X-over zero line and its MA, Turning points	Cyclical	Turning points
10. KKTD-7	Oscillator	Tick Data	Leading	X-over zero line and its MA, Turning points	Cyclical	Turning points
11. MTD-6	Oscillator	Tick Data	Leading	X-over zero line and its MA, Turning points	Trading range	Turning points
12. TDST	Oscillator	Tick Data	Lagging	X-over 50 line and its MA, Trend finder	Any	X-over its MA
13. TDRS	Oscillator	Tick Data	Lagging	X-over 50 line and its MA, Turning points, Trend finder	Any	Turning points
14. FSST	Oscillator	Any	Leading	X-over 50 line and its MA, Trend finder	Any	X-over 50 line, X-over its MA
15. FSRS	Oscillator	Any	Leading	X-over 50 line and its MA	Any	Turning points

PART 3

APPLICATION

11

Entering the Market

"All things come round to him who will but wait!"
—Henry Wadsworth Longfellow (1807–1882)
"The Student's Tale" from Tales of the Wayside Inn

All the previous preparation has made it possible for you to do two critical things: getting *in* the market and getting *out* of it. You may not realize it, but both those steps are equally critical. Although exiting the market is more difficult for some than entering correctly, the latter is ever so much more complicated. However, first things first. Entering comes before exiting, and the better your entrance, the easier and better your exit.

You've completed the preparatory step of finding a market with which you are comfortable—a market that has good volatility and sizable volume. You also have been monitoring the various important timeframes, such as weekly, daily, the 60-, 15-, and 5-minute bars, and perhaps even the 1-minute bars, as well as your favorite indicators. As you know, I will be following the Stochastic, RSI, TDAC, and FSRS, and using the last two as my critical timing indicators. I frequently overlay the Stochastic on the price bars in order to give the others more vertical "room to play" on the same page. The TDAC also is best seen when overlaid on the price bars. However, you must be careful and not lose track of an indicator line, as it can get obscured by a price bar, or vice versa. That could result in a costly mistake!

Remember that you do not enter the market on the basis of one indicator, or one pattern, or one of anything. You must train yourself to inspect all the critical factors and act only if there is a consensus. You must develop the necessary patience to wait until the odds are so stacked in your favor that you are bound to succeed. Some trades will be okay but risky; some will be tempting, and may work out; but we want the highest possible chance of success. Therefore, we must be very patient. No, we won't go days and days without trading; there will be many opportunities.

Longfellow said: "All things come round to him who will but wait!"

That is ever so true in trading, because if you don't like the trade you're looking at, just wait; there will be another one along shortly. It's just like waiting for a bus: If you miss one, another will arrive in a little while. Also realize that you don't need to trade continuously; you do not need to jump from one trade right into the next, and the next, and the next. Resist the urge to trade on a whim, tip, or rumor. This is serious business; don't be cavalier about it and set yourself up for a fall! If the entry signals are not clear, if they are ambiguous, contradictory, or in any way doubtful or suspicious, don't enter. **Wait!** There will be a time when the majority of signals are clear and in agreement. That moment will practically leap out at you and tug at your sleeve! You will know it. *That's when you enter.*

Getting down to specifics, what exactly are we looking for in order to enter a market? Let me say first that I rarely trade countertrends or reactions to the current trend. The reason is that in a strong bull market, a countertrend or reaction (or retracement) may not be large enough to be worthwhile, but that will naturally depend on the situation.

Suppose, for example, that you're looking at the Swiss franc, which may have gone from 66.00 to 66.70, and you see a retracement coming. Where will it take you? A 50-percent retracement equals 35 points, but don't think you'll get all those points! You'll be lucky to get 30. Now, that's okay; I'll take them. But what if there's only a 33-percent or 38-percent retracement? That's 26 points, and you probably will get only 16 to 18 of those. It's better than a loss, but we're not really after mere 16–18 point gains. We should be able to find better trades! Therefore, I mostly will take trades in the direction of the trend. The exceptions would be very large moves, either up or down, where any retracement would be significant. For example, if the move had occurred very rapidly with no brief consolidation periods along the way, I might give a countertrend a try.

To show you how to enter a market, I'll first describe a theoretical situation that illustrates the basics, then we'll move on to specific illustrations taken from actual trading.

You, the trader: You're wide awake and feeling fine. You have plenty of time to trade. You are free from distractions and can concentrate on your work.

Fundamentals: You have kept aware of current events in the financial world and see that the U.S. economy still is going from bad to worse. The employment figures due out this morning are likely to be worse, and will send a signal to the Federal Reserve that easing of interest rates would be appropriate. That would of course affect such interest rate futures as Treasury bonds, Treasury bills and eurodollars, but also the U.S. dollar, and therefore the foreign currencies. There should be good potential for an upward move in the T-bonds and the foreign currencies.

Monitoring: You have been monitoring the T-bonds and eurodollars, as well as the Swiss franc, Deutschmark, and British pound. You see that the bonds and euros already have anticipated the government data before it is released and have rallied to new highs; in fact, the bonds have risen as much as 9 points during the otherwise quiet evening session. The indicators show the bonds to be in the overbought region already. Can they go much higher? Perhaps yes, but how high? Four to five points or 20–30 points? The currencies are poised for an upward move, having broken out above a trendline and showing a double bottom on the daily charts. The Swiss franc appears to be the strongest and most volatile. The indicators are turning up from the oversold area. The Swiss franc looks like your first choice!

Timing: You are up and awake 20 minutes before the International Monetary Market (IMM) opens. You begin by checking the action on the overseas market during the night. The Swiss franc has already moved up 25 points from yesterday's close of the U.S. market, also anticipating that the dollar will be pressured by the upcoming government report. From this, you know that the Swiss franc will open higher, forming an opening gap. What do you do now?

Don't enter on the opening. Let the market sort itself out. That may take 10 or 15 minutes' trading. The market eventually will establish a trend, and that's when you want to enter. If you are absolutely convinced that the Swiss franc is going to move up, you can take advantage of several opening ploys. You can wait until the initial flurry of activity is quieting down and the price is taken down perhaps 10 or 15 points to "shake out the weak longs," so the floor traders can buy at the low prices that probably won't be seen again for a while. You must understand that the market is searching for prices where trading can take place. If no trading is generated at a certain level, the price must be changed to a higher or lower level till some activity occurs. Floor traders will anticipate where the price should go, and will try to bring it a little bit the other way right after the opening so they can get an even better advantage. You can too, but don't expect too much of an "exploratory" drop. If you see 10 points, take it!

In that case, buy at market. **Do not** place a limit order if you want to be sure to get aboard. If you are very experienced and have good anticipation ability, you may be able to place a limit order just a point or two above the current price, but why take a chance? By the time the order is in, the market will already be one or two points higher, possibly even 10 points higher in a fast market. By the time you have changed your order to a market order, you will have lost 15 or more points of profit. There is a place for limit orders, but this isn't it. We'll discuss when to use limit orders in the next chapter: "Stop-Loss Orders and Risk Control."

If you want to be certain that the trend is going to be up, you might want to wait until the price moves up past the opening price before you enter. You can also place a "buy stop" order 5 or 10 points above the opening price and just wait until the market catches up to your price. However, I prefer to enter on a market order, because I want to know *now* where I stand. In a busy market, you might not know *where* or even *if* you got filled for 20 or 30 minutes. By then it could be time to take profits—but are you long or what? I like to know for certain, and that means a market order.

So far we have talked about fundamentals and general technical considerations. You can do quite well with those alone. However, precise entry-point indicators can be very useful, not only in confirming the proper direction to take, but also the very best time to make your entry. You will recall our discussion in Part I of this book that we will be looking for a favorable *chart* pattern in all the time frames, and we will also look for specific *price bar* patterns indicative of a favorable trend in market sentiment. Finally, we will look at several indicators that graphically display the market sentiment and nature of price movements.

Take as an example a double bottom on the daily chart of the Swiss franc, with a breakout above a trendline (Fig. 11-1). Perhaps on the 60-minute bars we can see another chart pattern, such as a flag. The flag is typically a consolidation pattern, during which the market "takes a breather"; then it usually will continue in the same direction it was headed before the flag was formed. In our example, the flag has been forming for several hours and is now on the third bar. Perhaps a breakout to the upside is soon to happen. (We have not entered after the opening, as no clear signal was evident.)

The 5-minute bars (see Chapter 16: "Useful Real-Time Displays") show prices in a channel between 66.40 and 66.70; the franc has been up to 66.70 twice, and down to 66.40 twice, and it's now on its way up toward 66.70 for the third time. Experience has shown that if a breakout is to occur, the third "try" is the most likely to succeed. We get set for this likely possibility. We're also noting the bar patterns. The 60-minute bars are showing higher closing prices, and the present price is above the last close, indicating continued strength. Finally, we look at the indicators. The slow Stochastic on both daily and 60-minute bars have turned up from the oversold region and have entered the midzone, and on the 5-minute bars is nearing the overbought zone.

After the SlowK of the Stochastic indicator reaches the overbought zone, prices frequently will continue to move upward, sometimes explosively, until the SlowD part of the indicator reaches the same zone, sometimes even until the SlowK has turned down and is threatening to cross the upper reference line. This has been called the "Stochastic pop" by various authors.[25] Therefore, we might expect a sudden burst of upward movement as prices break out of the flag formation on the 60-minute chart and on the third swing upward on the 5-minute chart.

Looking at the FSK, we see that the fast Kurtosis line has crossed its 6-bar weighted moving average from the bottom of the range in an upward direction, giving a buy signal. Likewise, the TDAC has bottomed out and turned upward, also giving a buy signal. When the FSK crosses its zero line and the TDAC crosses its longer weighted moving average, they will give confirmatory buy signals. The odds are heavily stacked in our favor. We enter the market, buying two contracts "at market" and get filled at 60.68. Two minutes later, prices move to 60.74 and

Figure 11-1

Swiss Franc

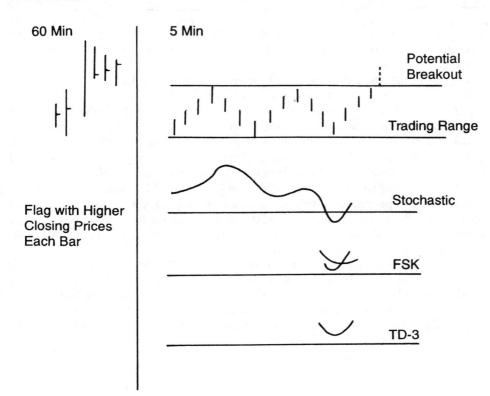

60 Min

**Flag with Higher
Closing Prices
Each Bar**

5 Min

Potential
Breakout

Trading Range

Stochastic

FSK

TD-3

then surge to 60.86, then 60.92. Successive bars gradually inch their way upward with higher closes to finally level off at 61.30, a 62-point move (Fig. 11-1).

If we are fortunate, we might see additional buy signals, such as bullish divergence between prices and Stochastics, or all three indicators; or others such as RSI, momentum, and even MACD, OBV, or %R. We've made an excellent entry, and now we face the next step: exiting the market. We'll tackle that step in the next two chapters. Chapter 12 is devoted to stop-loss and limit orders, where you give control of your destiny to the market. Then, in Chapter 13, you'll see how you can recapture that control over your own destiny when exiting the market.

Our example should show you how much positive evidence I like to have before entering the market. Would I ever take less? Perhaps, but I would realize that the risk of being wrong would be much greater, and the potential reward would have to be very large. In such a case, I should want additional insurance that I was entering on the right side of the market by placing a higher buy stop order—in the case under discussion, perhaps at 66.90, 20 points above the top of the current trading channel and breakout level. Although a move to that level would lend some support to the belief that prices would indeed move higher, I would also be prepared to exit the market very quickly should prices retreat back below the breakout level of 66.70. I'd be prepared for a loss of at least 24 points—that's a lot—and the potential reward would have to be far greater than it appears to be in the present example.

Now let's look at two examples from the Robbins System Trading Championship of 1992: Figures 14-1 and 15-1. Each example has a good many conditions and signals suggesting a good entry. How many can you find?

Note down all that you can find. Be precise, and number them. Compare each of your lists with that given for each example when you read Chapters 14 and 15.

12

Stop-Loss Orders and Risk Control

"There is no free lunch; but you can try bargaining!"
—*Ulf K. Jensen*

In this chapter, we'll examine ways to deal with the seemingly uncontrollable market and keep our heads above water. Then, in the next chapter, we'll deal with ways in which *you* can control your market position and profits. We've already laid some groundwork on this subject. We saw in Chapter 4 how your entire account is placed at risk whenever you take a position in the market. We discussed the conventional ways of attempting to minimize that risk and concluded that most of those are inadequate. One of the best ways of dealing with any bad situation is to avoid it in the first place!

I'm sure you've said: "I should have thought of that before I ... (did so and so)." By following the system in this book, you now have the advantage of thinking before you act. By doing so, you should be able to avoid all future "bad situations" in trading. Or, as another saying from the wisdom of the ages puts it: "An ounce of prevention is worth a pound of cure." The focus of most of this book is teaching you how to avoid entering the market at the wrong time or place. If you seriously follow those guidelines, you should not find yourself in any bad situations. Nevertheless, as we said early on, no person, system, approach, or anything else, is perfect. Therefore, you will have an occasional entry that suddenly turns against you. What can you do ahead of time to protect against that, and what should you do after the fact to protect your position?

Everyone is familiar with the stop-loss order that is placed either above or below your entry price to protect against a sudden move against you. It is also well known that you frequently get filled a few points further away from your entry price than you specified. The market may well move several points after your stop gets activated. It's *not* well known that it's possible to not get filled at all! If this happens because of an error or oversight on the part of your broker, he will probably guarantee you the correct fill. If the market gaps on the open, it will activate a stop order, but fill it only at the level where trading is taking place, and that could be quite far from your intended price. Such events are not unusual.

Much has been written about where to place stop orders. Your options are either a price level based on market behavior, or based on a dollar amount you are "willing to loose" or can "afford" to lose. In my opinion, if you want to be a successful trader, you cannot afford to lose **any** money ever! Likewise, I am not "willing" to lose any money ever! So we quickly can eliminate those options. The old argument of: "I can afford to risk $500 on this trade, because I hope to gain $3,000 (6-to-1 reward-to-risk ratio) is absurd. You may risk a lot more than $500, and you may never realize more than $30 in profit. Reminds you of gambling again, doesn't it?

As far as market behavior goes, there are as many places to put your stop as there are traders. The most common are: just beneath a trendline, just beneath a support level, just below the low of the day (not always a very good place), just beneath the lowest low of the past three days, or just below the last swing low (short-cycle low). Those stops make a lot more sense, but their value to the trader still is somewhat dubious. They make sense because their placement is based on market behavior, the only logical approach, rather than arbitrary dollar figures. But they are of dubious value, because they are all "invitations to a loss," some greater than others.

As prices move higher, the stop can be raised to lock in profits. Raising your stop to your entry price, or creating an *entry-level stop*, is your first objective. This is tempting to do, so that you will have no loss, but traders frequently do this prematurely in relation to market activity. If you place an entry-level stop too early, a natural swing low might easily stop you out of the market before it moves higher again and leaves you behind with no position. If the next swing low comes in above your entry price, it may be safe to place your stop at your entry price. But I prefer to wait until I can add a few points, not only for commission and fees, but also for a small profit. Four or five points will do. However, I only use a stop like that if I'm unable to keep a close eye on the market; for example, if I suddenly am called away from my trade station or have a prior commitment elsewhere. The most common mistake is to raise your stop too far too fast; that definitely will get you stopped out.

So your choices are staying in the market with a distant stop-loss order and risking a large loss; or protecting some profit or minimizing your potential loss, but with a much higher probability of being stopped out. If you believe that the market has embarked on a huge bull run that will take you to the moon in a few days, you would choose the more distant stop, or disaster prevention stop. If the market isn't that hot, a closer stop to minimize your potential loss would be more appropriate. The main problem with both choices and all the various placements discussed is that they are all invitations to a loss. Here's why:

First, stop-loss orders constitute the largest amount of "paper" held in the trading pits. "Paper" means orders waiting to be filled if certain conditions are met, usually the market reaching a certain price. You can readily see how these orders become *invitations* to floor traders who need the sales in order to make their living. A group of widely scattered orders wouldn't be enticing, but a large cluster of stops placed closely around a certain price could become irresistible if the market came close enough. You would be stopped out along with the whole gang. Therefore, *always* place your stops *several points below* the most logical place, and you may survive the "raiding party" by a couple of ticks (Fig. 12-1). Another tactic is to place your stop a little closer than the crowd. That way, you'll always get a better price than when you're trying to get an order filled in the middle of what might be a stampede.

Second, your broker loves stop-loss orders. Of course he wants you to be protected against being wiped out, or going into negative balance, something that is very disagreeable both to him and you. He also wants to protect himself from that situation. Furthermore, he also likes stops because he knows that most traders place them in the wrong place and frequently get stopped out. That means more transactions and commissions for him. Those who get stopped out have to get back in somewhere, if they want to trade, so the stop-loss order almost becomes a catalyst for generating transactions. The commissions can mount up rapidly, and are of course the mainstay of a broker's profits; so the more stops that get hit, the more he makes!

You've probably entered the market long and watched the price go up a little, only to see it back off, turn down and just barely "pick off" your stop, only to rise again, then really take off the way you had anticipated. The market left you behind cursing at the screen. Your stop was placed *too* perfectly; it was placed with an ideal market in mind. But we don't have ideal markets, *ever*. In the real world, you need to watch out for "stop runners." So if you must place a stop, place it below where you think all the others might be, or if you are trading multiple positions, split your stops: two here, two there, and two further down.

In day-trading, my policy is not to place stops, but to watch the market very closely and use a mental stop which will not tempt anyone. The trouble with that is that you need experience as well as discipline. You cannot get emotional and change your mind at the last second, thinking, "I'll just wait a little longer." The exception to that policy is a very volatile market, in which a stop really must be in place in order to avoid a huge slippage by the time your order gets filled; or when, as mentioned earlier, you must leave your trade station and cannot keep a close eye on the market. However, such mental stops are **not** recommended for beginners! *Beginners must use stops;* they have not yet gained sufficient control over their emotions to rely on mental stops.

The main reason I dislike stop orders for protection is that they will bring you losses, sometimes many, and all those small losses will add up to a big loss. You

Figure 12-1

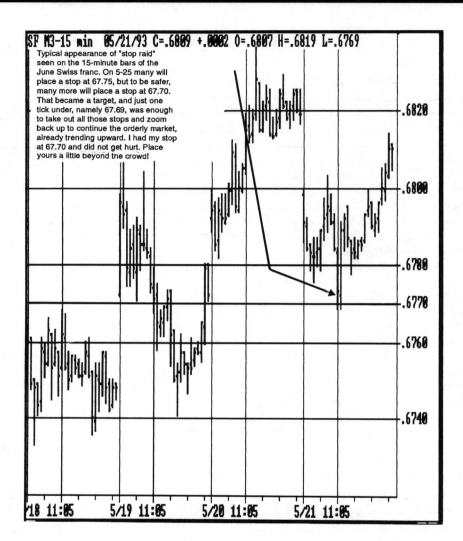

SF M3-15 min 05/21/93 C=.6809 +.0002 O=.6807 H=.6819 L=.6769

Typical appearance of "stop raid"
seen on the 15-minute bars of the
June Swiss franc. On 5-25 many will
place a stop at 67.75, but to be safer,
many more will place a stop at 67.70.
That became a target, and just one
tick under, namely 67.69, was enough
to take out all those stops and zoom
back up to continue the orderly market,
already trending upward. I had my stop
at 67.70 and did not get hurt. Place
yours a little beyond the crowd!

might even get a big loss. But what if you don't have a stop-loss? It really is a "Catch 22": If you place stops, you lose; if you don't, you lose more. What's a poor trader to do? **Prevention, prevention, prevention!**

You see, there's really only one good way to avoid those losses, big or small, and that's preventing them by proper entry. That's why I emphasize entry so much. You don't ever want to use your stop-loss as your *primary* defense against losses. You'll get killed! Famous trader and author Stanley Kroll puts it starkly: "The market doesn't take prisoners!"[5]

Believe me, you must learn to *prevent* losses, not just minimize them.

What about placing a stop-loss order far below your entry—in a place that probably will never get hit? Then at least you have some protection against a disastrous turn in prices. I guess that's okay, if it makes you feel better, but with proper entry and careful monitoring, you don't need it. Not only will you be in the profit zone quickly, but you will be *watching* the market closely. To be alert always is your best defense. Not placing stops also will make you a little more alert and anxious to exit the market quickly when you have a good profit (see next chapter).

Here's another defense: If you have a stop-loss order below the low of three days ago, and prices begin to move down and threaten to take out your entry price, don't wait for them to stop you out. Take control and sell out *at once!* That way, you can limit your loss to 10 or 12 points, not the 40 or 50 points that your stop-loss order would have allowed. Do minimize your loss if you can't prevent it!

We now come to the other way of using a stop order, as a means of market entry or exit, where the market decides your fate. You may decide to enter long on a breakout of significance and place a buy stop 20 points above a chart formation that is forming. The premise is that when prices break out and reach your stop order, their action will have demonstrated sufficient upward force that continued upward movement is quite likely, and it even may be with explosive force. If you had to react to that breakout by watching your screen and then placing an order, you and many others would get filled substantially higher than you wanted. There will be much paper at that level, which literally provides fuel for the fire of upward explosion. It is only logical and prudent to have your stop already in place *before* that explosion occurs; this is an *excellent* way to enter the market.

Of course, you also can exit the market in the same manner. If you place an order in anticipation that prices will eventually get up to that level, you cannot use a stop order, since a sell stop will be activated any time the price is at or below the stop. If you made the mistake of entering such an order, it would result in your position being sold immediately. You can, however, use a *limit order*. For example, "Sell two June Swiss franc limit 61.30," or more simply, "Sell two June Swiss franc 61.30." Some exchanges will take MIT, or "market if touched," orders; they are better than limit orders because they have more flexibility. An MIT order will become a market order when that price is "touched." A limit order is "limited" to the exact price, which sometimes may not be possible. You *can* give a range on your limit order, such as, "Sell two June Swiss franc limit 61.20 to 61.40." Limit orders are fine if you primarily want to get filled at a certain price, but I've found them useful only when I have a large number of contracts to buy or sell, when a market order might get me "killed" with 10 different prices over a large range.

My last aspect of risk management is adding contracts to your position. You discover that you are fortunate enough to have a profitable position that is beginning to trend; you want to increase your profits by adding on to that position. How do you do that safely? During day-trading there is seldom sufficient time for a long trend to get established, but it can happen. We sometimes see this in the currencies and T-bonds, and here a second contract could be added, if it is done fairly early in the day before the trend runs out of steam.

Perhaps you've experienced the frustration of adding a second contract and finding that no sooner have you hung up the phone than the price is moving against you. You now have a loss from the new contract, and, what is worse, your profits from the first one now are being wiped out. Most likely you entered the market at the top of a short cycle. You should have waited for the reaction to complete itself and then bought *just past the bottom* of that cycle. Even at that point, **don't** buy two or three contracts, which would create an upside-down pyramid. You must form a broad-based pyramid, or at least a rectangle, but **never** an upside-down pyramid. It can turn on you with a vengeance! For the most part, resist pyramiding; you will be able to make good profits without such risky maneuvers.

13

Exiting the Market

"I am the Master of my Fate; I am the Captain of my Soul."
—Invictus, *William Ernest Henley (1849-1903)*

We now come to the last but *most important* step on the way to steady profits. All the steps up until now have been *easy* compared to this last and essential step. Earlier steps may have been involved, fraught with pitfalls, and perhaps more demanding than you had imagined; nevertheless, they have been easy. True, many traders go awry during one or several of those steps, but many also traverse them unscathed, only to wind up with losses, because they failed this last step: **exiting the market.** "How can this be?" you ask. Read on, and I shall reveal the secret. It may well be a secret, since so many thousands of traders, both novice and professional, continually ignore it and either lose a good deal of their profit or lose it all! And yet, this "secret" is really no secret at all. Perhaps it's the application that is so difficult for so many. It surely is one thing to agree that a certain principle is worthwhile; it is quite another to bring it about or into play.

I am sure you've heard the saying: "No one ever becomes poor by taking profits early!" At the beginning of this book, I made reference to the "wisdom of the ages." This saying is yet another example of that wisdom. Taking profits in any venture obviously will add to your wealth, but taking them early implies two things:

1. You might have gotten more profits by taking them later.
2. You might have gotten less, none, or even a loss by waiting till later!

But how is it possible to lose profits by waiting for more? Very simple. The market does not respect your plans and goals; it's a dynamic medium, ever changing. Your profit at any given moment is just that: profit *at that instant in time on paper.* To actually have it, call it your own, and "take it to the bank," you must **take it!** *That is the secret!* Why is this so difficult to do? There are many reasons.

One is tradition. A trader is long two contracts at 80; two hours later the price has advanced to 100. But he is hoping for 110 or even 120. By using some method of projection (Fibonacci ratio of 1.62, the next cycle high, the next higher resistance level, or the next turnaround of his favorite oscillator) he has determined that the price target should be 120–130, so he holds onto his position. Remember, such profits are only paper profits. To count your money, you must **take those profit$ now!**

The second reason is greed. Most traders want more of the good thing they have just received. They can't let go. They are now starting to hope (that dangerous word in any business), but hope will not give it to them. The market suddenly decides to defy the neatly formed Elliott wave pattern[26, 27] and forego that expected fifth wave. It fails to go higher (a fifth-wave failure); it even fails to go anywhere … and goes back down. "But it can't do that!" you say. "Oh, yes I can!" the market says. Your nice profit has now evaporated, and in fact you are beginning to see a loss. You stare at the market with that incredulous look as if to say: "But I had a *profit!* What happened?" You merely neglected to take it. **It's that simple!** How many traders have not watched in such disbelief as their profits turned into losses time and time again? Don't feel bad if it's happened to you; it's a very common fate!

"Well, we can fix that easily," you say. "We'll just place a stop-loss order to lock in that profit." That's what tradition has taught all good traders. If you have a reasonable paper profit, this can be a workable method, because it will preserve *some* profit. However, we've seen that more than half the time you will be stopped out at a lower (or higher) value than you have set, and that such slippage can erode your profit significantly. Also, on that rare occasion when your stop is not filled at all (very fast markets, limit moves, etc.), you could have a disaster on your hands.

Let's look at an example of how a stop order can cut your profits. You've made a nice trade and have a paper profit, but you cannot place a realistic stop-loss at the current price, which is, say, 93, up from 80. To place a stop at 90 would be asking to get filled, and, considering the normal volatility of the market (nothing goes up or down in a straight line), it probably would be filled at 88. You can figure out what would have happened to your account. Exit at 88 minus entry at 80 = 8 points. Subtract 4, 5, or even 6 points for commissions and fees, and you've made perhaps 3 points—hardly an exciting trade. If the market had moved to 120, you might have thought you could have protected your paper profits by placing a stop at 105. You could have, but you would have accepted a profit of only 25 points rather than staying in the market and obtaining greater profits. You might have been stopped out at 105 by the next swing low that hits 103.

The market could have gone to 160, and if it had, you would have paid for the "security" of a stop order with lower profits: You got stopped out with only 25 points. The market could have gone to 160 without dipping to your stop order, but, believe me, more often than not it will stop you out unless your stop is placed so low that you have a larger margin of volatility between the market and your entry price. In such a case, you must have larger capital, and be prepared to take a much larger loss if you do get stopped out. There is a guideline that says: If you cannot afford the loss that a properly placed stop-loss order would allow, you can't afford to take the trade, and you should not take it.

Now, take a close look at what happened. In order to follow tradition, in order to satisfy your desire for more profits, in order to stay in the market, you **gave up control.** You paid a price for that, and that price was lost profits. You let the market decide how much profit you should have. Does the market like you? Does the market favor you in any way? Does the market hand you extra profits on a silver platter? Hardly. The market is relentless and treacherous. It "doesn't take prisoners"! It will take from you if you blink; it will kill you if you look away. If the profit is there, **take it now!**

Let's say the market went to 120, and we sold. We took 40 points of profit—a lot better than 25! At $12.50 per point, that's $500—vs. $312.50—per contract. Trading two contracts, we're looking at $1,000 instead of $625. If we do 10 such trades, the difference becomes $10,000 vs. $6,250, or $3,750 more. Remember, *steady* small profits do add up! Why is this so difficult to do?

The difficulty is that the trader is unwilling to accept the *present* paper profit because he feels he can squeeze more out of the market. He is too confident of his position in the market—a position for which the market has no "respect" whatsoever. Unfortunately, he is often wrong and when he is, he loses half his profit. He only rarely achieves his dream of the market's continuing to move higher.

You might say that you've had many trades where you entered the market at 80, and the price went to 120. You stayed with it, rode out the swing to 96, and when the price got to 145, you placed a close stop-loss order at 130. You were lucky not to get hit there, since the market soared to 170 before hesitating. You then advanced your stop to 160 and got stopped out on the next retracement. Had you sold out at 120, you would have missed the second 40 points of profit. Yes, this can happen. But if you're one of the very few traders who is both patient and selective enough to pick only those trades that are this successful, then you are indeed privileged, and you do not need to read this book, or any other for that matter. You can even write your own. But if you're not that shrewd or lucky, *my approach will assure you profits.*

Perhaps you feel you can modify my approach, or your own; combine them, or compromise by putting on two contracts, then taking moderate profits with just one contract and letting the other ride. Yes, that could work out very well.

As you know, almost anything "could" work out very well—but then again, it might not! Just as you sell that one contract, hoping the other will go higher, what happens? Prices go down, and you're losing profits. You get out just before you start to lose real money. When you look at your decisions, try the test of logic. If an action is good for half your contracts, it must by definition also be good for the other half! If it is risky to leave *two* contracts in the market, it's equally risky to leave *one*. From a dollar standpoint, of course, you've cut your risk in half, but one contract is still there. If you think it's time to sell, don't straddle the fence: **sell all!** Don't get caught up in the diplomacy of hedging. You're not a politician, you're trying to be a trader. Don't let the market control you; it controls itself. You cannot control the market, but you can and should control yourself and your position.

If you're already a winning trader, I'm not trying to tell you anything. If you incorporate some or all of my principles in your strategy, I'd be flattered, but my main purpose in writing this book is to help all the traders who are losing money week after week, month after month. Look at your balance sheets for the months. Do they show a profit? If not, *you need this approach!*

All right, we take the profits early. What does that mean? When exactly is that? To begin, let me repeat the credo of the day trader: **Be out of the market by the close!** If you have a small profit building up by the close, be happy; take it, and *it's yours.* You may find that, the next day, market sentiment will be entirely different, and if you had stayed in the market, your paper profit might have evaporated on a lower opening, or would soon have been wiped out by declining prices. If everything looks good the next day, you may want to re-enter. You will have lost a commission, but commissions are cheap compared to most trading losses. Never be afraid to lose a commission in order to be on the safe side and protect your capital. If you have a loss by closing time, definitely get out! Such a "small" loss could mushroom into a great loss on the opening the next day. So whatever you do, according to the main principle of day-trading, get out by the close. Yes, there are exceptions, as mentioned earlier, when a very strong trend is evident, and you want to ride it another day or perhaps more, but barring that, **get out by the close!**

There are two ways to take profits early. One involves setting minimum, target, and maximum price areas; the other involves recognition of market behavior. We'll look at both.

To set a minimum price for your profit, you obviously must be above the price necessary to pay for commissions and fees, so the number of points required for that is the absolute minimum. Your *practical minimum* will be 10–20 points higher; if you cannot expect to achieve that, you definitely should not enter the trade (see Chapter 11: "Entering the Market").

To set a target area or zone for prices to get to, you can decide on a dollar figure such as $300—$500 per contract or $500—$1,000 total for your entire position. However, I dislike exact dollar figures, because they are so arbitrary and artificial. The market really doesn't care about dollar figures as they may relate to your profit or loss. Even the better idea of setting your target profit at half or all of the margin requirement for a single contract is too rigid for the excursion of prices. However, such dollar values can give you a rough idea of where you would like to be. Unless you have good reason to expect further price advancements, take your profit when you've reached about $1,000 per contract; you could call that a good maximum value. It absolutely will nail down significant profits!

To set a maximum price for your profit, you'll need to employ techniques of projection from the various chart formations. For example, as prices come out of a flag formation, they usually will move in the same direction as before, and go the same distance as they did before, or the length of the flagpole. In a head-and-shoulders top formation, the distance from the top of the head to the neckline subtracted from the neckline gives a reasonable projection. Fibonacci ratios are also very helpful, such as the projection of 1.61 times the previous move before the retracement added on to the new swing low. Arthur Sklarew discusses these in good detail.[16]

The method based on market behavior is my favorite. I've found the best place to take early profits is *where the market begins to hesitate*. It's about to meet a minor or major resistance level, and will either consolidate or turn back and "retrace" a little—or perhaps more than a little! You want to be out of the market *before* either of those happens. Try to sell while there is still some momentum to the price advance; while there still are some buyers out there. Once the market stalls, there will be no more buyers. Your order, along with a handful of others, will drop the price, and you will see slippage. But if you sell while the market is still rising, you will more likely get the current price, and sometimes even a better one.

Does this mean you should sell out at the first sign of minor resistance? Yes and no. You must have a realistic idea of where the market is and where it is going. For example, if you are looking at a major bottom on monthly, weekly, and daily charts, as well as a bottom on the 60-minute bars, that's one thing. If you're looking at a market that has gone through two good rallies, and is halfway up a third rally on the daily chart, the 60-minute bars show consolidation, and you are reaching a resistance level on the 10-minute bars, don't expect miracles! Don't hope for a huge rally to follow the next retracement on the 10-minute bars. The market probably is ready for a bigger retracement. You don't have much basis for expecting further advancement of prices, so take those profits *before* the retracement. This calls for perspective. You must know where the prices are. Are they at the bottom of a range at the beginning of an intermediate cycle, or are they near the top of both. Remember, nothing goes to the moon in a straight line except astronauts. "Get real," as the saying goes.

If the market should surprise you by heading further upward (or downward, if you're shorting) after you've taken your profits, and the minor retracement is over, *get back aboard*. You may have lost a few points of profit, but 9 out of 10 times, you will have made the right decision and be very happy with your profits as the market turns down (or up).

There you have it! The incredible "secret"; the "wisdom of the ages" simply is the well-known but much-neglected saying: "No one ever becomes poor from taking profits early!" But for this remarkable principle to work for you, you must shed yourself of all your previous habits and expectations that are based on the "ideal" market, and accept the reality of a marketplace far from the ideal. You must forget the illusions of huge one-time profits and accept lots of small profits. This doesn't mean you must deny yourself huge profits when they come knocking on your door; just don't be expecting them every day. You must wrest control of the trading away from the unpredictable market and take that control into your own hands! You must become the master of your fate!

You must learn to take "profit$ now"!

I shall try to illustrate this in the following examples taken from last year's Robbins System Trading Championship, shown in Figures 13-1 and 13-2.

Figure 13-1

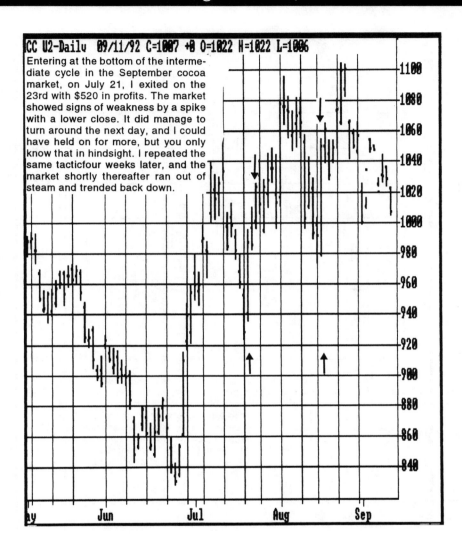

CC U2-Daily 09/11/92 C=1007 +0 O=1022 H=1022 L=1006

Entering at the bottom of the intermediate cycle in the September cocoa
market, on July 21, I exited on the
23rd with $520 in profits. The market
showed signs of weakness by a spike
with a lower close. It did manage to
turn around the next day, and I could
have held on for more, but you only
know that in hindsight. I repeated the
same tacticfour weeks later, and the
market shortly thereafter ran out of
steam and trended back down.

Figure 13-2

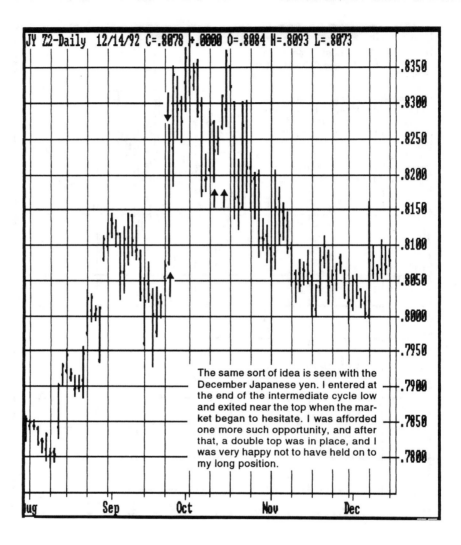

JY Z2-Daily   12/14/92 C=.8078 +.0000 O=.8084 H=.8093 L=.8073

.8350
.8300
.8250
.8200
.8150
.8100
.8050
.8000
.7950
.7900
.7850
.7800

The same sort of idea is seen with the December Japanese yen. I entered at the end of the intermediate cycle low and exited near the top when the market began to hesitate. I was afforded one more such opportunity, and after that, a double top was in place, and I was very happy not to have held on to my long position.

Aug   Sep   Oct   Nov   Dec

PART
4

BUILDING A
TRADING SYSTEM

Having discussed the various forces that move prices, and developed methods to recognize these forces at the earliest possible moment, we are now presented with the challenge of finding profitable ways to act on them. So-called mechanical systems have been developed to meet the need to find some "thing" that is more objective, or less emotional, than human beings. If a pure robot or computer could not only figure things out, but also act on them, you could just press a few buttons and wait for it to tell you to pick up the phone, dial your broker, and place your order. But it's still not quite that simple ... yet.

There are a few good mechanical systems; then there are all the others. You no doubt will enjoy making your own or using others, and eventually you'll find your comfort zone among them all. I'll present two simple systems developed from a few of the concepts we have discussed. Both these systems produced good profits in the 1992

Robbins System Trading Championship, helping me win first place. What's even better, you don't need a computer, "live" data, or real-time data to use these systems. They are extremely simple to work from ordinary price charts that have a Stochastic indicator displayed along with other information. That means you can get started immediately using these systems to earn money. Obviously, without real-time data you'll be limited to trading from daily charts, but with workable systems such as these, trading in any timeframe can be profitable.

14

The Trendline
Breakout System

The first system I used was the Trendline Breakout System. Some people say that trendlines don't work in the futures markets and are only reliable in the stock market. Those people are missing certain considerations. Obviously additional factors influence the movement of commodity prices as compared to stock prices. If we can identify these and deal with them, trendlines still apply.

The basic concept of a trendline is equally valuable whether you're dealing with commodities or, say, athletes running a marathon. There are both *reasons for* and *implications from* prices falling below an established trend, as with athletes falling behind an established pace in a marathon. They both are ominous developments.

Can they change? Can they turn around? Yes, of course they can, given certain circumstances, but most likely not. What are those circumstances, or, more to the point, what makes a trend-break a reliable predictor of continued weakness (or strength)? We'll try to answer that question with the help of our understanding of market sentiment as reflected in price-bar patterns and the indicators we've developed.

Where do we start? If we look at a market in a long uptrend, we can draw a nice trendline *under* all the *intermediate lows* and then wait for a "breakout"—or actually a "break**down**"—of prices below that trendline, particularly a *closing* price. But we might have to wait a month or two, perhaps even three, before that happens. A faster way is to find a market that already has corrected 38 or 50 percent and is putting in an intermediate low, and probably will resume its upward trend very shortly. Is it really a low, or is the early rally merely a short covering rally, soon to fizzle with prices heading south again? Well, let us see. First we draw a trendline connecting the tops of the *short* cycles of the *reaction*. This will be our main trendline that needs to be broken for us to have a buy signal. I'll bet you can begin to see prices already climbing out on top of that line and almost waving a flag, shouting, "Hey, we're outta here!" and enticing you to follow. Well, it may look good, but is it really? What else would you like to see before you send your hard-earned money after those prices?

1. Higher closing prices, indicating buying strength.
2. Rising volume, indicating more interest in rising prices.
3. Rising values of our newly developed indicators, reflecting not only more buying than selling, but predominance of buying with the passage of time.
4. Buy signals from various standard indicators.
5. Prices breaking out over a resistance level (horizontal line).
6. Perhaps even a break-away gap.
7. Formation of a chart pattern such as a flag or triangle, which frequently forces prices to react explosively in either direction.
8. Stochastic pop imminent.

If one or more of those signs are present, we can be increasingly confident that prices will move as predicted. Having tested these with TradeStation's system analysis capability, I have arrived at the following conclusions:

If the trendline break is accompanied by the following four conditions, it is very successful in predicting that prices will continue in the direction of the break. For a breakout to the downside, these conditions are:

1. Falling SlowD(9)
2. Falling Kurtosis
3. Falling FSRS
4. FSRS<50

The opposite will be true for a breakout to the upside:

1. Rising SlowD(9)
2. Rising Kurtosis
3. Rising FSRS
4. FSRS>50

Figure 14-1 shows a daily chart of the December British pound just before the currency crisis of late 1992. It appears to be topping out at very high levels and

Figure 14-1

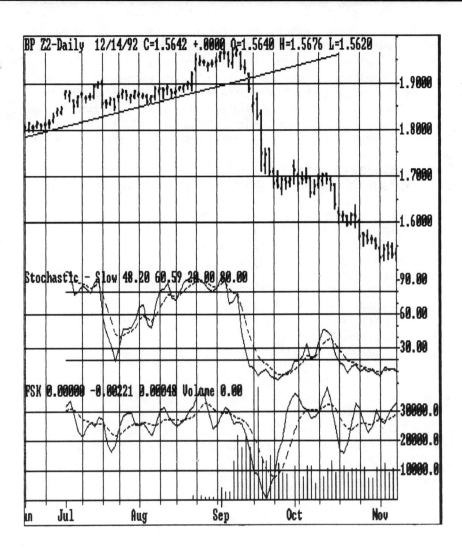

behaving rather unpredictably (choppy and volatile). We can see that when the *FSRS* crossed the reference line at 50, prices were starting to break below the rising trendline. The *SlowD(9)* and *Kurtosis* were falling, and a good sell signal was generated. Prior to that, we had seen a widening formation, or *"megaphone"* pattern on the price chart. That is decidedly bearish. In addition, *closing prices were quite low* two days in a row, with a confirmatory low close after the break. There was also a *Stochastic pop* to the downside imminent, and a *breakaway gap* almost formed on the break, but actually appeared *following* the day of the break. *Volume* increased considerably, indicating good interest in entering the market in the downward direction by short selling. We got almost all that we wished for, didn't we? Wouldn't it be nice to get such a plethora of signs every time we take a trade?

To formulate the five critical elements of the system so the computer can find them, we write as follows (We must first define our indicators.):

```
VALUE1=@MOMENTUM(C,3);
VALUE2=@MOMENTUM(C,3)[1];
VALUE3=0.3*(VALUE1-VALUE2)+(1-.03)*VALUE3;
VALUE4=WAVERAGE((VALUE3),6);
VALUE5=@RSI+VALUE4;
CONDITION1=SLOWD(9)[1]<SLOWD(9);
CONDITION2=VALUE4[1]<VALUE4;
CONDITION3=VALUE5[1]<VALUE5;
CONDITION4=VALUE5>50;
CONDITION5=CRITERIA FOR TRENDLINE BREAK UPWARDS.*
CONDITION6=SLOWD(90[1]>SLOWD(9);
CONDITION7=VALUE4[1]>VALUE4;
CONDITION8=VALUE5[1]>VALUE5;
CONDITION9=VALUE5<50;
CONDITION10=CRITERIA FOR TRENDLINE BREAK DOWNWARDS.*
IF CONDITION1 AND CONDITION2 AND CONDITION3 AND
CONDITION4 AND
CONDITION5 THEN BUY ON CLOSE;
IF CONDITION6 AND CONDITION7 AND CONDITION8 AND
CONDITION9 AND
CONDITION10 THEN SELL ON CLOSE;
```

You don't need to use the above proprietary criteria in your formula, and you do not even need a computer to use this or the next system. You can draw your own trendlines and look for the breakout; then see what the indicators show at the current and previous price bars.

---

* These criteria comprise a proprietary formula from TradeStation software, and cannot be reproduced here; they are of course available to users of TradeStation.

15
The 1-2-3
Reversal System

The second system we shall consider is the 1-2-3 Reversal System. It is based purely on price bar analysis rather than on chart patterns. This system also created good profits in last year's Robbins System Trading Championship. We have seen how our logic in analyzing market sentiment produced several indicators that we could incorporate into a profitable system. We should be able to continue using that logic to do the same with price-bar analysis, again keeping a firm foundation of market sentiment to guide us.

When jumping on a train, isn't it easier to get on right after it's slowed down, while it's stopped to change direction, rather than waiting until it takes off again, and then trying to jump on as it roars down the tracks away from you? You probably haven't literally had such an experience with trains; but if you've traveled outside the U.S., you may have done just that, if not with trains, then with streetcars or trolleys. At any rate, I know you can *imagine* the effects. The analogy has its basis in price turnarounds.

We frequently see an up-close (where the closing price is higher than the opening price), followed by another up-close, and then the third price bar becomes a down-close. What's happened? Sentiment obviously has changed. What was predominantly buying interest now has become predominantly selling interest. Prices followed suit and declined. The question is: Will this change persist or will it suddenly change back again to its original direction? More to the point, when will the change be sustained and constitute a reliable entry point?

Again, letting TradeStation do the analysis, we arrive at the following conclusions: If the reversal has been preceded by a significant price move, more than a single up-close (or down-close), a subsequent reversal is significant as it reflects some degree of exhaustion of the sentiment that prevailed. We might look for three, four, or five such up-closes (or down-closes), but that would unnecessarily limit our trades, so I go with only one bar before the reversal bar.

Although it is the minimum number possible, this has been shown to be significant and workable. Two such bars preceding the reversal bar is safer, but finds fewer trades, and might miss a good top or bottom. However, three such bars, being the safest signal, constitutes the 1-2-3 Reversal System. There are a good many such 1-2-3 reversals, but not all of them are desirable for our purposes, as some of them occur in the mid-cycle region. Those would have us in and out of the market excessively. So we'll add our filtering devices, the indicators.

When accompanied by the following criteria, the 1-2-3 Reversal System is successful in predicting the continued movement of prices in the direction of that reversal. The conditions for an upward reversal are:

1. One (or two) down-closes followed by an up-close (Two will produce fewer signals.)
2. Rising SlowK(9)

Of course, the opposite is true for a downward reversal:

1. One (or two) up-closes followed by a down-close (Two will produce fewer signals.)
2. Falling SlowK(9)

You can see that I like to employ an indicator or two as a filtering device for the signals, leaving the price-bar pattern as the critical timing device. The main reason I like this system is that it is so incredibly simple, both in concept and in its application.

Figure 15-1 shows a daily price chart of September 92 cocoa. We can see that each 1-2-3 reversal that is taken as a signal has followed an intermediate cycle low, and prices on that day are threatening to break out above the trend of the intermediate cycle (the cycle trending downward). What else can we say about it? We see strong high closing prices. A buy signal has been given by the upward crossing of the SlowK over the SlowD, the SlowK is emerging from the oversold zone, and volume is rising. Thus we have several confirmatory signals that prices are likely to continue upward.

To formulate some of these concepts and criteria into a system, we can write as follows:

Figure 15-1

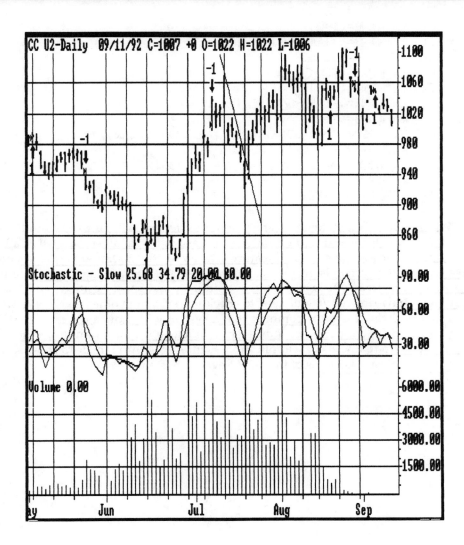

```
VALUE1=@SLOWK(9);
VALUE2=@SLOWD(9);
CONDITION1=C[2]<C[1];
CONDITION2=C>C[1];
CONDITION3=VALUE1>VALUE1[1];
CONDITION4=VALUE2<50;
CONDITION5=C[1]>C[2];
CONDITION6=C<C[1];
CONDITION7=VALUE1<VALUE1[1];
CONDITION8=VALUE2>50;
IF CONDITION1 AND CONDITION2 AND CONDITION3 AND
CONDITION4 THEN BUY AT MARKET;
IF CONDITION5 AND CONDITION6 AND CONDITION7 AND
CONDITION8
THEN SELL AT MARKET;
```

We now ask TradeStation to analyze our system, and Figures 15-2 and 15-3 show a very extensive and informative summary of that analysis, as well as a list of each individual trade, a great feature when you start to fine-tune the system. We see that the system is profitable, holding a single contract at a time in a limited number of trades. It is profitable in both long and short positions and has a very low draw-down. We will need to check this system in other markets as well as other periods. It is quite common that a system will show a different performance in a different period or a different market, so it's important to test it in a variety of both to find its best application. Figures 15-4 through 15-13 show some very profitable applications of the 1-2-3 Reversal System.

Figure 15-2

```
123-REVERSAL-RSC   CC U2-Daily    04/01/92 - 09/11/92
                 Performance Summary:  All Trades

Total net profit         $   1460.00    Open position P/L       $   -430.00
Gross profit             $   2280.00    Gross loss              $   -820.00

Total # of trades               6       Percent profitable           67%
Number winning trades           4       Number losing trades          2

Largest winning trade    $   1340.00    Largest losing trade    $   -430.00
Average winning trade    $    570.00    Average losing trade    $   -410.00
Ratio avg win/avg loss         1.39     Avg trade(win & loss)   $    243.33

Max consec. winners             2       Max consec. losers            1
Avg # bars in winners          11       Avg # bars in losers         21

Max intraday drawdown    $   -890.00
Profit factor                  2.78     Max # contracts held          1
Account size required    $    890.00    Return on account           164%
```

```
                 Performance Summary:  Long Trades

Total net profit         $   1040.00    Open position P/L       $   -430.00
Gross profit             $   1470.00    Gross loss              $   -430.00

Total # of trades               3       Percent profitable           67%
Number winning trades           2       Number losing trades          1

Largest winning trade    $   1340.00    Largest losing trade    $   -430.00
Average winning trade    $    735.00    Average losing trade    $   -430.00
Ratio avg win/avg loss         1.71     Avg trade(win & loss)   $    346.67

Max consec. winners             2       Max consec. losers            1
Avg # bars in winners          11       Avg # bars in losers         13

Max intraday drawdown    $   -850.00
Profit factor                  3.42     Max # contracts held          1
Account size required    $    850.00    Return on account           122%
```

```
                 Performance Summary:  Short Trades

Total net profit         $    420.00    Open position P/L       $      0.00
Gross profit             $    810.00    Gross loss              $   -390.00

Total # of trades               3       Percent profitable           67%
Number winning trades           2       Number losing trades          1

Largest winning trade    $    730.00    Largest losing trade    $   -390.00
Average winning trade    $    405.00    Average losing trade    $   -390.00
Ratio avg win/avg loss         1.04     Avg trade(win & loss)   $    140.00

Max consec. winners             1       Max consec. losers            1
Avg # bars in winners          10       Avg # bars in losers         29

Max intraday drawdown    $   -890.00
Profit factor                  2.08     Max # contracts held          1
Account size required    $    890.00    Return on account            47%
```

Figure 15-3

```
123-REVERSAL-RSC   CC U2-Daily    04/01/92 - 09/11/92
Date      Time     Type  Cnts    Price  Signal Name       Entry P/L   Cumulative
05/04/92  2:15pm   Buy    1       988
05/21/92  2:15pm   LExit  1       945                   $   -430.00 $   -430.00
05/21/92  2:15pm   Sell   1       945
06/15/92  2:15pm   SExit  1       872                   $    730.00 $    300.00
06/15/92  2:15pm   Buy    1       872
07/08/92  2:15pm   LExit  1      1006                   $   1340.00 $   1640.00
07/08/92  2:15pm   Sell   1      1006
08/20/92  2:15pm   SExit  1      1045                   $   -390.00 $   1250.00
08/20/92  2:15pm   Buy    1      1045
08/28/92  2:15pm   LExit  1      1058                   $    130.00 $   1380.00
08/28/92  2:15pm   Sell   1      1058
09/04/92  2:15pm   SExit  1      1050                   $     80.00 $   1460.00
09/04/92  2:15pm   Buy    1      1050
```

Figure 15-4

123-R-BP-DAILY BP M3-DAILY   01/11/93 - 05/20/93

Performance Summary: All Trades

Total net profit	$ 11075.00	Open position P/L	$	1562.50
Gross profit	$ 11300.00	Gross loss	$	-225.00
Total # of trades	6	Percent profitable		67%
Number winning trades	4	Number losing trades		2
Largest winning trade	$ 4087.50	Largest losing trade	$	-200.00
Average winning trade	$ 2825.00	Average losing trade	$	-112.50
Ratio avg win/avg loss	25.11	Avg trade(win & loss)	$	1845.83
Max consec. winners	2	Max consec. losers		1
Avg # bars in winners	15	Avg # bars in losers		5
Max intraday drawdown	$ -1700.00			
Profit factor	50.22	Max # contracts held		①
Account size required	$ 1700.00	Return on account		651%

Performance Summary: Long Trades

Total net profit	$ 8712.50	Open position P/L	$	1562.50
Gross profit	$ 8712.50	Gross loss	$	0.00
Total # of trades	3	Percent profitable		100%
Number winning trades	3	Number losing trades		0
Largest winning trade	$ 4087.50	Largest losing trade	$	0.00
Average winning trade	$ 2904.17	Average losing trade	$	0.00
Ratio avg win/avg loss	100.00	Avg trade(win & loss)	$	2904.17
Max consec. winners	3	Max consec. losers		0
Avg # bars in winners	15	Avg # bars in losers		0
Max intraday drawdown	$ -1700.00			
Profit factor	100.00	Max # contracts held		1
Account size required	$ 1700.00	Return on account		513%

Performance Summary: Short Trades

Total net profit	$ 2362.50	Open position P/L	$	0.00
Gross profit	$ 2587.50	Gross loss	$	-225.00
Total # of trades	3	Percent profitable		33%
Number winning trades	1	Number losing trades		2
Largest winning trade	$ 2587.50	Largest losing trade	$	-200.00
Average winning trade	$ 2587.50	Average losing trade	$	-112.50
Ratio avg win/avg loss	23.00	Avg trade(win & loss)	$	787.50
Max consec. winners	1	Max consec. losers		2
Avg # bars in winners	12	Avg # bars in losers		5
Max intraday drawdown	$ -1087.50			
Profit factor	11.50	Max # contracts held		1
Account size required	$ 1087.50	Return on account		217%

Figure 15-5

```
123-R-BP-DAILY   BP M3-Daily   01/11/93 - 05/20/93
Date       Time     Type   Cnts   Price  Signal Name      Entry P/L    Cumulative
02/04/93   3:00pm   Buy    1      1.4292
03/22/93   3:00pm   LExit  1      1.4780                $  3050.00 $   3050.00
03/22/93   3:00pm   Sell   1      1.4780
03/26/93   3:00pm   SExit  1      1.4784                $   -25.00 $   3025.00
03/26/93   3:00pm   Buy    1      1.4784
04/14/93   3:00pm   LExit  1      1.5438                $  4087.50 $   7112.50
04/14/93   3:00pm   Sell   1      1.5438
04/22/93   3:00pm   SExit  1      1.5470                $  -200.00 $   6912.50
04/22/93   3:00pm   Buy    1      1.5470
04/27/93   3:00pm   LExit  1      1.5722                $  1575.00 $   8487.50
04/27/93   3:00pm   Sell   1      1.5722
05/17/93   3:00pm   SExit  1      1.5308                $  2587.50 $  11075.00
05/17/93   3:00pm   Buy    1      1.5308
```

Figure 15-6

```
123-R-CURRENTS  DM M3-DAILY        01/11/93 - 05/20/93

                 Performance Summary:  All Trades

Total net profit       $    9400.00   Open position P/L      $     475.00
Gross profit           $    9400.00   Gross loss             $       0.00

Total # of trades              5      Percent profitable           100%
Number winning trades          5      Number losing trades            0

Largest winning trade  $    3537.50   Largest losing trade   $       0.00
Average winning trade  $    1880.00   Average losing trade   $       0.00
Ratio avg win/avg loss       100.00   Avg trade(win & loss)  $    1880.00

Max consec. winners            5      Max consec. losers              0
Avg # bars in winners         15      Avg # bars in losers            0

Max intraday drawdown  $   -2012.50
Profit factor                100.00   Max # contracts held          ①
Account size required  $    2012.50   Return on account            467%
```

```
                 Performance Summary:  Long Trades

Total net profit       $    4250.00   Open position P/L      $     475.00
Gross profit           $    4250.00   Gross loss             $       0.00

Total # of trades              2      Percent profitable           100%
Number winning trades          2      Number losing trades            0

Largest winning trade  $    3062.50   Largest losing trade   $       0.00
Average winning trade  $    2125.00   Average losing trade   $       0.00
Ratio avg win/avg loss       100.00   Avg trade(win & loss)  $    2125.00

Max consec. winners            2      Max consec. losers              0
Avg # bars in winners         11      Avg # bars in losers            0

Max intraday drawdown  $    -175.00
Profit factor                100.00   Max # contracts held            1
Account size required  $     175.00   Return on account           2429%
```

```
                 Performance Summary:  Short Trades

Total net profit       $    5150.00   Open position P/L      $       0.00
Gross profit           $    5150.00   Gross loss             $       0.00

Total # of trades              3      Percent profitable           100%
Number winning trades          3      Number losing trades            0

Largest winning trade  $    3537.50   Largest losing trade   $       0.00
Average winning trade  $    1716.67   Average losing trade   $       0.00
Ratio avg win/avg loss       100.00   Avg trade(win & loss)  $    1716.67

Max consec. winners            3      Max consec. losers              0
Avg # bars in winners         19      Avg # bars in losers            0

Max intraday drawdown  $   -2012.50
Profit factor                100.00   Max # contracts held            1
Account size required  $    2012.50   Return on account            256%
```

Figure 15-7

```
123-R-CURRENCIES   DM M3-Daily   01/11/93 - 05/20/93
Date       Time     Type  Cnts   Price  Signal Name        Entry P/L    Cumulative
01/26/93   3:00pm   Sell  1      .6214
02/08/93   3:00pm   SExit 1      .5931                   $   3537.50 $    3537.50
02/08/93   3:00pm   Buy   1      .5931
02/18/93   3:00pm   LExit 1      .6026                   $   1187.50 $    4725.00
02/18/93   3:00pm   Sell  1      .6026
03/16/93   3:00pm   SExit 1      .5945                   $   1012.50 $    5737.50
03/16/93   3:00pm   Buy   1      .5945
04/02/93   3:00pm   LExit 1      .6190                   $   3062.50 $    8800.00
04/02/93   3:00pm   Sell  1      .6190
05/19/93   3:00pm   SExit 1      .6142                   $    600.00 $    9400.00
05/19/93   3:00pm   Buy   1      .6142
```

Figure 15-8

123-R-CURRENCIES <u>DM M3-DAILY</u>   01/11/93 - 05/20/93

Performance Summary: All Trades

Total net profit	$	16862.50	Open position P/L	$	475.00
Gross profit	$	16862.50	Gross loss	$	0.00
Total # of trades		10	Percent profitable		100%
Number winning trades		10	Number losing trades		0
Largest winning trade	$	3537.50	Largest losing trade	$	0.00
Average winning trade	$	1686.25	Average losing trade	$	0.00
Ratio avg win/avg loss		100.00	Avg trade(win & loss)	$	1686.25
Max consec. winners		10	Max consec. losers		0
Avg # bars in winners		14	Avg # bars in losers		0
Max intraday drawdown	$	-5887.50			
Profit factor		100.00	Max # contracts held		Ⓢ
Account size required	$	5887.50	Return on account		286%

Performance Summary: Long Trades

Total net profit	$	5387.50	Open position P/L	$	475.00
Gross profit	$	5387.50	Gross loss	$	0.00
Total # of trades		3	Percent profitable		100%
Number winning trades		3	Number losing trades		0
Largest winning trade	$	3062.50	Largest losing trade	$	0.00
Average winning trade	$	1795.83	Average losing trade	$	0.00
Ratio avg win/avg loss		100.00	Avg trade(win & loss)	$	1795.83
Max consec. winners		3	Max consec. losers		0
Avg # bars in winners		9	Avg # bars in losers		0
Max intraday drawdown	$	-400.00			
Profit factor		100.00	Max # contracts held		2
Account size required	$	400.00	Return on account		1347%

Performance Summary: Short Trades

Total net profit	$	11475.00	Open position P/L	$	0.00
Gross profit	$	11475.00	Gross loss	$	0.00
Total # of trades		7	Percent profitable		100%
Number winning trades		7	Number losing trades		0
Largest winning trade	$	3537.50	Largest losing trade	$	0.00
Average winning trade	$	1639.29	Average losing trade	$	0.00
Ratio avg win/avg loss		100.00	Avg trade(win & loss)	$	1639.29
Max consec. winners		7	Max consec. losers		0
Avg # bars in winners		16	Avg # bars in losers		0
Max intraday drawdown	$	-5887.50			
Profit factor		100.00	Max # contracts held		5
Account size required	$	5887.50	Return on account		195%

Figure 15-9

```
123-R-CURRENCIES  DM M3-Daily   01/11/93 - 05/20/93
Date       Time    Type  Cnts   Price  Signal Name     Entry P/L   Cumulative
01/26/93  3:00pm Sell  1       .6214
02/08/93  3:00pm SExit 1       .5931               $   3537.50 $    3537.50
02/08/93  3:00pm Buy   1       .5931
02/18/93  3:00pm LExit 1       .6026               $   1187.50 $    4725.00
02/11/93  3:00pm Buy   1       .5935
02/18/93  3:00pm LExit 1       .6026               $   1137.50 $    5862.50
02/18/93  3:00pm Sell  1       .6026
03/16/93  3:00pm SExit 1       .5945               $   1012.50 $    6875.00
03/16/93  3:00pm Buy   1       .5945
04/02/93  3:00pm LExit 1       .6190               $   3062.50 $    9937.50
04/02/93  3:00pm Sell  1       .6190
05/19/93  3:00pm SExit 1       .6142               $    600.00 $   10537.50
04/14/93  3:00pm Sell  1       .6219
05/19/93  3:00pm SExit 1       .6142               $    962.50 $   11500.00
04/27/93  3:00pm Sell  1       .6285
05/19/93  3:00pm SExit 1       .6142               $   1787.50 $   13287.50
04/30/93  3:00pm Sell  1       .6269
05/19/93  3:00pm SExit 1       .6142               $   1587.50 $   14875.00
05/05/93  3:00pm Sell  1       .6301
05/19/93  3:00pm SExit 1       .6142               $   1987.50 $   16862.50
05/19/93  3:00pm Buy   1       .6142
```

Figure 15-10

```
123-R-CURRENCIES   SF M3-60 min     04/22/93 - 05/20/93
                    Performance Summary:  All Trades

Total net profit      $    7075.00   Open position P/L    $    -25.00
Gross profit          $    7175.00   Gross loss           $   -100.00

Total # of trades            8       Percent profitable          88%
Number winning trades        7       Number losing trades          1

Largest winning trade $    2300.00   Largest losing trade $   -100.00
Average winning trade $    1025.00   Average losing trade $   -100.00
Ratio avg win/avg loss      10.25    Avg trade(win & loss) $    884.38

Max consec. winners          6       Max consec. losers            1
Avg # bars in winners       17       Avg # bars in losers         10

Max intraday drawdown $   -1037.50
Profit factor               71.75    Max # contracts held         ①
Account size required $    1037.50   Return on account          682%
```

```
                    Performance Summary:  Long Trades

Total net profit      $    2300.00   Open position P/L    $      0.00
Gross profit          $    2400.00   Gross loss           $   -100.00

Total # of trades            4       Percent profitable          75%
Number winning trades        3       Number losing trades          1

Largest winning trade $    1125.00   Largest losing trade $   -100.00
Average winning trade $     800.00   Average losing trade $   -100.00
Ratio avg win/avg loss       8.00    Avg trade(win & loss) $    575.00

Max consec. winners          3       Max consec. losers            1
Avg # bars in winners       17       Avg # bars in losers         10

Max intraday drawdown $   -1037.50
Profit factor               24.00    Max # contracts held          1
Account size required $    1037.50   Return on account          222%
```

```
                    Performance Summary:  Short Trades

Total net profit      $    4775.00   Open position P/L    $    -25.00
Gross profit          $    4775.00   Gross loss           $      0.00

Total # of trades            4       Percent profitable         100%
Number winning trades        4       Number losing trades          0

Largest winning trade $    2300.00   Largest losing trade $      0.00
Average winning trade $    1193.75   Average losing trade $      0.00
Ratio avg win/avg loss     100.00    Avg trade(win & loss) $   1193.75

Max consec. winners          4       Max consec. losers            0
Avg # bars in winners       17       Avg # bars in losers          0

Max intraday drawdown $    -675.00
Profit factor              100.00    Max # contracts held          1
Account size required $     675.00   Return on account          707%
```

Figure 15-11

```
123-R-CURRENCIES  SF M3-60 min   04/22/93 - 05/20/93
Date       Time    Type   Cnts   Price  Signal Name      Entry P/L   Cumulative
04/26/93 10:20am Sell   1        .7015
04/27/93  3:00pm SExit  1        .7003                  $    150.00 $    150.00
04/27/93  3:00pm Buy    1        .7003
04/29/93 11:20am LExit  1        .6995                  $   -100.00 $     50.00
04/29/93 11:20am Sell   1        .6995
05/03/93 10:20am SExit  1        .6951                  $    550.00 $    600.00
05/03/93 10:20am Buy    1        .6951
05/04/93 10:20am LExit  1        .7041                  $   1125.00 $   1725.00
05/04/93 10:20am Sell   1        .7041
05/10/93 12:20pm SExit  1        .6857                  $   2300.00 $   4025.00
05/10/93 12:20pm Buy    1        .6857
05/14/93  3:00pm LExit  1        .6890                  $    412.50 $   4437.50
05/14/93  3:00pm Sell   1        .6890
05/18/93  2:20pm SExit  1        .6748                  $   1775.00 $   6212.50
05/18/93  2:20pm Buy    1        .6748
05/20/93  1:20pm LExit  1        .6817                  $    862.50 $   7075.00
05/20/93  1:20pm Sell   1        .6817
```

Figure 15-12

```
123-R-CURRENCIES   BP M3-60 min      04/22/93 - 05/20/93

                    Performance Summary:  All Trades

Total net profit       $    9175.00   Open position P/L   $  -1200.00
Gross profit           $    9312.50   Gross loss          $   -137.50

Total # of trades            13       Percent profitable        92%
Number winning trades        12       Number losing trades       1

Largest winning trade  $    3012.50   Largest losing trade  $  -137.50
Average winning trade  $     776.04   Average losing trade  $  -137.50
Ratio avg win/avg loss        5.64    Avg trade(win & loss) $   705.77

Max consec. winners           7       Max consec. losers         1
Avg # bars in winners        22       Avg # bars in losers      24

Max intraday drawdown  $   -4712.50
Profit factor                67.73    Max # contracts held      ⑤
Account size required  $    4712.50   Return on account        195%
```

```
                    Performance Summary:  Long Trades

Total net profit       $    4350.00   Open position P/L   $      0.00
Gross profit           $    4487.50   Gross loss          $   -137.50

Total # of trades             9       Percent profitable        89%
Number winning trades         8       Number losing trades       1

Largest winning trade  $    1012.50   Largest losing trade  $  -137.50
Average winning trade  $     560.94   Average losing trade  $  -137.50
Ratio avg win/avg loss        4.08    Avg trade(win & loss) $   483.33

Max consec. winners           5       Max consec. losers         1
Avg # bars in winners        28       Avg # bars in losers      24

Max intraday drawdown  $   -4712.50
Profit factor                32.64    Max # contracts held       5
Account size required  $    4712.50   Return on account         92%
```

```
                    Performance Summary:  Short Trades

Total net profit       $    4825.00   Open position P/L   $  -1200.00
Gross profit           $    4825.00   Gross loss          $      0.00

Total # of trades             4       Percent profitable       100%
Number winning trades         4       Number losing trades       0

Largest winning trade  $    3012.50   Largest losing trade  $     0.00
Average winning trade  $    1206.25   Average losing trade  $     0.00
Ratio avg win/avg loss      100.00    Avg trade(win & loss) $  1206.25

Max consec. winners           4       Max consec. losers         0
Avg # bars in winners        10       Avg # bars in losers       0

Max intraday drawdown  $   -1300.00
Profit factor               100.00    Max # contracts held       2
Account size required  $    1300.00   Return on account        371%
```

Figure 15-13

```
123-R-CURRENCIES  BP M3-60 min   04/22/93 - 05/20/93
Date      Time     Type  Cnts    Price  Signal Name      Entry P/L   Cumulative
04/26/93 10:20am Sell  1        1.5824
04/27/93 12:20pm SExit 1        1.5716                  $    675.00 $    675.00
04/27/93 12:20pm Buy   1        1.5716
05/07/93 10:20am LExit 1        1.5770                  $    337.50 $   1012.50
04/27/93  3:00pm Buy   1        1.5722
05/07/93 10:20am LExit 1        1.5770                  $    300.00 $   1312.50
04/28/93 11:20am Buy   1        1.5666
05/07/93 10:20am LExit 1        1.5770                  $    650.00 $   1962.50
05/07/93 10:20am Sell  1        1.5770
05/10/93 12:20pm SExit 1        1.5288                  $   3012.50 $   4975.00
05/10/93 12:20pm Buy   1        1.5288
05/14/93 12:20pm LExit 1        1.5340                  $    325.00 $   5300.00
05/10/93  2:20pm Buy   1        1.5290
05/14/93 12:20pm LExit 1        1.5340                  $    312.50 $   5612.50
05/11/93  9:20am Buy   1        1.5362
05/14/93 12:20pm LExit 1        1.5340                  $   -137.50 $   5475.00
05/13/93 11:20am Buy   1        1.5214
05/14/93 12:20pm LExit 1        1.5340                  $    787.50 $   6262.50
05/13/93  3:00pm Buy   1        1.5178
05/14/93 12:20pm LExit 1        1.5340                  $   1012.50 $   7275.00
05/14/93 12:20pm Sell  1        1.5340
05/18/93 10:20am SExit 1        1.5252                  $    550.00 $   7825.00
05/17/93  9:20am Sell  1        1.5346
05/18/93 10:20am SExit 1        1.5252                  $    587.50 $   8412.50
05/18/93 10:20am Buy   1        1.5252
05/19/93 11:20am LExit 1        1.5374                  $    762.50 $   9175.00
05/19/93 11:20am Sell  1        1.5374
05/20/93  1:20pm Sell  1        1.5554
```

PART 5

GETTING THE MOST OUT OF YOUR COMPUTER

Even when calculations were done with pencil and paper, it was possible to do research on many relationships between price action and an endless number of patterns and sequences of prices. Calculators made that task simpler, but it still was laborious. With computers, the task became considerably easier, and a vast new area of interest opened up for many traders. However, lack of good analytical software was a great handicap, since only some of us were able to write our own analytical computer programs. This great need was filled by many of the so-called "data vendors." In addition, Bill Cruz of Omega Research, Inc., of Miami, first produced System Writer and later TradeStation, which has the ability to do everything also in real time. TradeStation has saved me massive amounts of time in analyzing various aspects of the markets. It comes supplied with a manual that is very thorough and not only has excellent disclosure of the built-in analytical tools, such as functions, indicators, and systems; but also information on the background and development of those tools. The available videotapes on using the program are also very helpful.

Nevertheless, and not with the intention of outdoing the manual or videos, I believe a user's guide to getting the most out of TradeStation, and any other analytical software, would be helpful to many traders. Some may be intimidated by the required steps needed to develop their own analytical tools, and some may not have the mathematical background to "squeeze" all the "juice" out of what they have created. This section will attempt to provide a hands-on user's guide to making the most out of what you are doing with TradeStation, or any other software. The emphasis will be on those aspects critical to trading, rather than on exploration of more esoteric aspects of the programs. Other software—such as may be supplied by CQG, Ensign, Future Source, Signal, CSI, Computrac, Bonneville, and others—also can be supplemented by this guide insofar as they permit user input and modification of functions, and as long as the language of the individual software is used.

Of course we'll use the "Easy Language" that is used by TradeStation. The emphasis will be on five aspects of the program:

1. Useful Real-Time Displays
2. Constructing Mathematical Functions
3. Constructing Indicators
4. Analyzing Price-Bar Patterns
5. Creating Systems

This section should be considered as a *supplement* to existing manuals.

16

Useful Real-Time Displays

There are an endless number of ways to set up your real-time displays. You can choose from an enormous number of colors for the background, price bars, opening and closing prices; pick from hundreds of fonts for text, as well as various degrees of boldness (thickness) for each of them. In addition, up to 50 windows of varying sizes can be displayed on each of many pages. If they are overlapped in specific ways, a tremendous amount of information can be viewed at one time. In fact, it's probably more data than is possible for us mortals to assimilate in our minds at the rate it is displayed! You can also add several indicators, some superimposed on the price bars, as well as a system. So where do you begin, or, more important, where do you **stop?** Let's begin with a basic display, then add onto that in the next chapters.

To set up your initial pages with an assortment of windows on each page, you will need to have set up the portfolio of markets you'll be following. Here, at the very beginning, you must be careful to select *at least* those that interest you, even only slightly. If next month you suddenly hear about a development in a market that you've not been following, you cannot "bring it up," because there will be no data in your portfolio. So make sure your portfolio collects data for all the markets you *might* be interested in. Even if you don't trade live cattle now, go ahead and include it anyway, You never know; you might want it later.

What delivery months do you include? This is also very important. You always must have the current or active month *plus the next* delivery month, and probably the *one after that* as well. That makes at least two, or, better yet, three delivery months. The reason is that when the current month stops trading (actually, most traders stop trading a contract on the "first notice day"; that's when brokers get nervous if you are holding positions that could come up for delivery), you need to have sufficient data on the next month to make intelligent analysis. At that same time, the month that becomes the new next month (the third contract) will start to show significant data, and collecting it from that day will give you the most data to use when the new current month expires. When your current month contract is no longer traded by you, then add another third contract—the one following your final contract month—and so forth, always staying ahead.

If you are into using spreads, such as front month vs. back month, another set of three contracts of later delivery months must be included. If you are allocating some funds for investment purposes and follow contracts with delivery dates one year or longer into the future, such as December 94 eurodollars while the current month is December 93, such far-out contracts should also be added to your portfolio.

The worst mistake is to have too few contracts and suddenly realize that you have no data on the current month. Of course, you can always call your data vendor and request three or six months' data on such missed contracts and paste it in according to the directions for your software. But your best course of action is to collect your own!

Having filled your portfolio properly, the next step is to organize your markets in a manner that makes sense to you. This could be according to the time of day you start trading. If you start at the opening of the currency markets, you might have the currencies, T-bonds and bills, eurodollars, and precious metals on your first page; you will have another page with markets that open later, such as foods and fibers, grains and livestock. On the other hand, you may need only one page with five or six markets that you're following closely.

I've found that I need a lot of periods displayed for each market I follow, and consequently I have a lot of windows on a page. If you also have a lot of indicators, the computer cannot process all that data (which is enormous) fast enough to allow you to work quickly between pages. The more data you display, the slower the "turning of pages" will be. It could become a chore to go from a page heavy with windows on currencies to another page heavy with windows on T-bonds and related financial contracts. My solution to that problem has been to create several different pages as follows:

First, I have a "Quote Page" displaying all the significant markets (Fig. 16-1). This page comes up quickly and gives me an instant view of what they are all doing. This tells me essentially what's going on in the world today. I also have a similar page with Globex quotes of the foreign currencies, T-bonds, and eurodollars; this page includes windows with daily charts of all those markets. That page keeps me abreast of what is happening overseas after the U.S. markets have

Figure 16-1

Symbol	Open	High	Low	Last	Net	Volume	Description
DM M3	.6211	.6239	.6211	.6242	+.0041	43	Deutsche Mark (IMM
AD M3	.7125	.7129	.7067	.7073	-.0056	450	Australian Dollar (IN
BP M3	1.5500	1.5536	1.5500	1.5530	+.0060	21	British Pound (IMM)
CD M3	.7916	.7917	.7891	.7894	-.0030	2962	Canadian Dollar (IN
SF M3	.6870	.6890	.6870	.6880	+.0018	8	Swiss Franc (IMM)
JY M3	.9100	.9103	.9070	.9070	-.0024	52	Japanese Yen (IMN
DX M3	90.51	90.60	90.50	90.55	-.34	2032	US Dollar Index
CC N3	923	928	917	924	+6	3827	Cocoa
CT N3	62.60	62.85	61.60	61.88	-.62	4134	Cotton #2
KC N3	54.15	55.50	54.15	54.95	+.75	9171	Coffee
SB N3	11.75	12.27	11.75	12.25	+.59	9229	Sugar #11
HG N3	85.70	85.80	83.45	83.95	+.50	4806	Copper-high grade
GC M3	339.0	342.0	338.9	341.2	+.5	13381	Gold
PL N3	365.5	371.0	365.5	369.9	+1.7	2681	Platinum
YX M3	244.20	246.20	242.05	242.35	-2.55	3809	NYSE Composite In
SP M3	442.75	446.30	438.30	438.55	-5.30	57655	S&P 500 Index
S N3	590^4	595^2	590^2	593^6	+2^0	86910	Soybeans
TB M3	97.13	97.14	97.11	97.13	+.00	1790	Treasury Bills 90 d
US M3	112^08	112^13	111^15	112^11	+^04	189026	Treasury Bonds
W N3	309^4	309^6	308^0	309^0	-1^6	31055	Wheat
ED M3	96.78	96.79	96.77	96.78	+.00	17541	Eurodollar (IMM)

closed. This helps fill in the gaps frequently seen on the currency charts from the U.S. markets.

Next, I have a page called "Watching Now." It consists of 12 or 16 windows covering 3 or 4 contracts. I will usually have a position in only one market at a time, or at most two, so 3 or 4 closely watched contracts will include the one or two I am currently trading and two or three others that are candidates for trading within a short time. I watch four periods: the daily, 60-minute, 15-minute, and the 5-minute bars.

I can get an overview of what is happening by looking at the daily bars (I also check out the weekly and monthly bars, which in the latest version of TradeStation can be seen by a click of the mouse on an "Easy Icon" that represents weekly or monthly bars; you return to the daily bars by another click of the mouse.) I then get a little closer look at the real-time action with the 60-minute bars. Precise entry and exit points are best defined with an even shorter timeframe, such as 5- , 10- , or 15-minute bars. I like both the 5- and the 15-minute bars, the former fine-tune the entry or exit points of the latter.

The 5-minute bars are fairly fast, but not as fast as the 1- or 3- minute bars. You don't want another bar to start forming and perhaps even finish while you are still on the phone with an order; that can happen if you trade the very fast bars in a fast market. I overlap the four periods as follows: The 60-minute bars occupy the entire screen. That gives me a good perspective. The daily and 15-minute bar charts are downsized and inserted where they best fit in without obscuring critical parts of the 60-minute chart. Finally, I insert the 5-minute bar chart on the 15-minute bar chart in a harmless spot (Fig. 16-2). With that set of windows, it's easy to watch those three or four markets. Figure 16-3 shows another similar set of windows. If it's beginning to look like I should enter one of those markets, I just exit that page and go to what I call my two "decision-making" pages.

The first decision-making page is an overview of the entire group of related markets. If I were watching the D-mark, Jap. yen, and T-bonds, having, for example, a position in the T-bonds and seeing that the D-mark was turning a bottom and was becoming the next candidate for trading, I would bring up my "Currency Page." This is a page with all the foreign currencies on daily bar charts; it happens to include also the U.S., Canadian, and Australian dollars, as well as T-bonds, T-bills, and eurodollars. Here I can get an overview of what is happening to the currencies and the U.S. dollar.

Seeing that all patterns look favorable for an upside move in the D-mark, I then exit that overview page and bring up the second decision-making page. This is a more detailed page of the individual commodity, here the D-Mark. It is labeled D-Mark, and contains windows with 5- , 15- , 30- , and 60-minute bar charts as well as daily charts of the current and next contracts; it may also have a spread such as the D-mark/Jap. yen spread. This last page will be a heavy page with lots of indicators on many windows (Fig. 16-4), but that's okay, because I'll stay with that page until I've placed my order and followed the market for a little while. There's no need to change in and out of this heavy page.

So you see, this procedure is nice and easy and fairly quick, as it avoids shifting between heavily loaded pages and letting the market get away from me while I'm still sorting pages. Is this the only way to do it? Of course not, but this works best for me as an active trader.

Figure 16-2

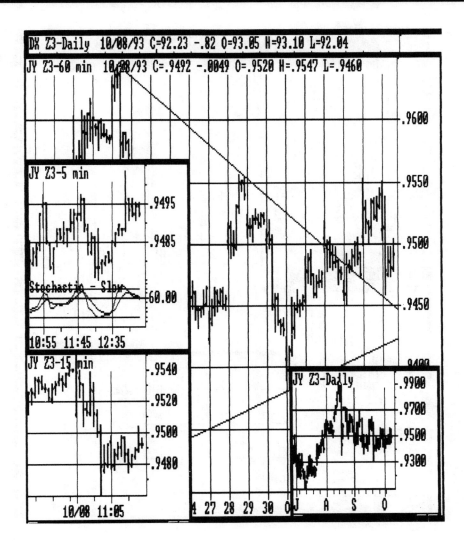

Figure 16-3

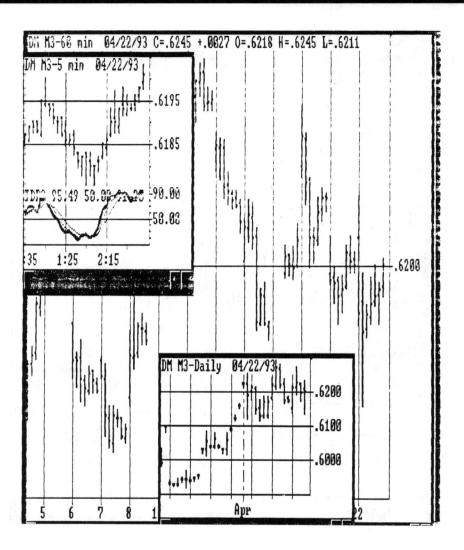

Figure 16-4

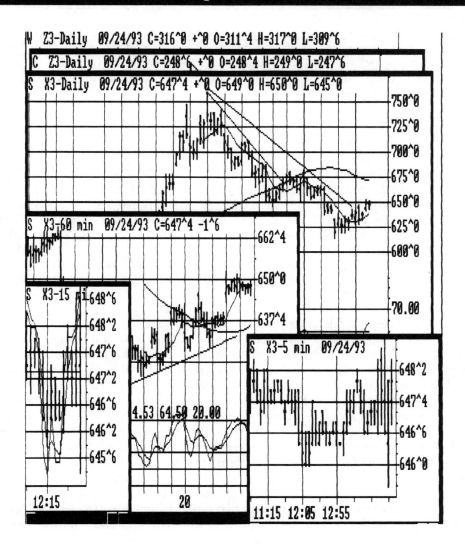

Having adequate space on your hard disk is important, but even more important is having enough RAM (random-access memory). If your computer is slow
handling your loaded pages, try doubling the amount of RAM. I found a *substantial* improvement in speed by upgrading from four to eight megabytes of
RAM. Finally, the newest add-on accelerator boards and fast video boards for
Windows graphics will also speed things up substantially.

Before I go any further, be sure you've invested in two important items that
nobody ever tells you about:

1. A good and comfortable office chair with adjustable height and a back
    rest that can be custom-fitted to your back. It will save your back,
    believe me.
2. You absolutely *must* get a radiation filter for your color monitor to pro-
    tect your eyes from radiation. A significant amount of radiation is emit-
    ted from these screens and will hasten the formation of cataracts,
    something your eyes don't need. Such a filter will also help reduce glare.
    A slight decrease in brightness is unavoidable but not of any conse-
    quence. These filters cost about $60 to $80 and come in two sizes; get the
    larger. It easily hangs on the front of your monitor and can be trans-
    ferred to other monitors if you use several. In other words, keep it where
    your eyes are.

Another suggestion is to keep the height of the screen fairly low, so you don't
need to bend your head back in order to see it (Fig. 16-5). Likewise the angle
should be adjusted to optimize your posture. If you wear bifocal glasses, and
need to view the screen through the lower lenses, that will make you bend your
neck backward and cause neck strain. Investing in a pair of reading glasses, in
which your reading-power lenses make up the entire glass, is well worth the cost
in preventing neck and eyestrain.

Sorry for the brief digression, but, as a physician, I feel the need to warn you
of potential hazards to your health and show you how to minimize them.

As far as colors go, it is important to make screens that are easy on the eyes,
since you'll be watching them a lot. Use dark colors such as black or dark blue
for the background, because the background color is the dominant one displayed. This doesn't mean you can't use pink or light blue for an occasional
chart in a window here and there, but your eyes will appreciate mostly darker
colors. The bars and other items can be almost any color, but the opening and
closing prices should have their own separate and easily distinguishable color.
All these—bars, opening and closing prices—should have consistent colors in all
your windows, so that you won't make a mistake in interpretation.

If you print some of your charts, pay attention to how your printer handles
various colors in terms of shades of gray, or perhaps doesn't handle them at all.
Two very different colors may turn out to be identical when printed in black and
white. Therefore, you may want to change the "texture" of such lines from the
standard solid line to a dotted or dashed line to distinguish, for example, the two
lines of the Stochastic indicator. If you're printing in color, be aware that such
light colors as yellow and light blue are almost invisible on white paper, since
the background color of the chart as you see it on the screen is not transferred to

Figure 16-5

the paper and shows up pure white. Check the color saturation of the ribbon you have; perhaps you have a very dark yellow color that you can see better than most. You easily can change the bar colors of a chart you suddenly want to print; just change the yellow bars, if those are what you have on the screen, to cyan (a strong light blue), and they will print much better.

Be sure the colors of your indicator lines are different from the background color of your windows. That sounds rather basic, but if one of your lines doesn't want to show up on the screen, it may be that its color is identical to your background. Also, it could be a bad scaling of the indicator or a problem with the calculation of the formula. Likewise make sure that the two twisting lines, such as those of the Stochastic indicator, have colors that are far apart on the spectrum of colors so you can readily distinguish one from the other. Don't use red and pink, or blue and black; go ahead, be holiday traditional and use red and green, they work well! If the default color (the color pre-set by the program) is the same or close to the same as your background color, then go to the editor and bring up that indicator and go to "Properties" and then to "Style" and change the color permanently to one that is more suitable. That way you don't waste a lot of time painting when making charts and selecting indicators. You will probably use several favorite indicators repeatedly, and you don't want always to be changing their colors.

Chose a weak color for your grid. Some of you may never use grids, but they can be helpful in providing a frame of reference for prices. There's a handy Easy Icon for choosing the grid design and another for the color of the grid. If these Easy Icons are not on your selection rows, at the top and the side of your screen when using TradeStation charting, then follow the directions to place them there, as they will save you a lot of time. You do this through the "Power Editor" and "Customizing Icons." Now choose a design that is not very outstanding or overbearing; that way the grid lines won't detract from the price bars or cause confusion. I usually choose a grid with four horizontal lines in a shade of blue that is pretty close to the background shade, so it will appear more like a shadow. Nevertheless, it will give you a point of reference. Such a weak color won't draw your attention away from the price bars. Again, you may like to do it differently, but this way has worked very well for me.

Finally, your eyes also will appreciate large charts. Don't crowd too many charts onto a screen. Even if you can fit a large number of small charts in there, allow at most three or four to a screen as mentioned earlier (Fig. 16-2). Now that we've set up the necessary charts and made them easy on the eyes, let's move on and become more creative.

17

Constructing Mathematical Functions

Here comes the more difficult part: keeping those beautiful displays from becoming too cluttered as we add other things to them. TradeStation has a large library of mathematical functions and relationships such as averages, median price, absolute value, and many more. You must familiarize yourself with all the listed functions, so that you know exactly what goes into each of them. You may ask "Why should I learn how to create any of those functions when they already exist in the TradeStation library and can be applied by a few clicks of the mouse?"

The answer is that, for the most part, they are single functions. In other words, if you want to display a composite of functions such as a 6-day moving average of the high minus the mean price, you couldn't find that in the library of functions, and would need to set it up yourself. If you wanted the mean value of the 6-day weighted moving average of the high and the same average of the low price, you would need to know how to construct the formula for the mean or median value, since the built-in function of "MedianPrice" refers only to prices, not to any other value such as an average of prices.

Let's begin by constructing a display of the high minus the mean price of the 5-minute bars of the June 93 Swiss franc. We want to see if there is any correlation between the behavior of that function and future price movement. That is, of course, the underlying purpose of all technical analyses. We will also want to see how this function differs from the simple mean price. We'll want to display these functions in a useful way. There are essentially *three ways* to display them. *First* is a series of dots (or dashes, or x's); *second* is a continuous line; and *third* is a series of bars of varying heights. We can then modify such displays by putting the formula through various mathematical manipulations, such as multiplying by a factor, dividing the figure 1 by the result (called the inverse of the function), subtracting the formula from the figure 1, and so on.

To display the formula we can use the "Custom One Line" selection under indicators. The quickest way to enter the library of either indicators or systems is to use their Easy Icons. If you don't already have those two icons on your row of icons at the top and left side of your screen, go to Power Editor and then to Customizing Easy Icons. Find the two icons you want and drag them over to the display rows, either at the top or side of the screen. Then all it takes is a click of the mouse, and you can scroll through the entire library and simply click on your selection. Having done that, we need to click on "Inputs"; then erase any default wording present and type in your own formula. Click on OK, and then click on "Style" to choose the type and color of the display. Don't forget to click on "Options" and set the "Max Bars Back" to 10 (see below). The formula is derived as follows:

H = High price; L = Low price; M = Mean or Median price;

$$M = \frac{H + L}{2} \text{, or as written for computers: } (H + L)/2$$

It's important to write the formula correctly, so the program can read it properly. When a computer looks at a set of tasks, it performs multiplication and division first, and then addition and subtraction. Therefore, we place brackets to indicate that the *sum of the high and the low prices* must be divided by 2, rather than just the *low price*. Since we now want to subtract that entire result from the high price, we need another set of brackets to make sure that it gets done properly. The formula then becomes:

H − ((H + L)/2)

Now we'll go to TradeStation charting. You'll see how easy all this is if you take this book right now, place it in front of your computer and follow the directions. Before plotting your function, indicator, or system, be aware of the Max Bars Back setting. The default number set by TradeStation is 50; this is so that you won't be getting a lot of error messages if your indicator requires more bars for analysis than have been set. However, if you let that figure stand, your function will not show up on the screen for the first 50 bars! That may eliminate half the screen from your study! Therefore, always set that number to the lowest possible number, so you can see your function as early as possible. If you set it too low, you will of course get an error message asking you to increase it. I've found that setting it to a number two higher than what my indicator needs works fine. Thus, if you are using a 6-bar average, set the Max Bars Back to 8.

Open the page with the current Swiss franc, then click on "Windows."

Click on the 5-minute bar window. If none exists, click on New Window and create a 5-minute bar chart.

Click on the Easy Icon representing Indicators.

Click on Add, and scroll to the Custom One Line, click on that, and click on OK.

Click on Inputs.

Press Backspace key to erase the word Close.

Type in a formula (right now, type in the formula for the median price).

Click on Options.

Press Backspace key to erase 50 from the Max Bars Back setting.

Type in 10 and click on the box for Update study value every tick.

Click on OK.

Click on Style.

Click on Red and on Line and on Very Thin and on Solid.

Click on OK.

Click on Scaling.

Click on Screen and on OK.

Make sure that the Status switch is on. If not, click on Status to turn it on. It usually goes to the off setting only if an error has been detected.

Click on the little box next to 2 under Plot Custom One Line so it will not take the default setting and be plotted superimposed on the price bars.

Click on OK.

The result is the heavy solid line shown in Figure 17-1.

Now let's produce a graph of the formula we developed two pages ago.

Click on the Easy Icon for Indicators, click on Add.

Scroll to the Custom One Line and click on that, and click on OK.

Follow the directions above except for three items:

1. The formula to be typed in is:

    H − ((H + L)/2)

2. The color for the display should be Green, and select Dotted Line.
3. Be sure to click on the little box #3 before clicking OK to bring it up on the screen. That will place the second plot beneath the first in a separate section of the screen.

You now can see the different characteristics of the two functions. If they look very similar, you'll need to plot them on the same screen to be able to see exactly how they differ. You simply click on the Easy Icon for Indicators and change the little box referred to above, so both functions will appear on the same sub-screen (Fig. 17-1).

You also can superimpose one or both on the price bars to accentuate their amplitude (see below). Superimposing them on the price bars allows them to "unfold" better and allows more space for other plots beneath the price bars.

Figure 17-1

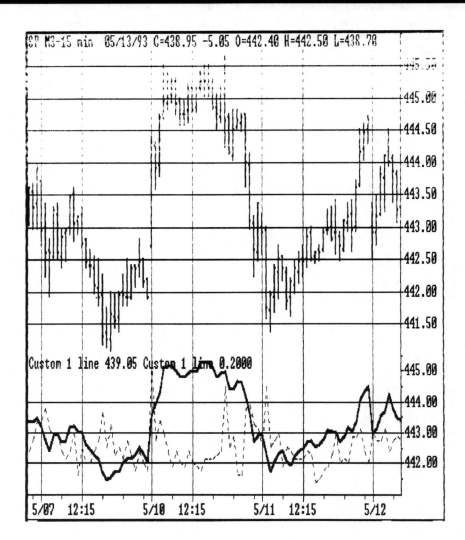

If you don't think your graph is dramatic or volatile enough, it can be modified in several ways to become more outstanding.

1. The first is changing the scale. The program automatically scales the data according to the extremes of high and low of the entire data series. For any specified period, the high and low of that section of data may be quite far from the extremes of the entire series, and so it will be plotted with a small amplitude. The program thinks it needs room on the screen to plot the extremes present elsewhere in the data (Fig. 17-2). Changing the scaling to Screen will cure this low amplitude, as now only the small section of data you're viewing onscreen is used to set the extremes of high and low. The screen is filled from top to bottom (Fig. 17-1). The difference is quite dramatic, isn't it?

2. A second way, though it's not always possible while still retaining proper clarity, is to give the graph as much amplitude as possible by superimposing the plot on the price bars, then using as few additional plots beneath that screen as possible. The more additional plots or screens you add, the smaller your first or price-bar screen becomes. With no additional screens, you'll get the maximum amplitude possible (Fig. 8-13). Be careful of the indicator line obscuring part of a price bar or vice versa; this could lead to an error if a critical value goes undetected.

3. A third way is to use a mathematical computation, somewhat the opposite of differencing, namely a cumulative expression of a series of numbers. Each successive number is added to the previous, with or without respect to the sign (positive or negative). This produces very interesting and useful curves; such established functions like accumulation-distribution index and on-balance volume are expressions of this technique.

   In simple computer language this is expressed by a "counter" such as $X = X + Y$, where Y is the next figure to be added, and X is the sum of all the previous figures. The X changes constantly with the addition of each new Y. In TradeStation language, we shall use "VALUE1" and "VALUE2" as our variables, thus we can write:

   VALUE1 = VALUE1 + VALUE2

   where VALUE1 is the accumulated sum and VALUE2 is the ever-changing value of your function. With the numbers reversed below, the formula for a simple tick difference is as follows:

VALUE1=(UPTICKS-DOWNTICKS);	(The basic function)
VALUE2=VALUE2+VALUE1;	(VALUE2 is the summation)
VALUE3=WAVERAGE((VALUE2),3);	(Smoothing by short moving average)
VALUE4=WAVERAGE((VALUE3),9);	(Longer average for comparison)
PLOT1(VALUE3,"ACCUMO");	(Curves are labeled by words inside quotation marks)
PLOT2(VALUE4,"MATD");	

Figure 17-2

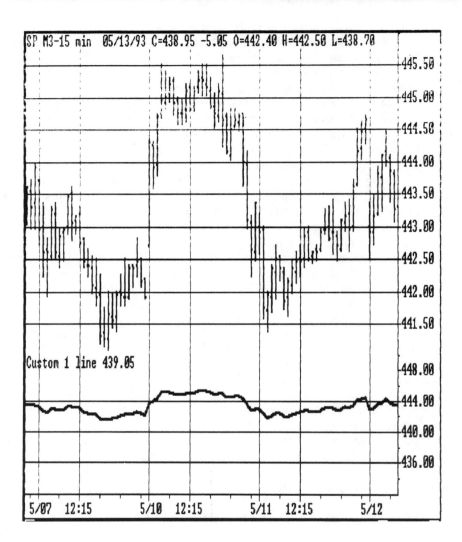

We have thus constructed a new indicator, one having a fast and a slow moving average of itself, based on the net buying and selling sentiment, or market sentiment, expressed in a cumulative fashion. It's interesting to compare this indicator with the others we have created (Fig. 8-12).

I might mention at this time that if you need to enter the formula for a known function that already exists in the library of TradeStation, you need only mention it by name, rather than retyping the entire formula. Just place the character "@" in front of the name of the function. For example "@RSI" tells the computer to employ the *formula* for the RSI indicator whenever it finds that sequence of characters in your statements. This obviously will save you loads of time in constructing systems.

A common problem in plotting a function is that it appears too volatile or jagged, that is, it has too many ups and downs in a short period. This can be cured by a smoothing treatment that will make interpretation easier.

One way to do that is to take an average. This could be a 3-bar, 6-bar, or even an 18-bar simple average or weighted average. The weighted average gives a little more weight to the later values and thus gives a better representation of what is happening *now* as compared to 18 bars ago. A 6-bar weighted moving average of our function (high - mean) is shown in Figure 17-3.

A second way to smooth a curve is by differencing. Functions such as momentum are calculated this way. We can subtract a previous bar's value from today's or the present bar's value and get a whole set of differencing curves. For example, we can take the value of the above function nine bars ago and subtract it from the value of the present bar. This will be written as:

@MOMENTUM((WAVERAGE((H-L)/2),6),9);   (shown in Fig. 17-4)

When you've created a function, or other formula, you'd be wise to save it. It might be very valuable, or it might serve as a stepping stone to further development of a better formula. You don't need to save everything you write, but do save what looks most interesting and useful. You can simply write it down carefully before you delete it, or better yet, if you are using TradeStation or similar software, click on File, then on Save as ... , and you will be prompted for a name under which it will be saved. You can also let the program print a hard copy for you. That is done with a click on File and then on Print.

If you've created your function through the Custom One Line pathway, you'll need to write down your formula, then go to Power Editor: Click on File, then Open, then select Indicator and you will be prompted for the name of your function as well as a short description. Once you've typed that in, click on OK and a text box in which you can type the formula appears. Click on File and then Verify, and, if all is okay, you will see the little blue sign: Excellent. If all is not okay, the program will advise you of what errors you might have made. You then will need to correct them before you can proceed. You need to get that Excellent!

Click on Properties.

Click on Options, and select the shortest possible Max Bars Back setting.

Click on Style to select your format and colors.

Click on Scaling to select Screen.

Figure 17-3

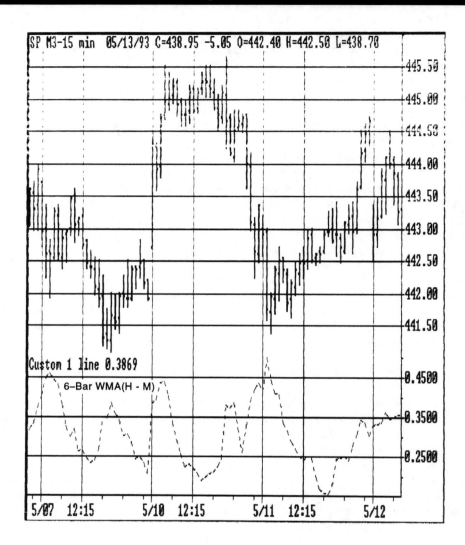

Figure 17-4

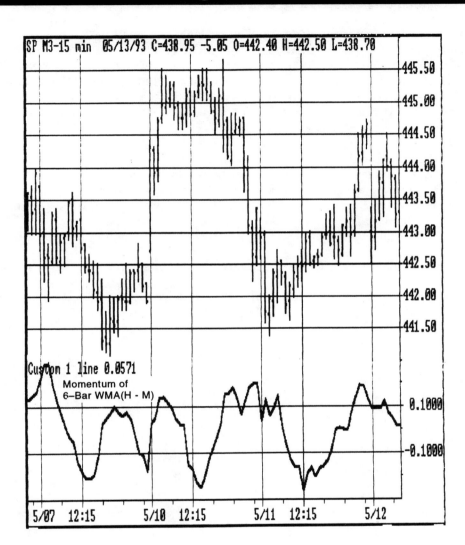

SP M3-15 min   05/13/93 C=438.95 −5.05 O=442.40 H=442.50 L=438.70

Custom 1 line 0.0571
Momentum of
6−Bar WMA(H − M)

Click on OK.

Click on Utilities, and Go to Charting. You'll be back to your price bars, from where you can now select your verified function via the Easy Icon by scrolling through the library looking for the name you gave it. Bring it up in order to check that the display is what you had in mind, and if so, you're finished. If it is not exactly what you wanted, simply click on the Easy Icon again, delete the function, return to the price bars, and then click on Power Editor. You'll be back at the text dialog box and can revise as you see fit. Return again to the price bars (follow this paragraph again) and test your work again.

You have now learned how to:

1. Construct a mathematical function;
2. Combine two or more such functions into a formula;
3. Display the graph of such functions in a useful fashion;
4. Modify the functions in three different ways to give the most dramatic display;
5. Modify the functions to be less jagged by smoothing in two different ways; and
6. Add such functions to the library of indicators which includes functions.

In the next chapter, we will apply what we have discussed so far to creating indicators.

18

Constructing Indicators

Constructing a function such as a mathematical relationship is fairly simple, provided you have some knowledge of mathematics—of course, the more the better. Constructing an indicator, however, involves a few more concepts derived from observing price action. It is true that a simple moving average can serve as an indicator with some predictive value, but the signals given are rather late, and, when the market is not in a trend, they can not only be false, but can change back and forth rather quickly. The primary purpose of an indicator is to attempt to give a signal indicating a useful and imminent upturn or downturn in prices. Once prices have turned, *they themselves*, along with moving averages and other lagging indicators, become indicators. But we need indicators that will give those signals *ahead of time*, not after the action already is underway.

To define such a signal, several concepts have been developed:

1. The crossing of a zero reference line.
2. The crossing of reference lines at the extremes of upper and lower limits of an oscillator.

3. The crossing of a short moving average of some sort over a longer moving average of either itself or some other function.
4. The tops and bottoms, or peaks and valleys, or turning points of an indicator.
5. The divergence of the trend of an indicator compared to the trend of prices.

We can use any one or a combination of these five methods to generate the sought-after signals. Our task is merely constructing the indicator in such a way that its plot or graph is a reasonable display (not too jagged nor too flat) that can be correlated with the direction of price movement.

We must be able to distinguish between those that *will* correlate and those that *will not*. Furthermore, it is not sufficient that they correlate over a short segment of data; they must correlate over lengthy segments. (Here TradeStation can provide you with huge amounts of data, going back as far as 10 years of daily data and 1 year of tick data. As you know by now, data is supplied as either daily data, which will produce your daily, weekly, and monthly bar charts, or tick data, which will produce your minute bars.)

We also must check the indicator in different markets, as each market has its peculiarities. The final test of a good indicator is whether it allows us to incorporate it into a mechanical system that provides profitable entry and exit points. This final test may not always be successful, and yet the indicator could still be reliable and valuable. But more about that in the chapter on systems. For now, we can make a list of all we want. Our task is *merely* to do *all* of the above! Let's go back for a moment and very briefly review what we discussed in earlier chapters.

1. We can make a function.
2. We can display it vibrantly.
3. We can modify it so it is dramatic.
4. We can smooth it if it is jagged.
5. We can build complex functions.
6. We can plot many functions on one or more graphs.
7. We can name and save what we have created.

Now we'll build on those abilities and add the following:

8. We must add a set of reference lines for the indicator to cross, or be compared to, for producing signals.
9. We must be able to identify turning points.
10. We must be able to identify the crossing of any of those lines.
11. We must be able to identify divergence between prices and the indicator.
12. We must be able to build complex indicator formulas if we need them.
13. Finally—and this will be taken up in the chapter on systems—we must be able to incorporate the indicator into a mechanical system.

Let's deal with each of the last six items in order.

To add reference lines, we either will add a 0 line in the center of the graph, or top and bottom lines. If we use the center line, the values of the indicator will be either positive and above that line, or negative and below that line. If we also add two lines, one will be near the top and one near the bottom of the range of the indicator, that is, near the extremes of the values. That works equally well whether we are using an oscillator than runs between 0 and 100, or an indicator whose value range is much wider. The various extremes are reached under the same circumstances of overbought or oversold conditions of prices. To do this, we first go to the dialog box or text window for the indicator we are about to construct, then we start typing the directions for these reference lines:

For the 0 line we type:

INPUT: BUYZONE (0);

This will tell the program to establish a line at the 0 level. To see that line on the screen, we must tell the program to plot it. Therefore, the second line of our directions becomes:

PLOT I (BUYZONE,"BUYZ");

The characters inside the quotation marks become the label that will identify the indicator when it is plotted with several others. You can use anything you want, but to keep things simple to remember, use characters that relate to the name of the indicator, and use names that reflect their nature. After you have typed in your directions for the indicator and have it verified, you of course will go to Properties and select your style (format and colors). Here you will select a modest color for the 0 line or "Plot1" above. Try green; it's a good reference line color, and I use it for all my reference lines, but you can use anything you like.

To add two reference lines, one at the top and one at the bottom, follow the same directions, except use the plural of the word "input" as follows:

INPUTS: BUYZONE(20),SELLZONE(80);

You can choose any set of limits for your extremes, such as 10 and 90, 25 and 75, or any other pair. You will also need to employ two plots such as:

PLOT I (BUYZONE,"BUYZ");
PLOT2(SELLZONE,"SELLZ");

When you select the colors, make both reference lines the same color. You also can employ all three reference lines, leaving one remaining plot for the indicator itself. Only four are possible. For example, an indicator might *dip down below* the lower extreme, then *turn around,* then *cross that same reference line* in an upward direction, and finally it may *cross the zero line* heading for the upper line. In the process described, we can identify no less than four buy signals, one right after the other, each subsequent signal confirming the previous one.

The crossing of a line is a very clear signal as it is highly visible, hence its popularity. This doesn't mean that you cannot get vague crossings where the lines "kiss" and jog along close together, or cross slightly and then twist and turn back and forth for a while, but for the most part, crossings are fairly clear.

We like to "see air" between the lines after they have crossed to make it a valid crossing! To identify the crossing of the various lines, whether they are the two lines of an indicator or a single indicator line crossing a reference line (or lines) depends on making each of them sufficiently different from all the others. This is why colors of maximum difference are so valuable. But, as mentioned earlier, be very careful when printing these indicators on paper. Some colors will print as shades of gray that appear indistinguishable. If you don't have a color printer, assign either a different thickness to one line or a different character, such as dots or dashes (or crosses or zeros) so they will print differently.

As mentioned above, another valuable signal is the **turning of a plot** from a downward direction to an upward direction or vice versa. Again, this could turn out to be vague, as when a downward direction turns to horizontal rather than turning up immediately, or forms a very flattened-out turn, such as a saucer shape. However, we are looking for a good *spike* or point that is easily identified as a bona fide turnaround. This is where our ability to dramatize these curves is helpful; we can turn a small "blip" into a dramatic spike, using the technique discussed in the previous chapter, so we really see that turnaround.

To identify **divergence,** we must be able to identify the peaks and troughs of both prices and the indicator. Again, we must be able to dramatize the turning points of the indicator enough to allow easy identification. A useful aid in this regard is the tool called the trendline (Fig. 8-18). You can draw a trendline connecting a pair or series of peaks of both prices and indicator. This readily will point out any divergence. Please note that even if one or the other trendline is flat, there still will be a divergence, as long as *either one is not flat.* In other words, the two trendlines do not *both* have to go either up or down. One of them can be horizontal; as long as the other is headed either up or down, there will be divergence. If the price trendline is flat, and the indicator trendline is rising, that is called *positive divergence* and is an equally valid signal, since the concept is one of relativity.

To build the kind of indicator that has meaning, you may have to combine several simple indicators, just as we combined several simple functions to form a more complex function. TradeStation allows us to do this by virtue of its generous capacity for a large number of logic statements. In order not to create repetition of huge formulas or logic statements, we can simplify a lot by using the expression "value," which can accept assignment of any value we want. We can have many such values, as long as we number them to keep proper track of them, such as VALUE1, VALUE2, etc. The program actually assigns a value to a variable, which here is not X or Y, but the same word with a number tag.

This lets us assign the result of a complex formula to VALUE1 and another to VALUE2; we then can integrate those two variables (VALUE1 and VALUE2) into further logic statements without having to re-enter their complex formulas. Furthermore, we easily can specify which bar on the price chart we are considering; thus VALUE1[1] refers to the value of the indicator at the previous price bar. We can further manipulate this value by taking a 6-bar weighted moving average simply by specifying:

WAVERAGE((VALUE1),6) **or even**
WAVERAGE((VALUE1[2]),6)

if we wanted that average two bars back in time. That value could then be assigned to VALUE2 and further formulation could be done, compounding and compounding. All that is easy for us to write, and thanks to powerful computers and TradeStation software, also easy for the computer to do.

Why would we want to do all that? Certainly not for the sake of creating fancy formulas! We may need to build up a series of logic statements that are related to each other as depicted above. However, such a need must arise out of our application of logic in our research. We must build gradually; take one observation and test it. Make a proposal or hypothesis; then test that, and so forth. There is no telling where we might wind up; hence the need to understand why you're doing it, know that you can do it, and especially know **how** to do it. Now, with what you've learned, you know how!

I've found it useful to plot each new step as a new indicator, and thus be able to compare it to the previous step, sometimes by superimposition on the previous one, sometimes by superimposition on the price bars. It can be interesting to have as many as three such indicators on the same graph, each giving a better signal than the previous one.

An important warning: To avoid loss or confusion, be sure to print the text of your indicator on paper before you start to modify it. That way you'll always have a record, a hard copy of what it was, as you may find yourself getting further and further away from what once was a useful formula. You may remember, "Five indicators ago, I had the best correlation; I want to go back to that one!" But if you didn't print it, you may have lost it forever. Sure, you can save it to your hard drive or a floppy disk, but that maneuver might fail if something happens to your power or the computer "locks up." Having a hard copy is a good failsafe. Always print out anything that appears to have value. Also, whenever you save it through the program, be sure to check that it really has been saved. Bring it up on screen and compare what you see with your printed version. Make sure it's the exact version that you meant to save under that name; you cannot be too careful.

19

Analyzing Price-Bar Patterns

Personally, I think that constructing indicators is the most fascinating part of doing research with TradeStation. It is very exciting to see these indicators respond in real time and undergo their dramatic contortions on the screen. However, price-bar analysis runs a very close second with two breathtaking features of TradeStation called "Show Me Anything" and "Paint Bar."

These unique and brilliant features allow you to ask the program to mark any price bar that you have designated in such a way that it stands out boldly on the screen, either with a marker on top of the bar or by painting the bar a different color than all the others. You then can scroll back through screen after screen of data and instantly identify your designated price bars that are part of a pattern you specified. You then can get an idea of their relation to subsequent price movements.

We mentioned that there are an infinite number of possible price-bar patterns, so there's ample room for research. Of course I can't illustrate everything in this chapter, but let me touch on a few basic concepts, as well as ways to get the most out of TradeStation's already vast capabilities.

As a starting point, we must return to logic. Market sentiment will determine direction of price movement, and this will be indelibly written into the price bars, so the price bars reflect that sentiment. As I mentioned in an earlier chapter, we must *extract* that sentiment from the price bar, utilizing not only its intrinsic makeup, but also its relation to neighboring price bars and *their* individual makeup. That's why it is crucial to have charts that show opening and closing prices. For example, this is essential to Japanese Candlesticks, as no candlestick can be fashioned without opening and closing prices.

We also mentioned that there are several dozen Japanese Candlestick formations, but there are many more price-bar patterns. How many more are significant? You'll have to help us there; only a fraction have been analyzed. So how do we begin?

Looking at the formation of a price bar, we might see an opening high above the previous high, or, in fact, a **gap.** There probably was a rush of buy orders with only a few sellers available. That required prices to be raised further until more sellers came forward. But, having achieved that, there are no further buyers. Suddenly a seller appears. What now? That lofty price must be lowered until a buyer is enticed to come forward. So we see the price bar extend down a few ticks. Another seller appears, and more, until the gap is closed. Perhaps the price bar is now ending, or closing, as its period is finished. The closing price, then, is at the lower limit of that price bar.

We have seen a high opening with prices at that level not sustained by sufficient support from buyers, and a gradual decline in prices to a low closing price—obviously a predominance of selling. The next bar might show the same decline in prices after an opening at the level of the previous close. In other words, it would indicate a continuation of the same selling activity. Thus we have the making of a pattern: a high that is lower than the previous high; a low that is lower than the previous low; a close that is lower than the previous close, and perhaps even an opening that is also lower than the previous close; or even the previous low, causing a small gap to the downside. We could interpret all this selling sentiment to be significant and wish to test this pattern in order to see its relation, if any, to subsequent price movements. Is it an ominous sign indicating more selling and price declines to come, or merely a small insignificant ripple in the great scheme of things? We'll simply ask the program to "show us" where those price bars are. We can use either of the two features I mentioned at the beginning of this chapter.

First, let's use the **Show Me Anything** feature:

Click on the Easy Icon for Indicators, and click on Add.

Scroll down to Show Me Anything and click on it and on OK.

Click on Inputs and Edit.

Type in your criteria for what you want to see. Here you would type:

H < H[1] AND L < L[1] and C < C[1]

The program gets unhappy with more than three criteria on a line, so limit the text to that number.

Now click on Style and choose how you want those bars marked. You can choose the *type* of marker as well as its *color* and *thickness*. The marker then will appear on top of the bars that fit your description or criteria. Click on OK and watch the screen light up!

All the bars having lower values for the high, low, and close than the previous bar have been marked at the top. You may have found hundreds of them. In that case, you'll need to be more selective and add other criteria. For example, you could choose an opening lower than the previous close. You can either choose the same feature (Show Me Anything) and have a different marker or color identify the bars that fit the new criterion, or you can choose the other feature (Paint Bar) for that purpose. Since there will be some overlap (at least we hope there will!), as we want to find bars that fit all four criteria, it will be much less confusing if we employ **Paint Bar.**

Click again on the Indicator Icon and on Add.

Scroll down to Paint Bar Custom, and click on it and on OK.

Click on Inputs and Edit.

Type in your criterion for what you want to see. Here you would type:

$$O < C[I]$$

Click on Style; now select the color and thickness you want your selected bars to have. Click on OK and again watch the screen light up with your new color on the selected bars. The newly colored bars will stand out clearly from all the rest, making it easy to find your price-bar pattern. You'll have some bars with markers on top, some of a different color, and a few of the latter also will have a marker on top. Those are the ones that fit all four criteria (Fig. 19-1).

If you now see that these select bars all occur *after* a top, they would indicate a good place to sell, and your next step would be to incorporate those criteria into a system. But before you do that, you'll want to test the opposite side of the coin, the buying patterns. Will two successive up-closes also be located just after a bottom? Or will it take three or four? You may find that more complex criteria will be necessary to "nail down" a consistent relationship between a pattern and an upward price movement. Perhaps the closing price has to be higher than the midpoint of the bar, perhaps higher than 75 percent of the bar or just the range between opening and closing prices. You could write that as:

$$C > L + (H - L)*0.75$$

Whatever you think might hold a clue, write it down so the computer will understand what you want to see; it then will search for it and show it to you if it's there.

If you are using Paint Bar to find your selected bars, and if you have many more criteria than will fit on one line, simply select the Paint Bar function again and type in the rest of your criteria on the second line provided. But you will need to use two colors, one for each study, that will produce a recognizable color when superimposed. If you've chosen blue for one study, you would need to select yellow for the other. That will cause the bars fitting both sets of criteria to be colored green—since blue and yellow mixed together form green. Give yourself a color lesson. Try out different colors, mixing them in that fashion and noting down the results for future reference. You probably will need to have

Figure19-1

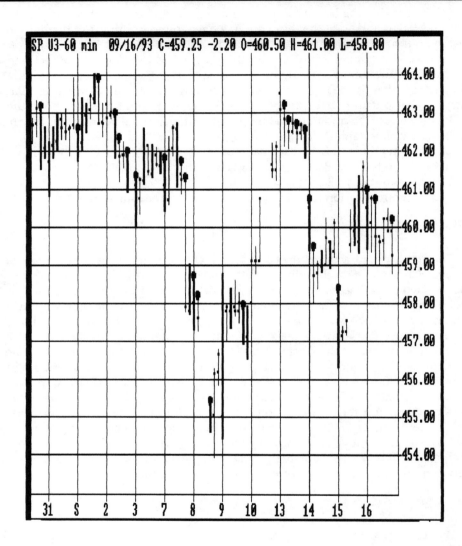

another such set of colors to mark the bars related to the opposite price movement. Here are some starters:

1. Blue + yellow = green
2. Blue + red = purple
3. Black + white = gray
4. Red + yellow = orange
5. Red + white = pink

There's a clever trick for color superimposition with computers. Since TradeStation does not allow superimposition of two colors as such, the color of the second Paint Bar indicator will prevail, wiping out or replacing any previous color. However, we can *fool* the computer by making the bars colored by the first Paint Bar indicator *twice as thick* as those of the second Paint Bar indicator! Then the second indicator bar's colors will occupy and wipe out only *half* of the bars with the first color. But the appearance will be very near that of superimposition!

Of course, you can make all kinds of fabulous pictures—a type of modern art, or maybe "financial art." However, if you are to make any kind of headway toward finding the Holy Grail of trading, you must proceed logically from the basis of market sentiment. Keep in mind that you're actually looking at that sentiment every time you look at a price bar. Try to see what it's telling you, and build on that. One of my successful systems was built just that way; if you don't recall the details, refer back to Chapter 15: "The 1-2-3 Reversal System."

20

Creating Systems

As mentioned in the previous chapters, a good test of an indicator is whether or not it can be incorporated into a mechanical system. There may be technical reasons why an indicator may not be able to become part of a system, but that does not necessarily diminish its value. The basic rule for creating systems is **Keep It Simple.** This is true of system writing as well as many other things in life, and certainly in regard to any approach to futures trading. If you have to observe 237 rules every time you make a trade, you know what will happen: You'll probably never find that perfect trade. When you do, it might well be fantastic, but to wait five years? That's a long time! The simpler it is, usually the better it is, even for computers.

Essentially, systems can be built on two bases:

The first basis is one or several simple logic statements referring to price action. This can be either in its simplest form, referring to characteristics of individual price bars; or more complex configuration of groups of bars or your position in the market in respect to current or past prices.

Basically, you must tell the computer:

1. *What to look for;* and
2. *What to do* once it has found what it was looking for.

In its simplest form, we can illustrate a system using TradeStation Easy Language as follows:

CONDITION1=C>C[1];
IF CONDITION1 THEN BUY ON CLOSE;

Adding a *second* logic statement, we either can extend the sentence with the word "and":

CONDITION1=C>C[1] AND C[1]>C[2];

or we can place the second logic statement in a second sentence by itself, where it becomes a second independent condition:

CONDITION2=C[1]>C[2];

Having added a second condition, the "IF-THEN" statement must include that, becoming:

IF CONDITION1 AND CONDITION2 THEN BUY ON CLOSE;

We can now add corresponding selling directions:

CONDITION3=C<C[1];
CONDITION4=C[1]<C[2];
IF CONDITION3 AND CONDITION4 THEN SELL ON CLOSE;

This system would then buy on two higher closes and sell on two lower closes. Since there are more than 100 different criteria possible based on prices alone; and since this software allows as many as 50 to be combined in a system, you can see that there is almost an infinite number of combinations possible. The total would be at least 100 to the 50th power; 100 to the third power is 1 million, so 100 to the 50th power is quite a big number—approaching infinity!

The second basis is one or more signals from one or more indicators. For example, take the slow Stochastic. We might create logic statements such as:

CONDITION1=@SLOWK(9)>@SLOWK(9)[1];
IF CONDITION1 THEN BUY ON CLOSE;

And we might add a second criterion:

CONDITION2=@SLOWK(9)<20;

The "IF-THEN" statement then becomes:

IF CONDITION1 AND CONDITION2 THEN BUY ON CLOSE;

We then would add two similar criteria for selling to complete a system that buys on a rising SlowK that is in the oversold zone below 20 and sells on a falling SlowK that is in the overbought zone above 80. See if you can write those statements to complete the system. Cover up the answer on the next lines until you have finished.

CONDITION3=@SLOWK(9)<SLOWK(9)[1];
CONDITION4=@SLOWK(9)>80;
IF CONDITION3 AND CONDITION4 THEN SELL ON CLOSE;

Did you get them right? If not, stop right here and go back over the previous page and even the previous two chapters. If it's still not clear, you'll need to study the TradeStation or other software manual, especially the chapters on Easy Language (or the language of your software) and system writing. I hope it's all very clear to you and we can proceed.

You've probably surmised that we now are able to combine criteria from both bases defined above. For example, we can use two criteria from the first type and two from the second type and produce a system that buys on the second higher close, provided the SlowK(9) is in the oversold zone (lower extreme), and sells on the second lower close, provided the SlowK(9) is in the overbought zone (higher extreme). This is all very simple, but now let's get a little more sophisticated.

We'd like the computer to be able to recognize all the various signals we discussed in the chapter on indicator construction. How can it do that? Actually it has a very easy time doing that. In fact, where we humans have to dramatize the appearance of these indicators, a computer can instantly recognize minuscule changes. If the value of an indicator is 0.15 two bars ago and -0.07 one bar ago, and at the close of the current bar it is 0.12, we would barely perceive that it had made a small spike downward and also had crossed the 0 line twice. A computer will see that in a flash. Therefore, we don't have to dramatize our indicators if the computer is the one that has to read them. However, in finding ways to filter out unwanted or insignificant signals, you'll see that we may still call upon our ability to dramatize the indicators in selective ways.

Now we'll look at how we can tell the computer to pick up the signals generated by the indicators. We discussed six different types of signals:

1. Crossing a 0 line;
2. Crossing a line at either extreme of top or bottom;
3. Crossing its own lines;
4. Turning around;
5. Rising or falling; and
6. Diverging from prices.

First let me emphasize that for any computer to plot any value permanently, it must not be subject to immediate change. In other words, the designated price bar must have "closed" or finished. For example, on a 5-minute bar chart, the current 5-minute price bar must finish, and the true closing value must be available to the computer. That goes for all associated data, indicators included. You will see, as mentioned in a previous section, that these indicators will wiggle and squirm up and down on the far right end of the screen as prices change up and down, but once a price bar has closed, that stops any further change at that point, and the changes now occur at the site of the *next* price bar.

In TradeStation language, variables are identified not by X or Y, but by the word VALUE and distinguished from each other by a number, such as VALUE1, VALUE2, and so on. Other software will have different specifications for variables. Here's how we tell the computer to recognize the signals.

1. Crossing a 0 Line If the indicator has crossed the 0 line in a downward direction, the value at the close of the present bar (current bar) is negative (written for the computer to understand as VALUE1<0), and the value of the indicator at the close of the previous bar must have been positive (written as VALUE1[1]>0). Therefore we can construct the following logic statement or "Condition":

CONDITION1=VALUE1[1]>0 AND VALUE1<0;

When the computer sees two consecutive price bars where the indicator was positive at the first and negative at the second (at the close), it is alerted and goes on to search for the instructions for what it should do. Your instructions might be:

IF CONDITION1 THEN SELL ON CLOSE;

This would constitute a sell signal, and a little red downward-pointing arrow would appear over the top of that price bar. For a crossing in the opposite direction, the logic statements would read:

CONDITION2=VALUE1[1]<0 AND VALUE1>0;
IF CONDITION2 THEN BUY ON CLOSE;

Combining those two sets of statements, you would have a system that buys when the indicator crosses the 0 line from negative to positive and sells when the indicator moves from positive to negative, crossing that 0 line in a downward direction (Fig. 20-1).

2. Crossing Lines Near Extremes Just as in the previous example, if the line to be crossed is near the upper extreme, for example 80, the value of the indicator at the close of the previous price bar would have to be above 80 and at the current price bar be below 80. This is written as:

CONDITION1=VALUE1[1]>80 AND VALUE1<80;

Crossing from below 20 to above 20 would be written as:

CONDITION2=VALUE1[1]<20 AND VALUE1>20;

Figure 20-1

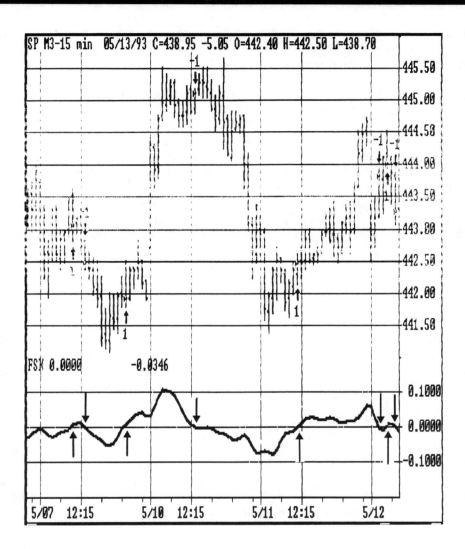

3. Crossing Its Own Lines This is very similar to the indicator crossing any one of the reference lines, except that the second line of the indicator becomes the reference line of the first example above. To do this properly, each of the indicator lines must be identified by assigning them to VALUE1 and VALUE2. The directions for the downward crossing of the first, usually shorter or faster, indicator line over the second indicator line are:

CONDITION1=VALUE1[1]>VALUE2[1] AND VALUE1<VALUE2;
IF CONDITION1 THEN SELL ON CLOSE;

This system will sell on the close of the bar where the indicator line assigned to VALUE1 crossed from above downward to below the second indicator line assigned to VALUE2. This frequently is seen in the slow Stochastic where the SlowK crosses the SlowD line for a signal.

You will now get a chance to prove your mastery of writing these instructions by supplying the ones needed for buying on the upward crossing of the two lines of an indicator. Cover the answer on the next line until you've written your own instructions.

CONDITION2=VALUE1[1]<VALUE2[1] AND VALUE1>VALUE2;

Did you get that right? Good, I'll assume you did, so we can move on together.

4. The Turnaround A turnaround has three rather than two points. Thus, an indicator would be turning around if the middle value were lower than the one on either side, thus forming the point of the bottom. The opposite would be true of a top. It's written as:

CONDITION1=VALUE1[2]>VALUE1[1] AND VALUE1[1]<VALUE1;

where VALUE1[1] is the value of the indicator one bar ago, and where the value of the indicator at the bar on either side is higher, and of course the value of the indicator one bar ago, VALUE1[1], is the low point, identifying it as the turnaround. Now you should be able to construct the language for a turnaround at the top. Cover the answer on the next line and see if you can get it right:

CONDITION2=VALUE1[2]<VALUE1[1] AND VALUE1[1]>VALUE1;

Did you get that right? If not, you know what you must do: Go back and review! This system will buy on the close of the 3rd bar of the turnaround at the bottom and sell at the 3rd bar of the turnaround at the top (Fig 20-2).

You can see that you must be very careful about the signs. It's easy to make an error and have one isolated sign be reversed from what it should be and have the whole system fouled up. That could ruin your day. Check and check again!

5. Rising or Falling This should be very easy as we've already seen it earlier in this chapter. We simply ask the computer to compare the values of the indicator at two consecutive price bars. If the value of the indicator is higher at the sec-

Figure 20-2

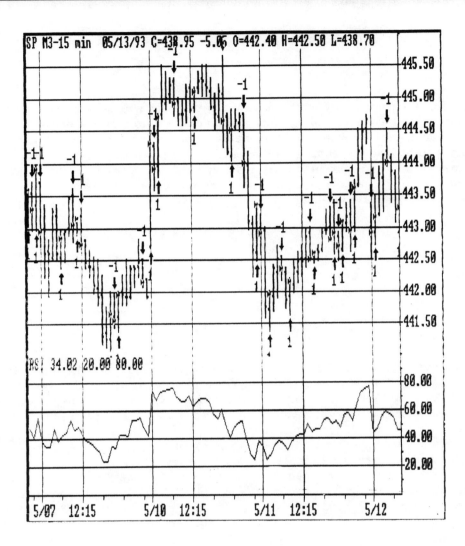

ond bar, the indicator is rising; if it is lower, the indicator is falling. In TradeStation language it is written as follows:

```
CONDITION1=VALUE1[1]<VALUE1;
IF CONDITION1 THEN BUY ON CLOSE;
CONDITION2=VALUE1[1]>VALUE1;
IF CONDITION2 THEN SELL ON CLOSE;
```

This system will buy on the close of any price bar where the indicator is rising, and sell when it is falling. Notice I didn't ask you to complete one of the sets of statements; I knew it would be too easy for you by now! However, I now will ask you to write the entire set of instructions for a system that buys on a turnaround of an indicator in an oversold zone, and sells at a top as the indicator turns around in an overbought zone. Be sure to cover the answer on the next lines until you have written your own.

```
CONDITION1=VALUE1[2]>VALUE1[1] AND VALUE1[1]<VALUE1;
CONDITION2=VALUE1[1]<20;
CONDITION3=VALUE1[2]<VALUE1[1] AND VALUE1[1]>VALUE1;
CONDITION4=VALUE1[1]>80;
IF CONDITION1 AND CONDITION2 THEN BUY ON CLOSE;
IF CONDITION3 AND CONDITION4 THEN SELL ON CLOSE;
```

I knew you could do it! (Fig. 20-3)

6. Divergence TradeStation has a built-in system that will detect divergence between the RSI oscillator and prices. You can access the text of that system via the Editor and substitute another oscillator for the RSI. To substitute *your* special indicator, the system will have to be rewritten so as not to wipe out the built-in one. We'll discuss that in some detail.

From Charting, click on Options, then Power Editor, then File, then Open. Check the box by System, scroll down to Divergence and click on it.

The text of that system will now be shown in the dialog box. You now can substitute any other oscillator for the RSI. It follows that it should be possible to substitute your own indicator for the RSI, and have the program detect divergence between prices and *your* indicator. Rather than fool around with the Divergence System in the library of systems, make your own new system. Give it the name of your indicator with "divergence" attached; this is so you'll know exactly what it is when you scroll through the contents of the library. Type in the criteria for your indicator and assign the final result to a variable like VALUE3 or VALUE4. Now type in the text of the divergence system.

Delete the Input line of the system.

Substitute VALUE3 for Osc in that system.

You now have a divergence system using *your own* indicator!

Using an indicator such as high-median price, the system would be written as:

```
VALUE1=H-((H-L)/2);
IF BULLISHDIVERGENCE(Close,VALUE1,2,30)=1 THEN BUY
```

Figure 20-3

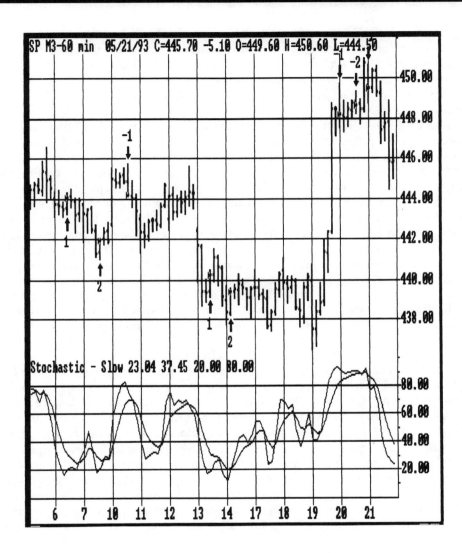

```
HIGHEST(HIGH,5)+1 POINT STOP;
IF BEARISHDIVERGENCE(Close,VALUE1,2,30)=1 THEN SELL
LOWEST(LOW,5)-1 POINT STOP;
```

You can further modify your instructions for acting on the divergence by changing the "If-Then" statements to "Conditions." Then you could combine those conditions with one or more others to form your system. That way, you will be making divergence only a part of, rather than the only, criterion for action.

I now will leave it entirely up to you to construct a system that relies on divergence between prices and an indicator you also have constructed in addition to recognition of a special price-bar pattern of your choosing. Of course you will proceed to weed out losing signals in both long and short directions by fine-tuning your indicator and perhaps even the price-bar patterns. No, there's no answer here on the next line to cover up while you write your system, as I have no idea of what you might design. But I trust that by now you have learned enough techniques to be able to do this with confidence. In case you have not yet achieved that level of confidence, reread these chapters. The info is all there. You'll learn a lot from your own mistakes, so try and try again until you get it right. When you have, we'll move to another aspect of system writing.

We've clarified how to make the computer "see" the signals generated by the indicators we create as well as signals generated by specific price-bar configurations. This gives you an almost endless number of components with which to build your systems and make them comprehensive and useful. However, we need to discuss a few more aspects of system writing.

The **first** is how to act on the signals given. We have a choice of accepting only one signal at a time in each direction—a sort of "purist" way to go—or accepting multiple signals. I find that the former is the first display to look at, since it's the simplest. Be sure to check the box next to the phrase "Accept only one signal" in the Properties dialog box. However, do not stop at that in your analysis. It may be that taking all possible signals will be very worthwhile too, or even much better. There are times when a system will show a small loss with solitary signals in each direction (that simply means that no sell signal is taken unless it is preceded by a buy signal, and vice versa), and be very profitable when all signals are taken. All possible signals are then displayed by the program. When you trade such a system, you don't have to take all those signals. You can use your judgment and take only the ones in the extreme zones, or you can limit yourself to taking a maximum of two or three contracts at a time. Anything more than that you forego. But if you are trying to create a mechanical system, it makes more sense to fine-tune it so it works well and then stick to it.

Second, in such a case you will need to "weed out" the undesirable or losing signals by adding more criteria to your system. That's the way to build or fine-tune a system. You start somewhere, then fine-tune it. Look at all the signals. First concentrate on the buy signals, then later return and concentrate on the sell signals. Note which signals are losers or only marginally profitable; those are the ones you need to weed out. Perhaps the indicator showed only a minuscule rise and could be called a weak signal. You now could specify a criterion for "strong" signals that would require the indicator to rise by a certain minimum before a signal is generated. To find out exactly how much that should be, click on Tools, and then Show Chart Status at the bottom of the list. Now scoot the cursor along to the price bar where the weak signal was given. Note the change in the indicator value from the previous bar. *That* is the number that must be exceeded in your filtering criterion in order to eliminate that signal. For example, the indicator might have gone from 14 to 14.5 and have given a signal based on a rising value. If that signal is a losing one, it can be eliminated by adding an additional figure to your criterion for a rising indicator. Instead of simply saying:

CONDITION I = VALUE I > VALUE I [I];

you can say:

CONDITION I = VALUE I > VALUE I [I]+2;

and now a signal is generated only if the indicator rises by at least 2 whole points. The indicator going from 14 to 14.5 is insufficient to generate a signal, and if you re-apply the system, the little blue arrow no longer will be present below that price bar. You'll also find that, when you check the system summary, your profits will have increased!

Third, one word of advice when editing indicators or systems: Always delete them from your chart before you go back through the editor to the text and revise further. When you're done revising, you can return and re-select your indicator or system and add it in once again. This will prevent error messages and a possible shutdown of the computer program. When you're all done with your research for the session, delete them again from the chart to prevent clutter and drag on your chart pages.

Fourth, another concept when designing systems is to use different types of criteria for buying than for selling. For example, it may be unreliable to create buy signals after only two up-closes, but quite reliable after *four* up-closes. However, it may be very successful to generate sell signals after only *two* down-closes. So you'll have slightly different criteria for buying than for selling. Don't be bound by tradition; let your creativity have free reign! You can then check the other boxes under the option of accepting more than one signal in the same direction. Of course, you can use many different signals for buying in the same system. You can make a system that will buy after four up-closes **or** after an upward gap of at least three points, and so on.

Fifth and finally, you need to know when to stop. You can go on and on, adding criterion after criterion in order to fine-tune your system; but in the process it will have become a veritable "novel" of several pages. The more complex it is, the more it will have to be tuned to *past* data, and the less likely it will be to work well on future data. This is the pitfall of all mechanical systems. Too close a fit to past data eventually will cause a failure on future data. Keep your systems as simple as possible, and the chance of continuing success is much greater.

By now, you've learned to modify your system in ways limited only by your imagination. You have also been advised that systems are best kept simple. Then what is your goal? Is it big profits? Is it consistent profits? Is it small drawdowns in your capital? Is it a small frequency of signals? Is it small numbers of contracts required? Is it successful application to all markets? In all periods? Right, it is all of the above, but which are more important? That's a decision I'll have to leave up to you. However, I *can* tell you what *my* priorities are, and along which lines I try to modify my systems.

First has to be profit. The system must show a modest profit per trade of at least $250. Larger profits then can be achieved in many ways, such as taking two or three contracts instead of one, modifying the exit signals to stay in the market a little longer if possible, and so on.

Second is the ability to be profitable while holding as few contracts as possible; preferably only one, but at most two or three.

Third is minimal draw-down of capital, since the lower the draw-down, the smaller the account can be. This is of course theoretical, since there is no guarantee written in stone that your system will not fail to get you out of a large losing position some day in the future. However, it's not very comforting to sit on the edge of your seat while your system allows a huge draw-down in between making small profits. I am basically very much against allowing much of a draw-down, so I do not favor this type of dubious loyalty to a mechanical system; hence the importance of finding one where the draw-down is absolutely minimal.

My **fourth** goal is consistency. You don't want to see huge profits in a long-trending bull phase, only to see slight profits or even losses during the bear phase of a market. Your system should be able to make profits both on the long as well as the short side, consistently, with only an occasional loss here and there.

After these four, it doesn't matter too much if you have to give up something like versatility. Your system may work well for the grains, but not in the soft commodities like sugar or cocoa. That's fine; use it where it works well, and develop another system for the other markets you're interested in. This goes for periods as well, but a good system usually will work well in several periods in the same market.

I also prefer a system that does not overtrade, or get in and out at every other price bar. To make profits, you must be able to allow the passage of time; prices have to be given a chance to move. Thus, a system that keeps you in the market at least four or five price bars is a must.

A few final words about mechanical systems:

Do not forget to check off the Stops and Commissions before you calculate the System Summary. If your system has a large number of trades, those expenses rapidly will mount up into the thousands and perhaps make the system unprofitable, in which case you must try to limit the number of trades. It's great if you can find a system that is totally mechanical and consistently profitable with a single contract at a time. You can always double or triple your position with each signal, all according to what your capital will allow. You also can pyramid your positions.

My experience, as well as that of many other traders, has been that few systems are that perfect. You'll very likely have to employ a certain amount of that old-fashioned human common sense once in a while. The above example of large draw-downs as a disadvantage is one such time; I would not accept that from **any** system. There might be very ominous developments taking place just when your system is giving a buy signal; and, unknown to you, the whole rest of the world might be preparing to sell. Don't make the mistake of being a robot and taking the trade. Just stand aside. You may lose profits if you're wrong and the system is right after all, but you will not lose capital!

I've given my views on trading in general in the first sections of this book, so you know how I take profits. I do not allow any mechanical system to let those profits slip away. With or without a system, golden principles still apply. No system ever will have a monopoly of the market. Remember: **Take your profit$ now!**

PART
6

❖

THE PAYOFF

21
Putting It All Together

"Nobody goes straight to the moon—except Astronauts"
—*Ulf K. Jensen*

Putting it all together involves several series of key steps. I shall now take you through each of those series of required steps in the order they should be taken. Here is the first series, the **Five Preliminary Steps** (discussed in detail in Part 1):

1. *Decide what timeframe* you wish to use. Are you going to be a *day-trader,* which requires a lot of time spent in front of your computer screen during market hours; or are you going to be a *short- or long-term trader,* in which your trading hours will be more compatible with a fulltime job.
2. *Gain control over your time* as well as your *environment.* Even more important, your state of *alertness* should be at its best.
3. *Select your markets* for trading, eliminating the ones with little opportunity or volatility, in which there is only minimal possibility for significant profits. Use the *volatility index* given in Chapter 2 until you become more

familiar with the various markets. Trade only the markets with a *VI more than 20*.

4. *Select the appropriate data displays* on your computer, so you can monitor your markets in all necessary timeframes (usually the 5- , 15- , and 60-minute; and daily bar charts). You will want to include the RSI and Stochastics, as well as the TDAC and FSK or FSRS indicators. But don't neglect to look at other displays such as volume and open interest, MACD, %R, ADX, and 4- , 9- , and 18-bar moving averages.

5. *Monitor your chosen markets,* observing the fundamentals as well as the technical patterns. You've already added a selection of indicators, combining both the classic ones with the new ones developed in this book; try to get some experience with both types. Your basic temperament will determine what signals you will prefer. If you are an aggressive trader, you may want to take the peaks of the indicators as a signal; whereas a more conservative trader will wait for the crossover of the indicator lines, or even the crossing of the indicator over a reference line. If you want to be even more selective, you may want to wait for a divergence or a failed swing sign, or both.

Those were the *easy* steps! Next come the *difficult* steps. You're now ready to consider entering the market. Here is the next series, the **Five Consideration Steps** (discussed in Parts 1, 2, and 3):

1. *Determine the risk to your account* if you enter a particular market. Use the formula given in Chapter 4 until you become so familiar with evaluating the markets from this point of view that you can determine the risk by a quick glance and a mental calculation.

2. *Determine the best time and place to enter* the market based on your assessment of its daily chart pattern. Closely examine the *cycles* and the *resolution of the various chart patterns*, getting familiar with their behavior, mainly their consistency. Evaluate the *price bar patterns* carefully and choose reliable configurations as guidelines. *Study the Japanese Candlestick charts* and learn to recognize the *top and bottom patterns*. Learn to recognize the *changes in market sentiment* that they display; then see if you can recognize such changes in sentiment in the regular price bars. Look for the higher or lower closes, the spike tops, the "Doji," "Evening Star," "Hanging Man," and "Hammer."

3. *Determine the probable extent of the expected price move.* Be realistic. Use classic techniques of cycles, trendlines, support and resistance levels, Fibonacci ratios, and Elliott wave counts. If the move is not large enough to generate significant profit, do not risk your account on it. Wait for the next wave! Commonly, the next upwave of the cycle will be comparable to the previous one, but it could also be 1.6 times as large (a Fibonacci ratio), or it might be a 50-percent retracement. Look at all the possibilities. Focus on the most likely, but be prepared for all!

4. *Determine precisely where your first stop-loss order should be placed.* Calculate the size of the possible loss in dollars if that stop gets hit. Determine whether you are willing to lose that amount of money in

your quest for the estimated profits, or whether your account can afford that loss. If not, don't take the trade!

5. *Confirm your impression* by using classic indicators as well as market sentiment indicators. We've already gone over the various signals to use.

You now proceed to enter the market. I cannot emphasize enough: **Don't be in a hurry to enter the market!** It really is *too easy* to enter the market incorrectly. All you have to do is pick up a phone and call in an order, and, presto, you're in! How many traders have not very soon thereafter regretted that quick phone call! As I said in Chapter 11: "Stack the odds in your favor before you enter."

If you're a day-trader, a *market order is best,* as it lets you know exactly where you enter. If you're a short- or long-term trader, *entering the market on a stop order* will greatly increase your chance of being drawn into the profit zone immediately, and is highly recommended.

You can *"bracket" a market* by placing an entry stop order on both sides of the market. Place a buy stop above and a sell stop below the last chart pattern. Give it a little room to "wiggle" so it can gather a little steam going in your direction before your stop gets hit; that will make it more likely that it will keep going in the right direction.

Do not enter the market on an opening gap. They represent exaggerated movements that frequently retrace themselves in whole or in part. However, they are superb spots for taking profits. *Wait for the gap to fill,* then reassess the market. If you do get sucked into such a gap, frequently the best thing to do is get out immediately. When your broker calls with the fill, and you realize it has been filled on a large gap, *liquidate before you get off the phone!* What is a large gap? Anything more than 20 points!

Do not pyramid your positions until you are wealthy enough to take the vicious losses that can occur. Starting with a small account, you'll do just fine trading one contract at a time.

If you are a short-term or long-term trader, you will want to *diversify* among the various market *groups* to give yourself the best chance of catching a good move in one of the markets. *To stretch those margin dollars,* and not to commit more funds than is prudent to margin deposits, you can take T-bonds, currencies, gold and soybeans on the *Mid-America Exchange,* where the margins are half or less than the regular exchange. The profits will be less, but so will the losses, and that is what is important.

You can further stretch those margin dollars by trading soymeal instead of the beans, as the margin is much lower, but the profits are still quite good; the meal moves pretty near in tandem with the beans. You already know not to take on more than one contract in any group of related markets to minimize the effect of adverse developments on your positions.

Time your entry by the signals given by the indicators (review Part 2), but remember, *there is more to trading than following indicators!* They serve best as timing devices, although some of them have other abilities as well.

Can you employ systems? Yes, of course you can. But I advise that you remain as the final arbiter. *Do not accept horrendous draw-downs in the name of being loyal to a system,* no matter how good it is. As mentioned before, if your system says "Buy" and your analysis says "Sell," don't blindly go by the system;

give some credit to your analysis. Pass the trade and see what happens. Discover which is right. That's how you gain that venerated commodity, experience.

Those were the *easy* steps and the *difficult* steps. Now come the *impossible* steps! *Getting out of the market involves impossible steps,* because it is virtually impossible to get out of the market at the place that will give you the maximum possible profit! You always will have to accept something less than perfection. Or do you think that the *only* trader who sells at the one tick that is the *very top of the day* will be **you**? If so, *good* luck! Here is the final series, the **Five Profit-Taking Steps** (discussed in Part 4):

1. *Gain perspective.* Find answers to these questions.
   What is the *cycle* that you are trading: short, intermediate, or long?
   Where is the price in relation to the *current cycle*?
   Where is the price in relation to significant *recent high and low points?*
   Where is the price in relation to *support and resistance* levels?
   In short, where are you? If the price is near a *top*, your expectation must be different than if it had just passed a *bottom*. In the latter case, be prepared to hang in there, but in the former, near a top, get ready to get out!
2. *Ask more questions.*
   How is the market behaving? Is it leaping upward along a steep *2x1 Gann line,* or merely crawling along a much less steep *1x2 Gann line?*
   Are factors such as *tick volume or daily volume,* open interest, and volatility increasing?
   Are the *price bars* characteristic of this move?
   Are the *indicators* confirming these observations?
3. *Ask still more questions* before you draw a conclusion.
   What is happening now at this very moment in time?
   Is the market moving steadily along as you expected, or do you see any early warning signs of a change?
4. *Repeat those first three steps often,* in fact at every new price bar! Do a complete reevaluation. Write that evaluation down and compare it to the previous one. It is a valuable exercise; you will learn a lot. It might produce clues as to why one trade turned out better than another, or why one failed. If you are holding a *profitable* position from the day before, and the market opens with a *large gap,* liquidate your position *immediately.* Take that profit now! It will soon evaporate. You've been handed a significant profit in a matter of a few minutes, by all means, **take it home!** On the other hand, if you are a short-term or long-term trader and have a loss in your position, **do not** take a significant loss home overnight! Anything more than $200 is significant, but a steadily *rising loss* could be significant at a lower dollar value. **Get out!** Do not risk that loss turning into an even bigger loss on the opening the next day. Day traders by definition never will have that problem—they *always* will be out by the close.
5. *Take your profit$ now!* Deciding whether or not to take your profits now is the most difficult of all decisions for many traders. Here is where you must be realistic. Don't fall in love with your position! Nobody goes straight to the moon—except astronauts! Certainly not prices!

From your perspective of your position, you must quickly estimate the probability of prices going further. *If the market is hesitating,* and you can see early warning signs on price bars and indicators, *take those profits **now!*** If the market then continues on, don't be afraid to get right back in. More often than not, the market will turn back, and you will be relieved. Your work has come to an end; you can breathe a sigh of relief. You can celebrate: You have turned paper profits into *real dollars!* All the steps have been taken. You have taken **profit$ now!**

Now you're ready to start all over again. Go ahead, take that first step again! It's easy now; you've done it before! You've seen where it can lead you. You're gaining confidence. There's another old saying (You knew that's how this chapter had to end!) that says: "Do it right. Do it well. Then do it again!" That's your winning formula; don't ever forget it!

22

Winning the Robbins System Trading Championship

Here's how it all began. I first started trading stocks in 1970, and soon discovered the wonderful leverage of options. That was before any of the exchanges had option trading; you merely purchased the option from your broker, provided he could find a stock owner who was willing to sell an option on his stock. I became impressed with William Hurst's research on the cyclical nature of the markets, and I was able to use that knowledge to great advantage by combining it with the leverage of options. Thus, three independent concepts were uncovered in my mind:

1. The cyclical nature of the markets;
2. The high leverage of options; and
3. The power of combining two separate principles into one approach. The last was like the one-two punch of a prizefighter: very powerful!

I then became interested in the commodity markets as an extension of the leverage principle, as well as from a fourth concept: that of seeing the results of your efforts quickly rather than many weeks or months down the road. I found that it was easy to make quick profits in the commodity markets by entering the markets on the right side of a cycle, but also that it was even easier to lose your money, and fast. The losses came from misjudging the direction of the market as well as from the lightning-quick changes in the commodity markets.

I spent many years doing market research with my trusty vintage IBM-PC, one of the first ones on the market. I had to write my own programs, since no software was available for a whole year. (Necessity is a good teacher!). I was trying to make some sense out of the seemingly capricious futures markets. I had many a tug-of-war with the floor traders, winning, losing, winning, losing, almost perpetually. I knew there had to be a better way. I also knew that, to study the markets better, I had to have better equipment and software. That meant acquiring intraday or real-time data. A bigger problem was where to find friendly software.

It so happened that the famous trader, author, and market researcher Larry Williams offered a seminar on how to take home profits using TradeStation, analytical software from Omega Research, Inc. Of course I went. I saw that TradeStation was a fantastic tool for doing market research. From Larry Williams I got a good deal of insight into the capabilities and limitations of mechanical systems.

Everyone at that seminar was encouraged to enter a Systems Trading Championship, sponsored by the Robbins Trading Company of Chicago. I entered casually, never seriously thinking that I had any chance of winning against so many other traders, many probably more experienced in writing systems than I.

It was early May 1992. When I came home, I immediately set to work. It took a few weeks to get set up, and even more weeks to get fully into the complex software and become comfortable doing such things as making and changing charts, periods, and colors, to say nothing of writing functions, indicators, and systems in a way that the computer would understand. Before I knew it, two months had gone by. It was already July! I had only five more months till the deadline of November 31. Who was I kidding? How could I prevail in such a short time?

Well, I did have a secret weapon! I had a weapon that most people do not have. I had a *plan!* In fact, I had *two* plans: Plan A and Plan B. It's not always enough to have a plan; without it you're lost, and if it fails, you're lost again. You also must have an *alternative* plan. In the contest, it was the alternative plan that enabled me to get to the top in the time required. Plan A was to devise a winning system with the help of all the wonderful state-of-the-art computer, software, and data service. Plan B was to devise a winning system that could be used by anyone who did not have access to a computer.

Under Plan A, I would rapidly increase my market research and find useful parameters and correlations. Then I would construct one or more mechanical systems that the computer could throw at the markets. Taking profits would be like "taking candy from a baby"! Naturally, it wasn't that easy!

Sure, I could use someone else's system and perhaps get some profits, but that wouldn't be *me*. If I were going to win, it was going to be because of my very own innovation and strategy, not someone else's! I've never been a copycat; I'm a very independent sort. I soon realized that by the time I found something use-ful, I would be out of time! That didn't stop me from pursuing my market research, which eventually led me down the right path during the last month of the championship. At last I had found the clues. I feverishly worked on their fur-ther development; and that more than anything gave me the inspiration for this book. I had unmasked the signs of changing market sentiment in real-time, the driving force behind the price movements!

This "behind the scenes" look at market sentiment actually became possible quite early, through my Plan B. I quickly had seen the time limitation in working things out on the computer, and therefore I devised a plan to do the same thing without the computer, using daily price charts as my only tool. I wanted some-thing simple; something that did not require expensive equipment or massive amounts of time to start up. Using this method, traders not having access to expensive computers and software could also "play the game." It's not very expensive to subscribe to a weekly chart service; for the price of a daily paper, a trader could then update his own charts.

I now began to analyze the price-bar patterns before and after every change in the direction of the markets. After some time, I found a seemingly obvious—yet hidden from many—recurring pattern, which became my most successful mechanical system: the 1-2-3 Reversal System. I soon found another correlation. It was actually a classic chart pattern and a classic technical analysis tool; togeth-er they formed the Trendline Breakout System. However, neither of these sys-tems was consistent enough for my purpose. They needed something more. My old discovery that combinations can be more effective than each item alone came to my assistance.

I combined each of my systems with the classic Stochastic indicator to elimi-nate the unprofitable signals that sometimes occurred. That was all they needed! I was able to put these systems into effect quite soon; however, I remained very selective in their application. Although I focused on day-trading, I chose trades that had a good chance of continuing past the next day.

I found some good trades in a variety of markets, such as copper, cotton, T-bonds, eurodollars, and currencies. It was my good fortune that the first of the European currency crises happened in late September 1992. I have pointed out elsewhere in this book that a crisis represents an opportunity, provided you can position yourself correctly. I realized that the British pound would continue to drop, and that investors would seek a safer currency in the Japanese yen, which should then rise. These assumptions proved correct, and these currencies proved excellent vehicles for trading through my two systems. I then realized that I had a shot at winning the championship.

It was now the end of October. I had relocated my home the last part of September and was still surfacing out of boxes. Out of the six months allowed for the championship, I'd probably had only three months in which I'd been able to trade. I now began to wonder where I stood in relation to all those other more or less sophisticated traders with all their state-of-the-art equipment and years of experience. I called Robbins. "Where do I stand compared to the other entrants?" I asked. His matter-of-fact reply absolutely floored me! "You're Number One. In fact, you're even way ahead of the leaders of both the amateur and the profes-sional divisions of the World Cup Championship!"

"Wow, thanks," I said. "You've made my day!"

I celebrated by getting my wife a much-needed car. We felt like we had won the $10 million lottery!

Now what should I do? If I simply stopped trading for the last month, I probably would still win. In fact, those who never even put on a single trade probably would come in ahead of 90 percent of all the others who *did* trade! It would be safer *not* to trade! But there would always be the chance that someone would catch up to me. Anyway, I am not one to win anything by doing nothing. I know that Jesse Livermore, the most famous trader of all time, states that, to accumulate profits, sit on your hands. But that refers to letting a profitable position grow unhindered by your repeated meddling. I could not just sit by and watch some turtle overtake me!

I continued to trade, and of course I took some losses by being careless and not following my own principles. I became a little worried. November 31 finally came. After the markets closed, I called Robbins. **"You've won!"** he told me. "*Hot Dog!* Who would have thought that back in May?"

Looking back, what trades served to put me over the top? There were a good number of winning trades that outpaced the fewer losing trades by far, but naturally a few trades stood out as true winners. There were three such trades:

On 9/16/92, I sold the British pound after it had broken down through a trendline and covered my short position before the end of the day for a profit of $2,250.

On 9/21/92, I bought the Japanese yen and sold near the end of the day for a profit of $10,950.

Finally, on 10/13/92 I again bought the Japanese yen, added on to that position on 10/15/92, and sold on 10/16/92 for a profit of $9,525.

Those three trades alone would have secured the championship; I could have avoided all the others! But such is hindsight. The first of those three resulted from the Trendline Breakout System, the last two from the 1-2-3 Reversal System.

That's all it takes: a few really good trades. You go through a lot of trades with small profits as well as a good number with small losses in order to catch "the big one." That time I caught three.

I then turned my sights to writing this book and developing a consistently profitable approach to the futures markets that would help novice traders stay alive in the jungle out there. I think this book will open eyes as to where the risks are buried, as well as how to haul in those profits before they disappear.

I subsequently have had the privilege of attending an advanced trading workshop given by legendary trader and author Stanley Kroll. I had the pleasure of exchanging ideas with Kroll for some time thereafter, all of which led to my publishing a daily fax market letter, consistent with the excellent guidelines Kroll emphasizes and employing most of the principles outlined in this book. That letter is a more active attempt to assist novice as well as seasoned traders in achieving success in the markets. A series of intensive one-on-two workshops also is available to show traders how to get the most out of their computer software along with the principles of my commonsense approach to futures trading called "PROFIT$ NOW!"

For more information on either the daily market letter or the workshops, please send me your name, address, and telephone number, or fill out and mail the coupon on the last page of this book.

Several of the indicators and systems discussed in this book as well as two new indicators and systems are now available on floppy disks, ready to add to your software's library of indicators and systems. Please see the last page for information on how to order these. **I sincerely hope this book will help your trading! Good luck.** —Ulf K. Jensen

Glossary

ADX An indicator designed to detect a trending market

Advance Generally refers to a rise in prices

Bearish The belief that prices will fall

Bear market A downward move in prices

Breakout Prices escaping out of a consolidation period

Bullish The belief that prices will rise

Bull market An upward move in prices

Bull run An exceptionally long upward move in prices

Candlestick Description of the Japanese way of viewing a price bar; the part between the opening and closing prices

Chart pattern Overall picture of a group of price bars

Chasing the market Attempting to enter a market that is moving away from you

Click Briefly pressing down a button switch on a computer mouse to send a command to the computer

Close Last price traded at end of session, sometimes a range

Condition Part of a logic statement in TradeStation Easy Language

Consolidation Area in which prices seem to congregate between moves

Contract In the futures market, a specific commodity contract

Convergence Two trend lines coming together through time

Current Present price

Cycle Time segment between two highs or two lows

Decline Generally refers to a drop in prices

Delivery month Month when a futures contract comes up for delivery

Dialog box Box on a computer screen (on a Macintosh or in Windows); it usually has two or more "buttons" to register a choice of actions

Divergence Two trendlines moving further apart through time

Downtick An executed sell order

Drawdown Trading loss that still is only on paper

Easy Language Language in the TradeStation program that lets the user enter customized formulas

Elliott wave Series of waves in all markets described by Elliott

Equity Amount of unencumbered money in your account

Functions Mathematical relationships varying in complexity

Fundamentals Supply and demand factors affecting a commodity

High Highest trading price during a session

Icon Tiny graphical representation of a computer program, file, or task; when clicked on with a mouse, it causes a specific task to be done

Indicator Mathematical formula plotted and correlating with prices

Investor Person who places funds long-term, anticipating growth

Kurtosis Indicator composed of sequential momentum

Lagging Curve that changes only after prices have changed

Leading Curve that changes before prices have changed

Limit move Maximum price move permitted during a session

Logic statement Words instructing computer to perform a specific task

Long Trader who has purchased a futures contract

MACD Moving average convergence divergence indicator

Margin Amount of money required as deposit to trade a contract

Margin call Request for additional money to satisfy minimum margin

Market Outcry auction where commodities are traded

Momentum An indicator comparing two prices by subtraction

Mouse Small plastic device with a finger switch that generates computer commands, and a ball on the bottom that moves the cursor across the screen when the mouse is moved across a surface

Moving averages
　Simple A number of similar prices divided by that number
　Weighted Same as simple, but each successive price is increased by a constant factor to "weight" later values
　Exponential Same as simple, but each successive price is increased by a constant power (exponent)

Open The first price traded in a session, usually a range

Option The right to buy or sell a futures contract or shares of stock

Order A direction given to a broker to buy or sell. Examples:
　Day Order that is good only for day entered
　GTW Good The Week: an order that expires at the end of Friday
　Fill or Kill Order that must be filled immediately; used to test market
　Limit Order that can be filled only at specified price. May not get filled if market moves away quickly
　Market Order executed immediately at available price
　MIT Market If Touched: activated as prices touch given price
　MOC Market On Close: market order filled only on the close
　MOO Market On Opening: market order filled on opening
　OCO One Cancels Other: used when bracketing a market

Oscillator A mathematical function whose curve oscillates between 0 and 100 or around a 0 line to indicate an overbought or oversold state of prices

Overbought Prices at a high level during a certain period

Oversold Prices at a low level during a certain period

Portfolio Collection of commodities or stocks one monitors or owns

Position Contracts owned at certain price, for example: "Long 2 Jul. Wheat at 330"

Price bar Line drawn connecting high and low of a period, usually with opening and closing prices marked on sides

Rate of change Comparison of prices by dividing current by previous

Ratio One figure divided by a second

Reward Amount of money that could be gained

Resistance Price level where previous top or bottom has occurred and prices are hesitating

Risk Amount of money that could be lost

RSI Relative Strength Indicator, compares up-closes to down-closes

Scalping Taking a profit of only a few points

Sentiment Attitude of traders, either bullish or bearish

Settlement Final price of session, frequently fixed 15 minutes after the close

Short Person who has sold one or more contracts

Short covering Repurchase of sold contracts expecting higher prices

Speculator Anyone who trades; the opposite of an investor

Spread Buying one and selling another related contract

    Intermarket spread Contracts are in different but related markets

    Intramarket spread Contracts are in same market but different delivery month

Stochastic Indicator comparing present price to a past range

Stop orders

    Buy stop Activated when prices move to or above your price

Sell stop Activated when prices move to or below your price

Stop close only Activated only on the close and only if prices reached your price

Trailing stop Some brokers will enter this order to let you exit a market a specified number of points above or below closing price

Support Price level where a previous top or bottom has occurred

Swing high Cycle high, usually short cycle

Swing low Cycle low, usually short cycle

System Set of computer directions to produce buy and sell signals

Technical Related to characteristic price-bar and chart patterns

Tick data Recorded transactions as they occur

Trader Someone speculating in the market by buying and selling

Trading range A range in which prices seem to congregate or oscillate

Trendline A line drawn under or over peaks or valleys of prices to emphasize the direction of price movement

Uptick An executed buy order

Value Word used by TradeStation software to indicate a variable

Velocity Speed

Volatility Magnitude of price fluctuation per unit of time

Williams %R An overbought/oversold indicator

Bibliography

1. Williams, Larry R. *How I Made One Million Dollars Last Year Trading Commodities*. Windsor, 1979.
2. Williams, Larry R. *Definitive Guide to Futures Trading*. Windsor, 1988.
3. Williams, Larry R. *Definitive Guide to Futures Trading II*. Windsor, 1989.
4. Angle, Kelly. *100 Million Dollars in Profits*. Windsor, 1989.
5. Kroll, Stanley. *Kroll on Futures Trading Strategy*. Dow Jones-Irwin, 1988.
6. Gietzen, Al. *Real Time Futures Trading*. Probus, 1992.
7. Chisholm, Michael. *The Taurus Method*. Windsor, 1985.
8. Lindsay, Charles L. *Trident: A Trading Strategy*. Windsor, 1991.
9. Howard, B. J. *The Price Spiral Method*. Windsor, 1988.
10. Goldberg, Harold. *The Power Index Method*. Windsor, 1986.
11. Dobson, Edward D. *The Trading Rule that Can Make You Rich*. Traders Press, 1985.
12. Duffy, Joseph T. *The Trading Advantage*. Windsor, 1991.
13. Chisholm, Michael. *The MegaTrade Method*. Windsor, 1987.
14. Appel, Gerald. *The Big Move*. Scientific Investment, 1982.
15. Murphy, John J. *Technical Analysis of the Futures Markets*. N.Y. Institute of Finance, 1986
16. Sklarew, Arthur. *Techniques of a Professional Commodity Chart Analyst*. Commodity Research, 1980.
17. Weiss Research. *Timing the Market*. Probus, 1986.

18. Brandt, Peter Lewis. *Trading Commodity Futures with Classic Chart Patterns.* Advanced Trading, 1990.
19. Steidlmayer, Peter J., and Koy, Kevin. *Markets and Market Logic.* Porcupine Press, 1986.
20. Belveal, Dee L. *Charting Commodity Market Price Behavior.* Dow Jones-Irwin, 1985.
21. Nison, Steve. *Japanese Candlestick Charting Techniques.* N.Y. Institute of Finance, Simon & Schuster.
22. Hurst, J. M. *The Profit Magic of Stock Transaction Timing.* Prentice Hall, 1971.
23. Lane, George C. "Lane's Stochastics." *Technical Analysis of Stocks and Commodities,* June 1984.
24. Barnes, Robert M. *Megaprofit Commodity Methods.* Windsor, 1983.
25. Bernstein, Jake. *Strategic Futures Trading.* Dearborn, 1992.
26. Frost, A. J., and Prechter, R. R., Jr. *Elliott Wave Principle.* New Classics, 1985.
27. Neely, Glenn. *Mastering Elliott Wave II.* Windsor, 1990.
28. Robbins, Joel. *High Performance Futures Trading.* Probus, 1989.
29. Wilder, Welles J., Jr. *New Concepts in Technical Trading Systems.* Trend Research, 1978.
30. Gann, W. D. *How to Make Profits in Commodities.* Lambert-Gann, 1951.
31. Marisch, Gerald. *The W. D. Gann Method of Trading.* Windsor, 1990.
32. Chicago Board of Trade. *Speculating in Futures.* CBT Literary Services, 1990.
33. Schwager, Jack. *The New Market Wizards.* Harper Collins.
34. LeBeau, Charles, and Luca, David W. *Computer Analysis of the Futures Market.* Business One, 1993.

Since some of these are put out by small, little-known publishing houses that specialize in financial books, here is some helpful contact information:

- Advanced Trading Seminars, Inc., Sacramento, CA 95875
- Business One-Irwin, Homewood, IL 60430
- Chicago Board of Trade Literary Services Dept., Suite 2210, 141 W. Jackson Blvd., Chicago, IL 60604
- Commodity Research Bureau, Inc., 1 Liberty Plaza, New York, NY 10006
- Dearborn Financial Publishing, 520 N. Dearborn St., Chicago IL 60610
- Dow Jones-Irwin, Homewood, IL 60430
- Harper Collins Publishers, Inc., 10 E. 53rd St., New York, NY 10022
- Lambert-Gann Publishing Co, Inc., Pomeroy, WA 99347
- New Classics Library, Inc., P.O. Box 1618, Gainesville, GA 30503
- New York Institute of Finance, 70 Pine St., New York, NY 10270
- Porcupine Press, 401 S. LaSalle St., #100, Chicago, IL 60605
- Prentice Hall, Englewood Cliffs, NJ 07632
- Probus Publishing Co., 1925 N. Clybourn Ave., Chicago, IL 60614
- Scientific Investment Systems, Inc., Toronto, Canada
- Traders Press, Inc., P.O. Box 10344, Greenville, SC 29603
- Trend Research, P.O. Box 450, Greensboro, NC 27402
- Windsor Books, P.O. Box 280, Brightwaters, NY 11718

Index